BORDER CITY BLUES

BORDER CITY BLUES

The Story of
Rugby League in Carlisle

Scratching Shed Publishing Ltd

First published by Scratching Shed Publishing Ltd in 2010
Registered in England & Wales No. 6588772.
Registered office:
47 Street Lane, Leeds, West Yorkshire. LS8 1AP

www.scratchingshedpublishing.co.uk

ISBN 978-0956478771

A catalogue record for this book is available from the British Library.

Typeset in Warnock Pro Semi Bold and Palatino

Printed and bound in the United Kingdom by
L.P.P.S.Ltd, Wellingborough, Northants, NN8 3PJ

This book is dedicated to Tina, my best friend and wife of 43 years. It was with her encouragement and support that I first got involved with rugby league in Carlisle. That support has never wavered and the preparation of *Border City Blues* was at her suggestion

Acknowledgements

The author is grateful to everyone who assisted him with the writing of this book, the majority of whom are named within its pages.

Particular thanks must go to Cumbria County Council's Carlisle Local Committee, who have supported the venture very generously, and Steve Ball of the Rugby Football League's Heritage Foundation.

With regard to the photography, my gratitude is extended to the following friends and colleagues, who each furnished me with images from their personal collections: Geoff Bland, Steve Raybould, Don McDowall, Allan Agar, Ken Laverick, Andrew Hogkinson, Elaine McCullough, Chris McManus, Trevor Easton, Dean Bell and the late Tom Clark.

Contents

Above: Carlisle legend Dean Bell, with wife Jackie and children Kurtis and Chloe

*

Foreword

By Dean Bell

WHY Carlisle? That is the question many people have asked me over the years. To them it was a strange choice; I can see why they thought so. Let's face it, Carlisle was a club with a one-year history in rugby league when I arrived there and it had a squad made up of ageing professionals in the twilight of their careers. More than that, the club was based in a football town! It didn't seem to add up as a destination for any young rugby league player trying to make the grade at the highest level.

In fact, for three young Kiwis (me, my uncle Ian and my cousin, Clayton Friend) it made no difference where we went at all. The fact someone was willing to pay us to travel to the other side of the world, while playing a sport that we played for nothing in New Zealand was unbelievable.

Back then, the three of us had been brought up in the game through the Manukau Magpies in Auckland. It's a club with a decent history and it's a place the Bell clan certainly has a strong connection with. It was a tough environment and a big part of our lives but there came a time when Ian, Clayton and I were looking for an opportunity and a chance to see something of the world while still being able to play our great game.

It all fell into place in 1982 after Clayton had made the Kiwis for the first time. Ian had already been a Kiwi by then, but he and I had both missed out on joining Clayton in the side that toured Australia and Papua New Guinea (another story completely).

This was the era when New Zealand players could take up off-season contracts with English clubs, but only once they'd completed their club commitments at home. They also had to be back for the start of the new season, so there was a window of about five or six months when you could head for Europe.

There were a couple of people who played a big part in making our trip to Carlisle possible. One of them was British-born David Robinson, a successful businessman in Auckland, who was then a director on the New Zealand Rugby League board. He had some contacts in England and started scouting around for a club that would take on three New Zealanders. Kiwi scrum-half Shane Varley, who had spent the 1981-82 season with Workington Town, recommended Carlisle to us, the club having earned promotion to what was then the first division in its debut campaign.

David sealed the deal and we were on our way, the beginning of a Kiwi link with Carlisle which was later revived when my dad, Cameron, was the coach there from February 1990 to April 1994. Future Warriors and Kiwis Hitro Okesene and Mike Dorreen also spent time at Carlisle, as did other New Zealanders, including Brad Hepi and Brett Iti.

There was a bit of trepidation when we arrived. There always is when you're striving to be accepted in a new place.

Above all, though, the dominant feeling was one of excitement as we were embraced by the locals. While my one season there was over all too quickly, I owe so much to Carlisle.

It wasn't about making money. Carlisle covered our air fares, gave us accommodation and provided a car between the three of us, but we weren't paid much at all, something like £1,000 after we'd played twenty games. That didn't matter at all to us. It was the catalyst for my professional career, the springboard for me to spend the 1983-84 season with Leeds and, ultimately, leading to my lengthy association with Wigan from 1986-87 through to 1993-94.

What mattered to me far more about Carlisle personally was that it was there that I met my wife, Jackie Parker from Harraby. It actually came about the very first day we were in Carlisle. There was a bit of media coverage about us on our arrival and we were fairly conspicuous in our tracksuits walking in the street. Apparently, one of Jackie's mates spotted us and Jackie said: 'Oooh, I'll have the blond one!' We met in a pub a couple of nights later and here we are still putting up with each other close to thirty years later.

Jackie had only just become interested in rugby league after Carlisle's success in 1981-82, but I'm not so sure my future in-laws were overly impressed when they saw me play for the first time. I was ordered off for fighting when we played St Helens!

I ended up playing twenty-three games that season, scoring eleven tries, and I have great memories playing alongside 'mature' pros like Mick Morgan, Denis Boyd, John Risman and company; it was a great introduction to the professional game. My very first outing for Carlisle was a Lancashire Cup match against Wigan, would you believe? Playing at famous venues like Headingley and the Boulevard was a particular highlight for me but I have rarely come across anywhere better than Brunton Park – the surface was like playing on carpet.

Outside of the game, Carlisle was a paradise for young males with pubs and nightclubs galore and, of course, lovely Cumbrian lasses! In fact, after closing time our house on Woodrouffe Terrace was the most popular place in town.

Little did I know that Carlisle would play such a big part in my own family's lives. Dad and my mother Janice have many fond memories of Dad's five years coaching in the Border city. While my parents eventually returned to New Zealand – as we did – my sister Tracey married local boy Paul Hill and they now happily live in Morton with their children Claudia and Nathan.

I went on to spend over half of my life in England and Carlisle was always a place that I felt comfortable visiting, which I did on many occasions when I found the time.

The big sadness for me, and for Dad, too, was seeing Carlisle struggle and watching their demise.

So whenever people say 'Why Carlisle?' my response is always: 'Why not?'

*

Preface

RUGBY league has, as far as I can recall, always played a major part in my life. Indeed, some of my earliest recollections as a very young boy are of being taken to Knowsley Road, St Helens, to watch the Saints. I can vividly remember the hero-worship I bestowed on the likes of Stan McCormack, Bill Finnon, Jimmy Stott and company in the late Forties.

A year or so later, I thought I'd die of happiness when Steve Llewellyn, the iconic Saints winger of the early-Fifties, visited our class at Knowsley Road Junior School and lectured us kids on the virtues of a healthy mind and healthy body – and for some strange reason (or maybe an obvious one since few of us had a bathroom at home) the importance of taking a shower after playing strenuous games.

A few years later, in 1956, my happiness was again boundless when I was taken to Wembley to watch Saints at last win the Challenge Cup by defeating Halifax 13-2 in a match that by today's standards was both dour and at times simply brutal. Apart from the game itself and the delight of seeing Saints captain Alan Prescott hoist the Cup aloft, my other memories of that day are my first experience of the tube and the disappointment of travelling to London and not seeing Buckingham Palace and the Tower of London. The uncle and aunt who took me, childless themselves, just didn't understand a young boy's yearning to see places that had only featured on pages in a book.

Fast forward a few years more and other indelible memories include the incomparable former Springbok international Tom Van Vollenhoven when he made his debut against Leeds in October 1957, at Knowsley Road. Nearly four years later I was back at Wembley with Tina, my wife-to-be, when Voll broke Wigan's hearts in the spring sunshine by scoring a decisive try after some quite imperious interpassing with his centre partner Ken Large.

Thereafter, the Saints memories followed thickly until, in 1971, disheartened by events at my workplace (Triplex, a division of Pilkington Bros) in the aftermath of a major strike, we decided that we should take a new opportunity in Carlisle. My wife and I, along with our one-year-old son, left behind our life in old industrial St Helens and moved to the vast emptiness of the Solway Plain in rural Cumbria.

Almost as soon as my son could walk I introduced him to the delights of the thirteen-a-side game and we took every opportunity when visiting my wife's parents and my own family to take in a trip to see the Saints.

We also discovered the delights of watching Workington Town and Whitehaven to the south west of us on the Cumbrian coast, especially when they were entertaining a Lancashire club.

A few years later, in a great blaze of publicity, Carlisle United, who were then, as now, just two divisions away from the equivalent of the Premiership, announced that they were backing a new venture at Brunton Park. The new venture was of course Carlisle RLFC. At a stroke, all interest in Workington and Whitehaven evaporated as my son and I threw our support into this new venture in the autumn of 1981.

Little did I realise it at the time but, from that point on, the die was cast for the extra-curricular part of my life and within a few years I found myself inextricably involved as a director and chairman in the management of the game, initially at Brunton Park, then when the club was reborn as Carlisle (1987) Ltd. at Gillford Park. That interest and involvement has never waned and, after a five-year spell as a director and then chairman of Barrow Raiders RLFC, in 2002 I joined Bev Risman and other RL enthusiasts, including former Carlisle Border Raiders director Dougal Kyle, highly-respected junior coach and former headmaster Trevor Easton, and Carlisle Saints former player-cum-secretary Andrew (Hodgy) Hodgkinson in forming Carlisle Centurions RLFC.

The love affair continues to this day with a role - with others now including another former headmaster, Malcolm Jackson, and retired GP Dr Ian Mackay - managing the affairs of the Centurions in the summer-based Co-operative Rugby League Conference.

During the nearly thirty years since Carlisle RLFC first burst onto the scene, I have experienced so many dramas, heartbreaks and moments of elation that I felt the story of rugby league in Carlisle needed telling while it was still a first-hand experience. Far better that than some sports historian's dry regurgitation of archived printed matter, spiced up with his or her speculation as to why various events occurred.

This book is an attempt to capture the history of our game in the Border City. The very early history of the code - i.e. the short-lived pro-club of 1928 and the Carlisle City Amateur Club of 1950-52 - is of necessity based on contemporary records – primarily from the *Cumberland News* and *Carlisle Journal*. The 1928 records were collated by the late Tom Parker, a Carlisle-based rugby league enthusiast. I am indebted to Graeme Harker of Carlisle who researched the records of the early Fifties team that played at Morton.

The statistical references from 1981 as regards scores, league positions etc are from the author's personal records, material loaned by Jackie Beech, or the relevant *Rothman's Rugby League Yearbook*, *League Express* newspaper or *Gillette Rugby League Yearbook*.

An attempt has been made to collate matters of interest relating to the various pub teams that sprang up in the wake of the 1981 pro club. Sadly, the last of these pub sides, the Carlisle Saints - originally born as St Nicholas Arms - finally died out in 2005, having made a brief one-year renaissance after a two-year absence.

Another team that has its history recorded in this book is the short-lived Rickerby Saints, an under-15s venture organised by Geoff and Chris McManus (uncle and father respectively of one of the players), who played in the winters of 2005-06 and 2006-07.

There was also a 'Ladies' team in Carlisle playing out of Dalston in the Nineties. While few, if any, playing records still exist, one of the players and organisers, Elaine McCullough, has recounted her own memories for us.

Wherever practical and possible I have interviewed the characters whose stories are so fundamental to this account of rugby league in the Border City. This has turned out to be a pure delight. I hope you enjoy it too.

ALAN TUCKER
OCTOBER 2010

1
*
1981-82

THE story of rugby league in Carlisle is the story of a dream. Or, to be more accurate, several dreams. The Board of Directors at Carlisle United dreamed of an extra revenue stream from Brunton Park to fund their promotion hopes. The RFL dreamed of the game expanding out of its narrow geographical boundaries. I simply dreamed of being able to take my son to watch the sport I loved without travelling to my hometown of St Helens, or West Cumbria. Within five years that club had taken over my life and, almost thirty years later, I'm still talking and writing about it.

Andrew Jenkins, long-time director and chairman of Carlisle United, gives an insider's account of the advent of rugby league at Brunton Park.

'The Carlisle United chairman at the time, the late Jim Bendall, was the driving force behind the formation of the RL club,' says Andrew. 'Jim had obviously heard all about the experiment that had started in Fulham (at Craven Cottage) and decided that this would be a worthwhile venture in Carlisle. It made good economic sense to profitably use Brunton Park for more than the twenty or so home fixtures that the Third Division of the Football League allowed at that time.'

Andrew, himself now chairman of the family concern Pioneer Foods, as well as the city's First Division football club, vividly remembers Carlisle United general manager Colin Hutchinson's incredulity when he related to him his chairman's vision of rugby league at Brunton Park. His incredulity wasn't shared by the Brunton Park faithful however, who responded to a poll of their members by indicating that 43 per cent (or around 2,000) of them would give the new game a trial. Nor was that incredulity shared by rugby league's ruling body, the RFL, whose member clubs, doubtless buoyed by the success at Fulham, voted unanimously to welcome the Cumbrians into the Second Division of their two-division structure.[1]

Andrew Jenkins recalls considerable opposition to the new venture at board level from directors Jim Monkhouse and Jimmy Johnston, mainly due to anticipated wear and tear to the turf. Notwithstanding this opposition, a majority of the board, doubtless swayed by the compelling economic arguments, supported their charismatic chairman. It was

---

[1]Bill Oxley, honorary RFL chairman of the RFL in 1981-82, wrote then that: 'As a fellow Cumbrian, I am delighted that my year of office is opening with the birth of two new clubs in Carlisle and Cardiff City.

'The Brunton Park application to join the Rugby Football League in this new era of expansion was given a unanimous send-off by the Rugby League Council. Our deputation who visited Carlisle on a feasibility study towards the end of last season brought back a very favourable report on the facilities and professionalism of the club. This has been proved further by the judicious appointment of Allan Agar as player-coach, along with his No. 2 Mick Morgan. Both these men have been exemplary professionals in their long and illustrious careers... Allan having experienced Wembley with Hull Kingston Rovers in 1980 and Mick having represented England down under in 1975.

thus that Jim Bendall, Ian Ward and Colin Hutchinson formed the nucleus of the rugby league board. The board was strengthened by the recruitment of three rugby league stalwarts in former Workington Town chairman George Graham, ex-Scottish RU International and Leeds RL player Ron Cowan and Geoff Holmes.

Geoff, a former director at Keighley RL in the 1970s and now living in Leeds with his Carlisle-born wife Lynn, recalls the start of his own involvement. 'I had read about the proposed developments at Carlisle,' he says. 'I remembered Colin Hutchinson from my time on the board at Keighley so I called him. Two weeks later he invited me to Brunton Park to meet the other directors. That was it. I joined.'

Interestingly, in the event that the club needed directors from outside the area, according to the club's minutes, the name Vince Karalius was suggested as being someone who should be approached. Whether or not the late Saints, Widnes and Great Britain legend was aware of this has gone unrecorded.

The new club thus had a strong board in chairman Jim Bendall, United directors Andrew Jenkins and Ian Ward, and three experienced RL men in Holmes, Cowan, Graham. The power and purse-strings were held by the

'Along with vice-chairman George Graham, drawing on his experiences as chairman of rivals Workington Town, Carlisle have brought together a side full of experience and potential without giving the bank manager too many headaches!

'Carlisle will compete in the Second Division of the Slalom Lager Championship for what promises to be the most competitive campaign since two divisions were introduced in 1973.

'The Rugby League Council have worked hard during the past seven years to ensure that rugby league has a future as a national sport. The game is proud of its 50 per cent increase in gates over the past five years and the birth of three new clubs over the past 18 months. We sincerely hope that Carlisle play a major part in the continued progress of the thirteen-a-side game.'

original investors Carlisle United (a 76 per cent shareholder) and their three directors on the board of the rugby league club. To all intents and purposes, the RL set-up was a division of the football club and thus totally controlled by them. Despite this, shares to the value of £18,500 were sold to 130 members of the public, mainly in Cumbria.

Thanks to the £4,000 signing of 32-year-old Allan Agar, formerly of Wakefield, Featherstone, Dewsbury and Hull KR, as player-coach and his assistant Mick Morgan (also 32), who came via Featherstone, Wakefield & York, it was inevitable that the team yet to be assembled would have a Yorkshire flavour.

And so it transpired, as a team of mature players and still-able veterans was assembled on a £115,000 budget. That team included Charlie Birdsall (31), a second-row forward signed for £6,000 from Hull; Denis Boyd (31), another second-rower signed for £16,000 from Wigan; Ian Crowther (26) a £4,000 hooker from Hull; Steve Davies (23) a centre from Wigan; Steve Ferres (27) a £6,000 half-back from Bradford; Terry Hollingsworth (28) a £10,000 loose forward from Wigan; loose forward Barry Limb (30) from Featherstone; Graeme Robinson (22) a £4,500 full-back from Featherstone; the veteran 32-year-old £8,000 prop Jimmy Thompson from Bradford Northern; Graham Evans (30), a £4,000 centre from Hull; £20,000 stand-off Nigel Stephenson (30) from Bradford; Wally Youngman (25) a winger on loan from Hull KR; Kevan Robinson (24), another loanee from Keighley; 32-year-old Tom Gainsford, a £10,000 loose forward from Barrow; Joe Bardgett (23) a £9,500 centre from Keighley; Steve Raybould, whose transfer fee was undisclosed and Carlisle's first ever signing from rugby union, the prop Martyn Ward, who had previously played with Morley RUFC.

In keeping with this white rose pedigree, the squad

trained at Featherstone Sports Centre and travelled to Carlisle together for each home game.

The wage structure was originally agreed at £80 for a win and £30 for a loss.[2] The marketing efforts included T-shirts, caps and eye-catching car-stickers sporting the slogan 'Rugby League at Carlisle, give it a try'. Posters with the theme 'Family Entertainment at Brunton Park' started to appear and season tickets incorporating special discounts on a wide range of goods and services were promoted

Considerable thought was given to team colours and it was decided to retain the blue, white and red of Carlisle United: '...to allow supporters following both codes to use the same scarves etc'; a spectator-friendly move that would be anathema to today's sports-marketeers, who have turned the sale of shirts and other memorabilia into a business rivalled only by the actual gate receipts from the turnstiles.

Eventually, the players came together with an off-the-record practice game at Featherstone against a local amateur side. There then followed a pre-season friendly against the previous season's new boys, Fulham, won by Carlisle 6-5 at Craven Cottage. A little known fact is that the club gave a trial to a very promising Scottish rugby union scrum-half in this game (under an assumed name, of course, in those days of prejudice against the thirteen-a-side code.) But the trial came to naught when the lad in question got word of a potential trial at Murrayfield. Geoff Holmes also recalls another Scottish union player who was in negotiation with the club at that time and who went on to get a full Scotland cap. Even after 29 years, their names are maybe still best kept under wraps.

---

[2]The omission of a wages sum for a drawn game was an issue that haunted the club for many years after. After several seasons of hiatus, the club eventually adopted the convention of treating a drawn game at home as a loss and a drawn game away as a win.

First Season under Way

THE first ever rugby league game at Brunton Park was against first division Wigan on 16th August 1981 in the Lancashire Cup. In those pre-Super League days, Wigan, like all other RL clubs, fielded a team of part-time professionals and, despite being a division above the Carlisle new boys, nearly went out in the first round as Carlisle just slipped to a 6-9 defeat in front of a very creditable crowd of 2,800. Graham Evans scored the new club's first ever try and goals were kicked by Steve Ferres, with Nigel Stephenson tagging on a drop-goal

Carlisle *News and Star*'s reporter Peter Hill commented: 'Wigan's clenched fist salutes at the final hooter seemed out of context with history. A club with a proud tradition stretching back into the last century surely shouldn't be elated with a three-point victory over a side playing its first ever competitive match.'

A narrow 10-4 victory at Bramley's McLaren Field followed, before the big one against local rivals Workington Town on 6th September 1981. And what an occasion that turned out to be.

The new code with its colourful players and equally colourful strip captured the imagination of the city and 5,900 turned up (to this day still an attendance record for the code in Carlisle). They were treated to a live band, freefall parachutists, first day stamp-covers ($13\frac{1}{2}$p) and all the razzmatazz the club could muster. Sadly, the Border City men were convincingly beaten 6-23 by the experienced Town, for whom John Jones scored a hat-trick and prolific goal-kicker Lynn Hopkins notched six goals, including one drop-goal. Carlisle managed just one try by Mick Morgan, with goals by Steve Ferres and Charlie Birdsall (drop-goal).

Despite the disappointing result, the city folk were taken by the strange game. One supporter, a Mr Ian Hodgson of London Road, was moved to write to the club: 'May I congratulate you on your venture to introduce rugby league to Carlisle. I personally was not too keen, but I was bitten by the bug at the Wigan game and so were many of my workmates. The main reason I am writing is to praise the way you promote family entertainment at Brunton Park. On Sunday at the Workington Town game, there was myself, my mam and dad, sister and fiancée. Not only did they go, but they enjoyed it and cannot wait for the next game.'

Even the Carlisle police were enthusiastic, commenting favourably on the crowd behaviour compared to the followers of the round-ball game. The telling statistic quoted at that time was that it took just three constables to police 3,000 spectators for a rugby game compared with thirty for a similar sized gate at the soccer.

A fairly mundane away win (7-13) - described at the time in the local paper as 'a bruising battle of the forwards before Allan Agar came on as substitute after 31 minutes to transform the game' - followed at Blackpool Borough. Next up, Swinton, in those days still a formidable side boasting stars such as Danny Wilson, Green Vigo and Norman Turley, came to the city. Carlisle won comfortably, 25-3, but officials were disappointed at the 2,000 gate, well below the 3,000 stated as a requirement for survival.

The following week, they undertook the long trip to Ninian Park. Cardiff, the other new boys that season, had kicked off their own professional debut with a 9,000-plus gate and were still unbeaten at home. They attracted an attendance of 3,200 to see them edge out the Cumbrians in a dour 11-7 victory in which Kevan Robinson (try) and Steve Ferres (two goals) were the Carlisle scorers.

Carlisle's season continued to prosper, on the field at any

rate, as their inability to consistently achieve their stated break-even gate of 3,000 was a constant worry. There were just a few blots on their playing record. Apart from the loss to Workington, these were being knocked out of the John Player Trophy, 16-10, at Widnes in October 1981 and when they suffered a 17-2 defeat to Castleford before a heart-warming crowd of 5,500 at Brunton Park in the first round of the Challenge Cup three months later.

Promotion to the top flight was achieved with an incredible seven games still to play when Carlisle narrowly beat Halifax 12-4 courtesy of two Mick Morgan specials (the second of which broke the try-scoring record for a prop forward of 18 tries in a season), a Nigel Stephenson try and goals from Agar (dg) and Ferres. The 3,500 attendance that day at Thrum Hall was one of Halifax's best of the season.

Carlisle then extended their unbeaten run to twenty-two consecutive league wins until their nemesis, Workington Town, pooped the party on Easter Monday 1982 with a 23-15 victory at Derwent Park, despite Carlisle scoring three tries (Stephenson, Ferres and James with three goals from the boot of Ferres). Town were as delighted with their 5,664 attendance for this game, their best of that season, as they were with a result that virtually guaranteed their own promotion alongside Oldham, Carlisle and Halifax, with Fulham, Wakefield, York and Whitehaven being relegated to take their places. The occasion was marked by the hilarious antics of a streaker who managed to stop play, with players of both sides reduced to laughter as referee Gerry Kershaw blew his whistle and gesticulated angrily at the culprit.

Andrew Jenkins remembers another aspect of that weekend. Carlisle had played Huyton on the preceding Good Friday and the players stayed together in the Gretna Hall hotel on the Thursday night, prior to the game at the run-down Alt Park ground on the outskirts of Liverpool.

Word reached him from chairman Jim Bendall, who had just been round to check the players were okay for the following day and found them all knocking back pints in the hotel bar, a situation that would have been condemned out of hand in the round-ball game. On questioning the sanity of the playing staff to be even in licensed premises on the eve of a game, he was assured that they'd be well sober come kick-off time. They were as good as their word and won 30-13.

My own personal memories of that first season are mixed. The excitement of the crowd seemed a little over the top for the quality of rugby on display compared with that at Knowsley Road or Wigan's Central Park. With hindsight, the Brunton Park faithful were maybe more used to the highly-strung histrionics of professional soccer players or the dour and endless scrums and kicks into the next parish of the fifteen-a-side game.

Certainly, fluent passing moves, sublime evasive skills, hard one-on-one tackles and the occasional toe-to-toe punch-up were cheered to the echo when in truth they were the bread and butter of professional rugby league. It's an interesting speculation as to what the supporters would have made of Tom Van Vollenhoven and Vince Karalius, two Saints legends of the Fifties and Sixties.

Mick Morgan rapidly became a personal favourite for his outright cockiness and uncanny ability to turn up at the right time and place to finish off a move with a touchdown. Veteran prop Jim Thompson and Steve Raybould soon became cult figures with the members of the farming community who took to the new code in abundance. Jim and Steve's no-nonsense approach and willingness to do the hard graft appealed to the farming work ethic.

However, such purist snobbery rapidly dispersed as the season went on. In fact it quickly turned to euphoria as we moved into early 1982 and promotion into the top flight started to turn from looking a distinct possibility into a racing certainty.

Bobby Shaftoe, a long-time supporter of the club and, being from the North East until he came to Carlisle in 1975, a Newcastle United fan, has some great memories of those days.

'In those days I was first and foremost a football supporter who'd watched a bit of live rugby union for years and only seen rugby league on BBC's *Grandstand*,' Bobby says. 'The main attraction, apart from the game itself, was the social scene and the approachability of the players. Unlike football players who, even at Carlisle United's level, apart from the notable exception of Irish international Paul Bannon, were aloof from the supporters, the rugby league players were totally at home with us and were happy to share a pint after the game. Apart from that first ever game against Wigan, I never missed a single match for the next two years.

'Even world-class players like Kiwis Dean and Ian Bell and Clayton Friend in the 1982-83 season would stand and chat to you in the street. This was brilliant for us supporters. I remember being in the old Stars and Stripes pub down Botchergate one night a few years later with my mates on a jam night, when there was a banging on the door. It was Clayton Friend with the entire Maori touring party. They'd parked their coach just up the road and were looking to get a taste of the Carlisle nightlife.

'Another time, the Australian touring squad[3] was in

---

[3] It was the invincible 1982 Australian touring party that not only whitewashed the best of British under the coaching of Johnny Whiteley, but redefined the standards of rugby league excellence for generations to come. The tourists beat Cumbria 40-2 in Brunton Park's only RL representative game on 9th November 1982, in front of nearly 6,000 appreciative supporters.

Carlisle to play a game against a Cumbrian team at Brunton Park. Afterwards, they were taken to the Malt Shovel pub. I can see them today... Mal Meninga, Wally Lewis and company all smartly dressed in white shirts, grey suits and Aussie ties. The doormen refused to let them in because they were wearing trainers!

'Boy, we used to enjoy our drink on matchdays. For a typical away game we'd meet outside the London Road Store in Carlisle and pick up a couple of bottles of sherry and a bottle of Bells whisky. We'd be drunk before we even got off the bus. For a home game we'd be in the old Carlisle Labour Club by nine-thirty, stop there until twelve and then get a taxi to Brunton Park, drink until the game, a couple of pints at half-time and then start again at full-time.

'An amusing memory from that first season was when we played Huyton at their vandalised Alt Stadium ground in a fairly rough area on the Liverpool outskirts. Afterwards we were chatting to their coach, player and groundsman Geoff Fletcher. Geoff had showered and donned his wig. We asked him where we should stop in Huyton for an after-match pint on the way home. I still smile at his answer: "Preston".'

Carlisle finished that inaugural season with some remarkable records. They achieved promotion at their first attempt. Mick Morgan had set a new world record of 25 tries by a prop forward in a season. Out of 32 league games, they'd won 29 and lost only three. They had recorded the highest-ever attendance for a Carlisle rugby league team and Steve Ferres had set a club record haul of 242 points in a season, a record that lasted until 1996, when Willie Richardson topped it with 254.

To add the icing to the city's cake, Carlisle United were also promoted to Division Two of the Football League. All in all, this was pretty unique for the old Border City and it spawned a massive interest in the thirteen-a-side code, not only with supporters but also with the numerous pub teams that sprang up around the city and which are covered elsewhere in this book.

However, even as the team were enjoying their moment of glory as conquering heroes, the financial storm clouds were gathering. The effect of over-optimistic budgeting for 3,000 average gates had started to unfold. The servicing of the club's bank overdraft, brewery loan, a loan from the football club and a Building Society loan also guaranteed by Carlisle United, plus transfer costs, wages and so on far exceeded revenue from gate receipts, sponsorships and ad-hoc raffles. It was plainly obvious that without a massive injection of funds or an equally massive reduction of the cost base, insolvency beckoned.

With the wisdom of hindsight after reading old board minutes, it is now clear that the club could not possibly live with the costs of a team of imported players and coaching staff. It is also clear that it needed to generate substantial revenue streams of its own and that the likelihood of achieving average gates of 3,000 without a mammoth six-figure investment in younger high-quality playing staff was remote, and even then far from assured. In short, an insolvent club had been promoted to the top level. Without a sugar daddy donating hundreds of thousands of pounds or some other modern miracle, it was bound to end in tears.

As Bobby Shaftoe recalls: 'We supporters expected a real struggle when Jim Bendall pulled out United's support. It was obvious to us all that the side needed new players. Allan Agar's closed-season resignation came as no surprise.'

I had a few conversations with Allan Agar during the writing of this book. In fact, he is partially responsible for it being written at all. Allan actually came to a Carlisle Centurions game at Gillford Park when we played Bradford in 2004 and presented me with scrapbooks and other memorabilia from his Carlisle days.

'I was 31-years-old and had played in what was probably going to be my last season with Wakefield in the First Division,' he says now, when asked about his memories of that time. 'I'd been contacted by Barrow and then Carlisle about coaching. It was George Graham, the former chairman of Workington, who called me. He also called Mick Morgan, so Mick and I travelled up to Carlisle together for interviews with Colin Hutchinson, Jim Bendall and George. I was offered the job there and then, and Mick was also engaged.

The conversation very much revolved around where the team would train etc. I still see some of the players from that first year. Mick Morgan is very much involved with Castleford. He had a pub about ten miles outside the town but recently retired. Mick does the video commentary for Castleford and helps them with their lottery.'

Of the rest: 'After resurrecting York City Knights, Steve Ferres went to Wakefield Trinity Wildcats as chief executive and now works for the Rugby Football League advising clubs on their commercial affairs. Charlie Birdsall has a newsagents in Hull. Nigel Stephenson went to Spain for a couple of years, and then Florida, and his son Francis is operations director at Wakefield. Jimmy Thompson has now retired from his insurance agency. Wally Youngman is a DCI with Humberside police and secretary of the Hull KR ex-players association. Graham Evans has had health problems and his wife has established a charitable foundation called "Second Chance". And while Ian Crowther is no longer involved in rugby, Martyn Ward and Kevan Robinson are involved with Upton and Kippax ARLFCs respectively. Joe Bardgett was signed by me for Featherstone Rovers after we'd won the Cup in 1983 and then he returned to Keighley.'

Peter Hill, the *Evening News and Star* reporter, was clearly impressed with the toughness of these characters.

He reminisces: 'Denis Boyd didn't so much tackle opponents as launch himself like a human exocet at anyone foolish enough to invade his territory. The former Wigan forward became a legendary figure among Carlisle supporters for tackles that often meant the recipient could take no further part in the game. He specialised in lurking behind the defensive line and taking out opponents who came through a gap, aiming himself at their chests. It was an awesome sight, except for the player on the receiving end.

'Boyd, who had built up a formidable reputation at Wigan, once told an RFL disciplinary hearing where he was accused of a late tackle: "I got there as fast as I could". Although he was a quiet man off the pitch, he once confided that there were occasions when men in Wigan pubs would challenge him to prove his hard-man reputation. "What do you do when that happens?" I asked. "I just hit them once," Boyd replied.

'Another legendary hard man, former Great Britain prop forward Jimmy Thompson, played out the twilight of his career at Carlisle. Although his dodgy knees meant he was unable to take the ball forward more than a few yards, supporters admired his dogged, uncompromising style. On a summer club trip to Majorca, a drunken British youngster decided it would be a good idea to pick a fight with Thompson in a bar. "He asked me to step outside," the Yorkshire miner recalled. "I didn't want to hurt him, so I just stared into his eyes. He changed his mind about fighting and went away."'

CARLISLE – 1981-82 – SEASON SUMMARY

Chairman: James Bendall
General Manager: Colin Hutchinson
Coach: Allan Agar (May 1981-June 1982), Mick Morgan (July 1982-)
Records: Attendance: 5,903 v. Workington T. (Div 2) 6 Sept, 1981
Goals: 113 by S. Ferres, 1981-82
Tries: 25 by M. Morgan, 1981-82
Points: 242 by S. Ferres, 1981-82
Highest score: 36-2 v. Batley, 1981-82, 36-10 v. Hunslet,
1981-82, 36-16 v. Blackpool B. 1981-82
Highest against: 27-7 v. Oldham, 1981-82

	App.	Tries	Goals	D/Gls	Pts
Agar, Allan	32	12	1	1	39
Bardgett,Joe	35	17	-	-	51
Birdsall, Charlie	33	6	-	1	19
Birts, Jimmy	5	1	8	-	19
Boyd, Denis	33	5	-	-	15
Brearley, Graham	4	1	-	-	3
Crowther, Ian	35	7	-	-	21
Davies, Steve	34	1	-	-	3
Evans, Graham	34	14	-	-	42
Ferres, Steve	33	6	111	2	242
Hollingsworth, Terry	26	3	-	-	9
James, Kevin	5	2	-	-	6
Limb, Barry	7	-	-	-	-
Morgan, Mick	35	25	-	-	75
Morgan, Terry	3	-	-	-	-
Raybould,Steve	17	1	-	-	3
Risman, John	5	-	-	-	-
Robinson, Graeme	25	8	-	-	24
Robinson, Kevan	20	7	-	-	21
Stephenson, Nigel	34	14	-	5	47
Thompson, Jimmy	21	1	-	-	3
Ward, Martyn	5	3	-	-	9
Youngman, Wally	31	10	-	-	30
TOTALS					
23 players		144	120	9	681

Allan Agar

1981-82 MATCH ANALYSIS

Date	Competition	Opponent	Result	Score	Tries	Goals	Attendance
16.8.81	LC(1)	Wigan	L	6-9	Evans	Ferres, Stephenson (dg)	2779
30.8.81	SD	Bramley	W	10-4	Evans, Morgan	Ferres, Stephenson (2dg)	
6.9.81	SD	Workington T.	L	6-23	Morgan	Ferres, Birdsall (dg).	5903
13.9.81	SD	Blackpool B.	W	11-7	Birdsall	Ferres (4)	
20.9.81	SD	Swinton	W	25-3	Agar (2), Crowther, Morgan,	Ferres (5)	2037
27.9.81	SD	Cardiff C.	L	7-12	Youngman K. Robinson	Ferres (2)	
4.10.81	SD	Batley	W	36-2	Morgan (2), K. Robinson (2), Boyd, Ferres, Evans, Stephenson	Ferres (6)	2104

Border City Blues

Date	Comp	Opponent	W/L	Score	Scorers	Goals	Att
11.10.81	SD	Hunslet	W	36-10	Stephenson (3), Evans (2), Birdsall, Brearley, Bardgett	Ferres (6)	2180
18.10.81	JP(1)	Cardiff C.	W	14-7	Youngman, Evans, Hollingsworth	Ferret (2), Stephenson (dg)	3224
25.10.81	SD	Doncaster	W	20-2	Agar (2), Evans, Morgan	Ferres (4)	
31.10.81	JP(2)	Widnes	L	10-16	Bardgett, Birdsall	Ferres (2)	
8.11.81	SD	Oldham	W	22-7	Crowther, Stephenson, Morgan	Ferres (6), Stephenson (dg)	
15.11.81	SD	Huddersfield	W	18-2	Crowther (2), Stephenson, G. Robinson	Ferres (3)	2807
22.11.81	SD	Batley	W	17-5	Crowther, Stephenson, Morgan	Ferres (3), Agar	
29.11.81	SD	Dewsbury	W	10-4	Evans, K. Robinson	Ferres (2)	
6.12.81	SD	Salford	W	21-18	Bardgett (2), Evans, Agar, Boyd	Ferres (3)	3107
17.1.82	SD	Keighley	W	9-3	Bardgett (2), Morgan		
24.1.82	SD	Rochdale H.	W	13-10	Hollingsworth, Morgan, Stephenson	Ferres (2)	
29.1.82	SD	Salford	W	19-7	K. Robinson (2), Morgan, Boyd, Bardgett	Ferres (2)	
7.2.82	SD	Doncaster	W	34-5	Agar (2), Birts, G. Robinson, Ward, Crowther, Morgan, Davies	Birts (5)	2583
14.2.82	CC(I)	Castleford	L	2-17	-	Birts	5452
21.2.82	SD	Halifax	W	20-0	Youngman, Evans, Bardgett, Raybould	Birts (2), Ferres (2)	2678
28.2.82	SD	Swinton	W	19-5	K. Robinson, Morgan, Ferres	Ferres (5)	
7.3.82	SD	Huddersfield	W	13-9	Birdsall, G. Robinson	Ferres (3, 1dg)	
14.3.82	SD	Blackpool B.	W	36-16	Morgan (2), Stephenson (2), Evans, Birdsall, Bardgett, G. Robinson	Ferres (6)	2498
21.3.82	SD	Keighley	W	28-5	Bardgett (2), Evans, Boyd, Agar, Hollingsworth	Ferres (5)	2668
26.3.82	SD	Rochdale H.	W	34-13	Agar (3), Morgan, Bardgett, G. Robinson, Youngman, Ferres	Ferres (5)	2793
28.3.82	SD	Huyton	W	30-13	Ward (2), Ferres, Youngman, Evans, Bardgett	Ferres (6)	2545
4.4.82	SD	Halifax	W	12-4	Morgan (2), Stephenson	Ferres, Agar (dg)	
9.4.82	SD	Cardiff C.	W	33.21	Morgan (2), Crowther, Agar, Stephenson, G. Robinson, Ferres	Ferres (6)	3232
11.4.82	SD	Huyton	W	19-5	Bardgett (3), G. Robinson (2)	Ferres (2)	
14.4.82	SD	Workington T.	L	15-23	Stephenson, James, Ferres	Ferres (3)	
18.4.82	SD	Bramley	W	25-10	Morgan (2), James, Bardgett, Youngman, Boyd, Thompson	Ferres (2)	2361
21.4.82	SD	Hunslet	W	14-8	Morgan, Youngman	Ferres (4)	
25.4.82	SD	Oldham	L	7-27	Morgan	Ferres (2)	5644
9.5.82	SD	Dewsbury	W	30-13	Youngman (3), Evans, Morgan, Stephenson, Birdsall	Ferres (4, 1dg)	2055

Above: An informal squad photo from 1981.
Back Row: Joe Bardgett, Jimmy Birts, Ian Crowther, Charlie Birdsall, Terry Kelly (timekeeper), Barry Limb
Middle Row: Wally Youngman, John Risman, Graham Evans, Jimmy Thompson, Allan Agar, Martyn Ward, Nigel Stephenson, Physio, Mick Morgan
Front Row: Asst. Kitman, Steve Ferres, Denis Boyd, Steve Raybould, Kitman

Left: Jimmy Thompson, Allan Agar, Mick Morgan and Nigel Stephenson in 1981

1981-82 SECOND DIVISION LEAGUE TABLE

	P	W	D	L	For Dg	Goals	Tries	Total	Agst Dg	Goals	Tries	Total	PTS
Oldham	32	30	-	2	2	147	146	734	11	71	41	276	60
Carlisle	32	28	-	4	7	114	138	649	8	66	52	296	56
Workington T	32	24	-	8	7	163	148	777	11	69	54	311	48
Halifax	32	22	-	10	19	97	101	516	12	68	64	340	44
Salford	32	20	1	11	-	130	132	656	10	78	89	433	41
Hunslet	32	18	1	13	4	102	91	481	11	87	89	452	37
Keighley	32	18	-	14	18	95	102	514	8	86	82	426	36
Cardiff C	32	17	1	14	7	110	113	566	11	116	102	549	35
Dewsbury	32	16	-	16	21	78	60	357	10	89	92	464	32
Swinton	32	15	-	17	13	102	99	514	10	81	82	418	30
Huddersfield	32	13	1	18	4	63	80	370	11	100	104	523	27
Bramley	32	13	-	19	6	66	81	381	8	104	99	513	26
Rochdale H	32	10	1	21	7	87	60	361	9	101	91	484	21
Batley	32	8	-	24	12	90	55	357	7	128	111	596	16
Blackpool B	32	7	-	25	5	54	76	341	7	116	123	608	14
Doncaster	32	5	1	26	17	76	50	319	4	147	165	793	11
Huyton	32	5	-	27	1	62	57	296	1	128	150	707	10

2

*

1982-83

THE summer close-season of 1982 was marked by money worries (partially alleviated by a very substantial written offer of £30,000 from Wakefield for Nigel Stephenson) and an ongoing debate re playing terms. There were numerous pleas to the RFL for financial assistance and, more positively, an approach from New Zealand offering the services of Dean Bell, his uncle Ian Bell, and cousin, Clayton Friend.

Dean was the unknown one when he arrived, while the serious signings were Ian (already an international with two caps to his credit) and Clayton, who had just achieved his first in a career total of 24 caps. Dean, of course, went on to enjoy a glittering international and domestic career with New Zealand, Leeds, Wigan and the Auckland Warriors. Clayton ended up joining his uncle Cameron Bell at Carlisle in 1990, before finishing his playing career with Whitehaven. Sadly, Ian died of cancer in 2003, having earlier settled in Newton-le-Willows, near St Helens.

Being young lads, work may as well have been the name

of a racehorse. They were found jobs in Andrew Jenkins's family business, Pioneer Foods, and at the soccer ground. Andrew still shakes his head at the recollection of the trio turning up for work in the refrigerated butchery department clad in shorts and flip-flops.

They were not without youthful cheek either as Andrew discovered upon buying them a Christmas tree for their Woodrouffe Terrace home in Carlisle, also provided by the club. They asked for some presents with which to adorn it!

Sports reporter Peter Hill recalls: 'When the Maori trio arrived from the other side of the world in 1982, they were a key part of strengthening the Carlisle squad before the club's one and only season in the top flight. And although they were new to the English game, they were already established big names in New Zealand. But their impact here extended far beyond their abilities on the field. These likeable mavericks made friends wherever they went and instantly felt at home in the Border City.'

Peter also recounts how, very often, it was hard to keep a straight face in the company of these three amiable young men who simply became known to everyone as the Kiwis. 'After they had spent about three months in the city, I interviewed them in the Caledonian pub on Botchergate – not exactly known as the Knightsbridge of the north – and I asked them what they thought of English rugby league and of Carlisle as a place,' remembers Peter. 'The Kiwis were not very big men by rugby league standards and had been taking some heavy hits against the likes of Wigan and St Helens, so I expected them to say they were finding it tough. Yet I was astonished when they said they found the English game soft. They explained that, in New Zealand, the first scrum of every match produced a mass brawl. The side who won the brawl usually won the match. By contrast, they found the English game rather polite.'

Likewise, the trio found the Botchergate pubs very genteel compared with those back home. For a start, women were allowed in pubs and beer was served in glasses instead of just drunk from crates piled on a table. The lads could not understand why there were so few fights. Fights broke out all the time in Auckland pubs. 'I could hardly believe what I was hearing,' says Peter, 'and thought they were winding me up. But I knew where they were coming from when I saw the film *Once Were Warriors*, which depicted the Maori way of life very graphically.'

The Kiwis, used to a culture where meat was cheap and plentiful, also astonished the locals with their prodigious appetites. Little Clayton Friend would often have a 'snack' of twelve lamb chops. If they ordered steak in a restaurant, one was never enough, so they asked for two or three. Every meal - even in Indian restaurants - was accompanied by a sidedish of six fried eggs each. Waiters gave them some very curious looks.

They also liked a beer - so much so that they had kegs of lager permanently on tap in their house near London Road. As a result, so many friends popped in that the house became known as the 'twenty-four-hour nightclub'. But the track-suited trio kept themselves fit and always made sure they were in good shape for matches.

And Peter Hill reveals how the late Ian Bell, brother of Cameron, was a skilful loose forward who had no respect for British traffic regulations. 'Ian was a lovely bloke,' says Peter, 'but he didn't like to be delayed when he was driving. He didn't see the point of traffic lights and simply drove through them, even when they were on red. I once shared a car with him and a couple of women, who screamed in terror every time Ian ignored a red light. He would leave his car right outside places such as the Twisted Wheel Club, even though no one was supposed to park there. He got loads of tickets, but I don't believe he ever paid any.[1] The Kiwis had this devil-may-care attitude as a result of their background. They were totally without malice and became good friends with many people in Carlisle. If you befriend a Maori you have a friend for life, but you wouldn't want one as an enemy.'

In July 1982, the inevitable happened and coach Allan Agar resigned. Agar had stated that survival in the First Division would be impossible without team-strengthening to the tune of £60,000. The cupboard was bare and owners Carlisle United, doubtless with an eye on the likely costs associated with their own survival in Division Two, declined his request.

The position of coach was given to Agar's assistant, Mick Morgan, while the assistant coach position was offered on a part-time basis to Jimmy Thompson, but he declined on account of work commitments. Steve Davis, Steve Ferres and Terry Hollingsworth joined Agar on the transfer list. Moving in the opposite direction, meanwhile, the club signed young goal-kicking amateur Andy Newton, together with Maurice Lucas and John Atkinson from Leeds, although, according to the minutes, there seems to have been a dispute among board members as to the latter's fitness.

John Sanderson from York and the three New Zealanders also signed in readiness for a new season that began hopefully enough with a narrow 10-7 home defeat to Wigan,

---

[1]Board member Don McDowall recalls a further anecdote regarding Ian Bell and Clayton Friend's devil-may-care attitude to British driving laws. 'On their second spell with Carlisle, I had to accompany both Ian and Clayton on separate occasions to the magistrates court, to answer drink-driving charges,' he says. 'On neither occasion did they have the money to pay the fine and the club had to step in. When they left, they both gave me their Maori tracksuits in lieu of parking fines incurred, in case the club was asked to settle these.'

in front of a 3,300 gate, a good attendance by lower league standards but woeful in the new higher division. Defeats away at Castleford and at home to Leeds followed before an optimism-inducing 16-8 victory at Brunton Park against Whitehaven, in front of 3,600 spectators.

An early highlight was reaching the semi-finals of the Lancashire Cup, where Carlisle managed a highly creditable 7-7 draw at St Helens. Less positively, that result saw the re-emergence of the argument over how to compute pay for an away-from-home draw, as it would again with monotonous regularity in the coming years. And the gate of 3,400 for the replay, which Carlisle lost narrowly by 9-5, whilst on the face of it not too bad, proved disappointing due to it having to be shared with the visitors.

Apart from some scintillating individual performances from Dean Bell in particular, who finished up with eleven tries, highlights were otherwise few and far between. Money problems, on the other hand, were always to the fore and prevented any further meaningful signings. Arguments with the club's owners, Carlisle United, were also close to the surface, especially when the main backer and proposer, chairman Jim Bendall, resigned from the rugby board. He was subsequently replaced by United's general manager, Colin Hutchinson.

As that wretched season wore on, disputes over finances and pitch concerns even forced the RL club to play a couple of home games in Yorkshire (versus Castleford and Bradford, at Wakefield and Huddersfield respectively). The logic behind such a move was that it would save on the travel and accommodation costs associated with bringing players to Carlisle, plus it held the prospect of increased gate revenue due to the matches being played in traditional rugby league areas.

Home gates, when they actually *were* played at home, fell

Above: The Horse and Farrier pub team, 1982-83. Back row: Tommy Jackson, Vic Hayhoe, Richard Edmondson, Peter Blackburn, Wilf Moorhead, David Armstrong, the late Ronnie Bowes, Brian Evans, Paul Lithgow, Tony Keyo. Middle Row: Raymond Hunter, 'Butch', Peter Mackay, Ken Laverick, the late Mally Norris, Stewart Hill, Tony Fell. Front row: Paul Kelton, Kevin Bell

away alarmingly to around 1,000, as the club registered just three league wins in the entire season before exiting Division One as rapidly as they entered it. Somewhat predictably, therefore, Mick Morgan left the club in the early months of 1983, to be replaced by John Atkinson.

As the season staggered to its inevitable and depressing conclusion, one of the few beneficial legacies was the formation of an amateur rugby league division in the city and the signing from it of the club's first local players, Steve Brierley from pub team Platform One and Paul Lithgow from the Horse and Farrier. Another lasting legacy was the capture of Hull-based Gary Peacham, a 23-year-old taxi driver. Gary - and, later, his brother Tony - would go on to play for Carlisle for several years. John Risman, signed from Fulham in another departure from the earlier Yorkshire player policy, afterwards took charge of the club's alliance team and remains an influential figure in the development of the game to this day, primarily with developing nations.

Steve 'Beast' Brierley remained a Carlisle favourite right to the end, too, and in fact still turns out occasionally for the amateur club, Centurions RLFC, alongside son Craig, an up-and-coming young half-back-cum-hooker. At 48 years of age, Steve, now a postman with the Royal Mail in Carlisle, is still a real handful with ball in hand. He tells an interesting tale about his recruitment in that fateful 1982-83 season.

'To us, in those days, rugby league was very much to do with the Carlisle drinking culture,' Steve reveals. 'We all belonged to our own pub-based social scene. Rugby league at Brunton Park became part of the Sunday afternoon drinking circuit. The pubs all shut at two o'clock on Sunday afternoons, so to carry on drinking and socialising involved a taxi to Gretna. That is, until the rugby started in 1981. All of a sudden we could just walk around to Brunton Park and drink and watch rugby all afternoon.'

Steve and his mates used to sit and take the mickey out of lads from other pubs. 'The Cally (Caledonian) lads would be at one table,' he recalls, 'with the Farrier (Horse and Farrier) lads at another, and the Scot (Border Scot) lads at yet another. We convinced ourselves that we could play this new-fangled game and that the Terrier lads could hammer the Farrier lads and so on. It was Rizzo [John Risman] who challenged us to form a sort of pub league and to play against each other. I played for Platform (Platform One Bar), and was spotted by the Carlisle Kiwi players and invited to Brunton Park, along with Paul Lithgow who was playing for the Horse and Farrier. To give me a crash course in how the game should be played, I was sent to play for Cockermouth ARL and then Workington's Alliance team.'

Steve must have impressed because by the end of that 1982-83 season he was given his debut and played the last seven games at number eleven ('I was quite fast then...') against the likes of St Helens, Castleford, Workington, Hull and Warrington. 'They were full games too,' he remembers, 'as the situation had deteriorated to the point where the struggle for numbers of players was everything. Injuries had to be really serious to excuse you from playing.'

Steve's Carlisle debut took place on 27th March 1983, when St Helens were the visitors. Carlisle were well beaten, 40-16, but Steve looked far from out of his depth and gained the following plaudit from *News and Star* reporter Peter Hill: 'Brierley held his own with a 34-minute stint and so made history as the first local player to represent the club.'

Steve continues: 'The older Leeds-based players were losing heart at the near certainty of losing-pay only and the club was looking to recruit from other areas, notably Hull. This was how we came to recruit Mick Sutton, Gary and Tony Peacham and Karl Portz. It also led, the following season, to the recruitment of Tony Scott, Dave Smith and Alan Todd from the West Cumbrian amateur scene. In those days I worked for Scott's Leather factory in Carlisle. I injured my knee ligaments at Barrow in 1983-84, was unable to work and was thus obliged, for fear of losing my job, to give up rugby until much later in the season. I actually went to play for Dalston ARLFC. When I eventually came back, the season was two-thirds over and I managed just twelve more games.'

Despite the start of the 'Cumbrianisation' of the club, the major factor in 1982-83 was the struggle for survival once Carlisle United FC effectively withdrew financial support. Scottish director Ron Cowan also resigned and it now fell to Geoff Holmes, George Graham and Colin Hutchinson to rally support. Geoff recalls that it all came to a head after the Lancashire Cup semi-final replay in September. Jim Bendall was bitterly disappointed at the 3,500 gate, and expressed the view that if this was the best the club could muster for a semi-final, then it had no hope and he was withdrawing financial support from the football club forthwith. Bendall further recommended that the club be liquidated. Given the state of the RL club's finances, he said, to carry on trading without the support of Carlisle United would leave the rugby league directors liable to prosecution.

At this, Holmes and Graham went into overdrive, announcing to the local media their intent to form a fighting fund. Immediate donations were received to the tune of £1,000 and this gave the two men enough confidence to attend a creditors meeting and persuade the creditors to hold back and give the club a chance. The Carlisle United board was also persuaded to maintain a semblance of support provided a nominal rent was paid and no further rugby league liabilities fell onto their shoulders. And so, from late 1982, the Carlisle RL club was cast adrift, with United's shares eventually going into a Supporters Trust - although the whereabouts and nature of that trust remains a mystery to this day.

As for the Rugby Football League in Leeds, it proved to be extremely supportive and advanced money that would have been due to the club at the end of the season anyway on an 'as-needed' basis, to ensure that the players were paid.

A public meeting was also convened at Brunton Park where, as is often the case on these occasions, there was an excellent turn-out, albeit of well-wishers who had little to offer but words, plus a heartening body of people willing and able to work on behalf of the game in general and the club in particular. One of those was Don McDowall, a keen supporter and planning officer on Carlisle city council. Don, who became chairman of the Carlisle RL Supporters Club and, later, a long-serving member of the club's board of directors, remembers it well.

He and council colleague Angus Kennedy went to the meeting together. They were both convinced that Carlisle Rugby League Club was a massive asset to the city and were determined to do their bit to save it. They volunteered to

Above: The Carlisle 1982-83 squad, pictured at Brunton Park. Back row: Steve Ferres, Wally Youngman, Graeme Robinson, John Risman, Andy Newton, Graham Evans. Middle Row: Jimmy Birts, Steve Raybould, Ian Bell, Kevan Robinson, Martyn Ward, Charlie Birdsall. Front row: Sammy Sanderson, Dean Bell, John Atkinson, Denis Boyd, Mick Morgan, Clayton Friend, Joe Bardgett

take an active role in the supporters club and weren't alone in that vision. Other such volunteers included newsagent Bob Rayson, ex-professional footballer Brian Tickell, and fans Alastair Goldie, Tony Braithwaite and Jean Pharaoh.

The very earliest task of this supporters' group was to establish a regular income-stream through a lottery that became known as the Thousand Club. This lottery quite quickly became established and, by the end of 1982, had already started to produce a regular income of several hundred pounds per week. It was a glimmer of light that grew in intensity as that grim season drew to a close.

Soon Don's abilities were recognised by Geoff Holmes who asked Don to join him on the actual board of the club. In 1983, they were joined by Dr Haworth GP (whose partner, the late Dr Tom Gardner, was at that time on the board of the soccer club). Then, Brian Whittaker, a keen Penrith-based supporter and, through his roofing business, active sponsor of the amateur league that had sprung up in those first couple of years, came in.

Back at the supporters club, meanwhile, a brave move was taken with which Don McDowall went along, despite his reservations. A lease was acquired from brewer Greenall Whitley for the Earl Gray pub on the corner of Botchergate and Rydal Street. The Earl Gray was, in essence, a failed pub when the supporters took possession of it. A previous tenant had tried to turn it into a gay bar called 'Casablanca'. Don recalls that the walls were adorned with murals of palm-trees and there were even huge drifts of sand on the floor. Soon, it was rather more prosaicly renamed Carlisle RL Supporters Club and, for a while, did become very popular, both as a pre and post-match venue for supporters and players alike. In its early days, at least, it was no quieter than other pubs at that end of town.

Personal memories of the place are of a pleasant enough venue that, once the initial novelty had worn off, became just another run-down and faded off-centre bar that suffered from lack of custom, other than on matchdays. When gameday came around, however, in the mid-to-late Eighties, the place was buzzing and much appreciated by all and sundry.

After a few short years, though, it sadly died the inevitable death that awaits such venues when there is neither the corporate management and capital investment nor bulk-buying power of the large chains to support it. Nearly twenty years on, after a couple of failed attempts to rejuvenate the place, this once busy but now forlorn building remains empty and boarded-up.

CARLISLE – 1982-83 – SEASON SUMMARY

Chairman:	George Graham
Coach:	Mick Morgan (July 1982-Feb 1983), John Atkinson (Feb 1983-)
Records:	Attendance: 5,903 v. Workington T. (Div 2) 6 Sept, 1981
Season	Goals: 113 by S. Ferres, 1981-82
	Tries: 25 by M. Morgan, 1981-82
	Points: 242 by S. Ferres, 1981-82
Match	Goals: No player has scored more than 6
	Tries: No player has scored more than 3
	Points: No player has scored more than 15
Highest score:	36-2 v. Batley, 1981-82, 36-10 v. Hunslet, 1981-82, 36-16 v. Blackpool B. 1981-82
	Highest against: 66-8 v. Castleford, 1982-83

	App.	Tries	Goals	D/Gls	Pts		App.	Tries	Goals	D/Gls	Pts
Agar, Allan	1	-	-	-	-	Netzler, Murray	2	-	-	-	-
Atkinson, John	18	3	-	-	9	Newton, Andy	21	1	33	-	69
Banks, Alan	6	-	-	-	-	Okulicz, Eddie	11	-	-	-	-
Bardgett, Joe	36	3	-	-	9	O'Rourke, Mick	4	-	-	-	-
Bell, Dean	23	11	-	-	22	Peacham, Gary	3	1	2	-	7
Bell, Ian	22	1	-	-	3	Penola, Colin	3	2	1	-	8
Birdsall, Charlie	23	-	5	-	10	Raybould, Steve	8	-	-	-	-
Birts, Jimmy	27	-	20	-	40	Risman, John	13	1	-	-	3
Boyd, Denis	12	-	-	-	-	Robinson, Graeme	4	-	-	-	-
Brierley, Steve	7	-	-	-	-	Robinson, Kevan	32	2	-	-	6
Crowther, Ian	20	2	-	-	6	Rowley, Allan	3	-	-	-	-
Evans, Graham	27	3	-	-	9	Sanderson, John	17	3	-	1	10
Ferres, Steve	28	5	4	-	23	Sutton, Mick	3	-	-	-	-
Friend, Clayton	20	3	-	-	9	Smith, Glen	1	-	-	-	-
Gaitley, Bob	14	-	-	-	-	Vickers, Dave	11	1	-	-	3
Glover, Alan	1	-	-	-	-	Warburton, Joe	7	1	-	-	3
Hobson, Ian	3	1	-	-	3	Ward, Martyn	11	-	-	-	-
Hollingsworth, Terry	10	-	-	-	-	Youngman, Wally	36	15	-	-	45
Limb, Barry	17	1	-	-	3	4 trialists	5	-	-	-	-
Lucas, Maurice	4	-	-	-	-						
Miller, Sean	6	-	-	1	1	**TOTALS**					
Morgan, Mick	22	3	-	-	9	44 Players		63	65	2	321

1982-83 MATCH ANALYSIS

Date	Competition	Opponent	Result	Score	Tries	Goals	Attendance
22.8.82	SLC	Wigan	L	7-10	Ferres	Birts (2)	3331
25.8.82	SLC	Castleford	L	18-20	Newton, D. Bell	Newton (6)	
29.8.82	SLC	Leeds	L	5-25	Risman	Newton	2724
5.9.82	LC(1)	Whitehaven	W	16-8	Bardgett, Friend	Newton (5)	3595
12.9.82	SLC	Hull K. R.	L	12-14	D. Bell (2)	Newton (3)	2833
15.9.82	LC(2)	Leigh	W	13-12	Sanderson (2), Youngman	Birts (2)	
19.9.82	SLC	Workington T.	L	10-25	Sanderson, Ferres	Birts (2)	
26.9.82	SLC	Barrow	L	11-12	D. Bell (2), Evans	Ferres	2747
29.9.82	LC(SF)	St. Helens	D	7-7	Friend	Newton (2)	
6.10.82	LC Replay	St. Helens	L	5-9	Evans	Newton	3406
10.10.82	SLC	Leeds	L	15-34	D. Bell (2), Ferres, Youngman	Birts, Sanderson (dg)	
17.10.82	SLC	Halifax	W	20-5	D. Bell (3), Ferret, Crowther, Morgan	Ferret	1966
24.10.82	SLC	Leigh	L	7-23	Limb	Birts (2)	2613
31.10.82	SLC	Oldham	L	14-17	Youngman, K. Robinson	Birts (4)	
7.11.82	SLC	Widnes	L	10-17	Youngman, Friend	Newton (2)	2201

Border City Blues

1982-83 MATCH ANALYSIS CONTINUED

Date	Competition	Opponent	Result	Score	Tries	Goals	Attendance
14.11.82	SLC	Hull	L	2-5	-	Newton	
21.11.82	SLC	Warrington	L	7-11	1. Bell	Newton (2)	
5.12.82	JP(1)	Doncaster	W	26-17	Youngman (3), Morgan (2), K. Robinson	Newton (4)	1413
12.12.82	JP(2)	Widnes	L	2-10	-	Birdsall	1905
26.12.82	SLC	Featherstone R.	L	10-20	D. Bell, Ferres	Birdcall (2)	
2.1.83	SLC	Featherstone R.	L	0-11	-	-	1410
9.1.83	SLC	Hull K.R.	L	3-25	Atkinson	-	
16.1.83	SLC	Bradford N.	L	7-15	Bardgett	Newton (2)	
15.2.83	CC(I)	St. Helens	L	0-52	-		
20.2.83	SLC	Oldham	W	16-3	Youngman (3), Vickers	Birts (2)	1390
27.2.83	SLC	Leigh	L	2-32		Bins	
6.3.83	SLC	Halifax	L	12-14	Crowther, Youngman	Birts (3)	
9.3.83	SLC	Widnes	L	0-52	-	-	
16.3.83	SLC	Wigan	l.	0-32	-	-	
20.3,83	SLC	Barrow	L	5-39	Peacham	Newton	
27.3.83	SLC	St. Helens	L	16-40	Atkinson (2), Youngman, Hobson	Peacham (2)	1500
3.4.83	SLC	Workington T.	L	13-30	Evans, Youngman	Birdcall (2), Ferres, Miller (dg)	1644
8.4.83	SLC	Castleford (At Wakefield)	L	8-66	Penola, Bardgett	Penola	1086
10.4.83	SLC	Hull	L	4-27	-	Newton (2)	1359
13.4.83	SLC	Warrington	L	8-33	Penola, Youngman	Newton	846
15.4.83	SLC	Bradford N. (At Huddersfield)	L	3-55	Warburton	-	1204
17.4.83	SLC	St. Helens	L	7-39	Youngman	Ferres, Birts	

1982-83 SLALOM LAGER CHAMPIONSHIP TABLE

	P	W	D	L	For Dg	Goals	Tries	Total	Agst Dg	Goals	Tries	Total	PTS
Hull	30	23	1	6	3	97	125	572	5	63	54	293	47
Hull KR	30	21	1	8	6	89	104	496	4	67	46	276	43
Wigan	30	20	3	7	5	90	99	482	5	50	55	270	43
St. Helens	30	19	1	10	14	89	108	516	3	79	78	395	39
Widnes	30	18	2	10	3	93	115	534	5	83	62	357	38
Leeds	30	18	2	10	2	86	102	480	7	92	84	443	38
Castleford	30	18	1	11	1	125	126	629	2	93	90	458	37
Oldham	30	15	2	13	3	77	63	346	2	75	56	320	32
Bradford N	30	14	2	14	8	80	71	381	7	59	63	314	30
Leigh	30	13	3	14	3	103	93	488	7	71	75	374	29
Warrington	30	13	2	15	3	99	74	423	3	82	81	410	28
Featherstone R	30	10	4	16	2	75	66	350	6	93	85	447	24
Barrow	30	11	1	18	3	89	97	472	1	90	108	505	23
Workington T	30	6	2	22	0	72	58	318	2	125	148	696	14
Halifax	30	5	1	24	6	55	35	221	4	112	141	651	11
Carlisle	30	2	0	28	2	50	50	252	1	135	160	751	4

46

3

✳

1983-84

THE bald statistics of the 83-84 season make grim reading. Carlisle's return to the Second Division resulted in fifteenth position in an eighteen-team league, just above the perennial basement clubs of that era, Huyton, Keighley and Doncaster. To make matters worse, closest rivals Workington Town who, like Carlisle, were relegated in 1983, finished in second place to book their own return to the top flight.

The Kiwi trio split up. Clayton Friend and Ian Bell hung around for a while but Dean Bell was snapped up by first division Leeds, where he went on to play twenty-two games before joining Australian club Eastern Suburbs for the 1985 season.

Dean, who enjoyed a most magnificent career with Easts, Leeds, Wigan and New Zealand before turning to coaching with Leeds and Wigan, is now a recruitment and development manager with the NZ Warriors club in Auckland, where he lives with his Carlisle-born wife Jackie and family. They still visit Carlisle from time to time to see Jackie's family in Harraby and Dean's sister Tracey, who has also settled to the west of the city with a family of her own.

When asked about those early days in England's north west, Dean reveals that Clayton's mum was a driving force behind the trio's arrival.

'Clayton's mum Cathy has always been heavily involved in League in Auckland and was on the committee of the main Auckland club at the time,' he says. 'She had a good contact in Dave Robinson, the chairman of the main sponsor of the Kiwis, a company called Autex. Being British, Dave had good contacts in the English game, had heard about the rapid rise of Carlisle and encouraged her to write to the club. Carlisle was also recommended to me by the NZ half-back Shane Varley, who was one of the first New Zealand players of that era to play over in England.

'Our time at Carlisle was a great opportunity to learn from playing alongside experienced people like Denis Boyd, Kevan Robinson, John Risman, Mick Morgan and company. We were never hammered in the First Division but really lacked that bit of polish to win tight games.

'It was also a great opportunity to be paid to see the other side of the world. We played hard too. The house provided for us in Woodrouffe Terrace became known as the best nightclub in Carlisle.

'It was a great time for me personally, as I met the woman who was to become my wife. It was very early on in our time there. She worked at Chapman's furniture store in the city centre. She later told me that she'd spotted the "Three Kiwis" strolling past in their green Maori tracksuits and fancied the blond one. We later met in the Kings Head and have been together since and married for twenty-six years.

'Another memory that sticks with me is the quality of the

playing surface at Brunton Park. It was far better than anything I'd been used to. It was like playing on a carpet.'

'I also remember our game against Leeds at Headingley. We lost but I had a good one and scored two tries. I think it was that game which caused Leeds to sign me in the New Zealand off-season, for the 83-84 English season. Another game that stands out was when we lost narrowly at home by 14-12 to a very good Hull KR.' Dean scored two tries in that game and Andy Newton kicked three goals.

Of more recent Carlisle players, Dean recalls Barry Williams from a testimonial game at Derwent Park. 'The boy had everything,' he says, 'athleticism, speed, power, skill the lot. I'd have snapped him up for Leeds like a shot, but he didn't want to leave West Cumbria.'

In 1983, training was still held in Yorkshire but was now switched to Eastmoor ARL ground in Wakefield, deemed to be more appropriate to Carlisle's needs at that time.

The club though remained heavily dependent on travelling players, mainly from the Leeds area, with a couple of notable recruits from Humberside in Karl Portz and Gary Peacham. A trickle of locals was beginning to come through. Tony Scott signed from Broughton Red Rose and David Smith (these days doing great work in drugs counselling) came from West Cumbria. Steve Brierley also returned late that season after recuperating with Dalston ARL from his ligament tear.

Outside the professional game, the Carlisle and District Amateur League was going from strength to strength and already comprised ten teams. The league had been affiliated into the Cumbrian division of BARLA, the amateur game's ruling body, who were imposing some order on the somewhat anarchic club affairs under the wise combined leadership of the newly-elected Carlisle League chairman John Risman and its player-secretary Andy Hodgkinson.

Reproduced below is the final league-table for that season[1]:

	P	W	D	L	F	A	Pts
Aspatria	16	16	-	-	829	152	32
Horse & Farrier	16	13	1	2	802	188	27
Caledonian	16	12	1	3	549	146	25
Platform One	16	7	2	7	536	336	16
Morton	16	7	1	8	378	328	15
Wigton	16	7	1	8	418	377	15
Board Inn	16	5	-	11	322	616	10
Friars Tavern	16	2	-	14	182	812	4
Malt Shovel	16	-	-	16	79	1130	0

The pro club's match-day programme developed a cult-following due to Frank Moor's quiz page. Frank, a colleague at Kangol Magnet in the city and father of future *News and Star* RL reporter Gareth Moor, was a 'star' of TV quiz shows with several major prizes to his credit. His quiz page enlivened many a half-time break. Sadly, Frank passed away very prematurely after our first few seasons at Gillford Park.

In November of that year a further keynote signing was made when Geoff Holmes captured the signature of young rugby union player Steve Langton, from Bradford and Bingley RUFC. Langton, who went on to form a devastating partnership with Steve (Rip) Kirby in later years (said by coach Roy Lester to have been rehearsed over the phone, as one lived in Yorkshire, the other lived in Barrow and neither of them trained) was an immediate hit and ever-present for the rest of that season, with seven tries to his credit.

Also that month, the Carlisle Supporters Club took the ambitious step of hosting the Slalom Lager League Roadshow at Harraby Catholic Club. It was a memorable

[1]Peter Hill, the Carlisle *Evening News and Star* RL reporter, exhibited a cruel streak in his nature when he congratulated the Malt Shovel on their improvement in form when they went down 72-2 to Aspatria after losing 126-0 to the Horse and Farrier in their previous game.

night full of comedy and fund-raising by all accounts and it featured the appearance of the Challenge Cup

In January, the loan arrangement with Hull for Karl Portz was formalised into a permanency, on payment of a £1,500 transfer fee. That brought the complement of ex-Hull players to six, with Ian Crowther and Graham Evans signed on the club's formation, Bob Gaitley signed in 1982-83 and Mick Sutton and Gary Peacham signed at the start of the 1983-84 season.

In March, as the club faced massive fixture congestion due to rearrangement of January's weather-hit games, Carlisle stumbled to an 58-18 reverse at Craven Park, Barrow. This defeat, other than a John Player Special 2nd round 68-17 loss to first division Leigh at Hilton Park in November, was the worst of the season. Ever the black-humourist, Peter Hill responded to Geoff Holmes's platitude that 'it was one to learn from' with the immortal line that his 'optimism in these dark days is the equivalent of General Custer cracking jokes at the Battle of Little Big Horn'.

With the season as good as dead, Carlisle demonstrated a perversity still common in the game at the dog-end of a bad season when results are largely immaterial - a minor rally with five wins out of eleven fixtures in the last crowded weeks of April and May. This ensured that Geoff Holmes and his board had the headache of finding five lots of winning bonus in just two months out of rock-bottom gates!

There were only two players with a tally of tries into double figures in that wretched season - Wally Youngman had fourteen and new boy Gary Peacham twenty.

One can imagine the mixed feelings in the boardroom when that season finally closed with a 25-22 win over Hunslet, in front of just 400 brave souls at Brunton Park. It was left to Geoff Holmes to figure out how to meet a three-

Left: Carlisle chairman
Geoff Holmes in 1983

game wage bill out of a sub-£1,000 gate. Nevertheless, despite the apparent bleakness of the outlook, there were several good things to come out of an otherwise miserable campaign:

- Penrith-based Brian Whittaker's sponsorship of the Carlisle and District Amateurs had put the spotlight on the amateur game in the city to the benefit of all players and the pro club.
- Brian was about to join the board and, in 1984-85, he became influential with John Risman in establishing a reserve or Alliance team, Carlisle-Penrith, playing out of Penrith FC's Southend Road ground.
- Two other new clubs, Mansfield and Sheffield were spawned. Mansfield soon afterwards disappeared, but the game remains as strong as ever in Nottingham, most certainly not a traditional RL area, with an amateur club Nottingham Outlaws currently a major force in the Co-operative RLC National Division.
- The small nucleus of Cumbrian players at the club who had begun to be noticed elsewhere in Cumbria were soon to be joined by others.

CARLISLE – 1983-84 – SEASON SUMMARY

Ground:	Brunton Park
Chairman:	Geoff Holmes
Coach:	John Atkinson (Feb 1983-)
Records:	Attendance: 5,903 v. Workington T. (Div 2) 6 Sept, 1981
Season:	Goals: 113 by S. Ferres, 1981-82
	Tries: 25 by M. Morgan, 1981-82
	Points: 242 by S. Ferres, 1981-82
Match	Goals: No player has scored more than 6
	Tries: No player has scored more than 3
	Points: No player has scored more than 15
	Highest Score: 38-16 v. Doncaster, 1983-84
	Highest against: 68-17 v. Leigh, 1983-84

	App.	Tries	Goals	D/Gls	Pts
Armitage, Des	6 + 5	1	-	-	4
Atkinson, John	2	1	-	-	4
Bell, Ian	4	-	-	-	-
Binder, Tony	33	7	-	-	28
Birts, Jimmy	14 + 1	2	-	-	8
Brierley, Steve	12 + 5	-	-	-	-
Crowther, Ian	30	2	-	-	8
Evans, Graham	9 + 4	3	-	-	12
Ferres, Steve	13	1	21	2	48
Friend, Clayton	2 + 1	1	-	-	4
Gaitley, Bob	18 + 2	2	25	1	59
Hardy, Alan	13	-	-	4	4
Hobson, Ian	11 + 6	8	-	-	32
Langton, Steve	20 + 1	7	-	-	28
Limb, Barry	4 + 1	-	-	-	-
Lucas, Maurice	5	1	-	-	4
McDonald, Ian	11	6	-	-	24
Miller, Sean	23 + 3	1	-	-	4
Newton, Andy	15 + 1	2	27	-	62

	App.	Tries	Goals	D/Gls	Pts
Peacham, Gary	36	20	-	-	4
Pearson, Alan	1 + 2	-	3	-	6
Portz, Karl	32 + 4	2	-	-	8
Risman, John	19 + 4	3	-	-	12
Robinson, Brian	3 + 6	1	-	-	4
Robinson, Graeme	32 + 2	1	7	2	20
Robinson, Kevan	33	5	-	-	20
Sanderson, John	9 + 2	3	-	-	12
Scott, Tony	0 + 1	-	-	-	-
Smith, David	4	-	4	-	8
Starbuck, Paul	0 + 2	-	-	-	-
Sutton, Mick	32 + 1	3	-	1	13
Tissiman, Les	9 + 9	1	-	-	4
Todd, Alan	0 + 1	-	-	-	-
Ward, Martyn	7 + 4	3	-	-	12
Youngman, Wally	32	14	-	-	56
TOTALS					
35 players		101	87	10	588

1983-84 MATCH ANALYSIS

Date	Competition	Opponent	Result	Score	Tries	Goals	Attendance
21.8.83	SD	Workington T.	L	10-36	Youngman, Atkinson	Ferres	2613
28.8.83	SD	Keighley	L	14-18	Youngman	Ferres (5)	-
4.9.83	LC(1)	Leigh	L	10-52	Peacham, Newton	Ferres	-
10.9.83	SD	Cardiff C.	L	16-21	Peacham, Binder, Robinson	Ferres (2)	-
18.9.83	SD	Batley	W	21-14	Youngman, Ferres, Risman	Newton (4), Ferres (dg)	931
25.9.83	SD	Halifax	L	16-25	Youngman, Newton, Binder	Newton (2)	-
5.10.83	SD	Dewsbury	L	30-39	Hobson, Miller, Gaitley, Evans, Binder	Newton (5)	-
9.10.83	SD	Bramley	L	6-22	Tissiman	Newton	912
16.10.83	SD	Swinton	L	4-22	Youngman	-	-
23.10.83	SD	Hunslet	L	13-28	Peacham, Lucas	Ferres (2, 1 dg)	
30.10.83	SD	Rochdale H.	L	22-24	Peacham, G. Robinson, Sanderson	Ferres (5)	725
6.11.83	JPS(1)	Workington T.	W	10-5	Youngman, Risman	Ferres	1297
13.11.83	SD	Kent Invicta	L	12-28	Youngman, Hobson	Ferres (2)	
20.11.83	JPS(2)	Leigh	L	17-68	Risman, Youngman, Langton	Ferres (2), Sutton (dg)	2152

Border City Blues

1983-84 MATCH ANALYSIS CONTINUED

Date	Competition	Opponent	Result	Score	Tries	Goals	Attendance
27.11.83	SD	Huddersfield	W	15-6	Sutton, Langton	Newton (3), Robinson (dg)	687
4.12.83	SD	Batley	L	15-22	Birts, Langton, Hobson	G. Robinson (1, 1 dg)	-
18.12.83	SD	Rochdale H.	W	14-10	Friend, Langton	Newton (3)	-
26.12.83	SD	Workington T.	L	4-11	-	Newton (2)	-
5.2.84	CC(P)	Widnes	L	12-20	Portz, Sutton	Newton (2)	1271
19.2.84	SD	Huddersfield	W	14-10	Hobson, Peacham	Newton (3)	-
26.2.84	SD	Halifax	L	10-12	Ward, Youngman	Newton	883
4.3.84	SD	Swinton	L	4-26	Binder		804
11.3.84	SD	Doncaster	W	14-5	Gaitley, B. Robinson, Evans	Gaitley	524
18.3.84	SD	Barrow	L	18-58	Youngman, Peacham, Sanderson	Gaitley (3)	-
23.3.84	SD	Blackpool B.	W	16-14	Armitage, Evans	Gaitley (4)	452
25.3.84	SD	Huyton	W	27-26	McDonald (2), Crowther, Pearson (3), Hardy (dg) Peacham, Langton		447
28.3.84	SD	Barrow	L	8-43	McDonald, Peacham	-	599
1.4.84	SD	York	L	24-26	Peacham (2), Birts, McDonald	Gaitley (3), Newton	350
4.4.84	SD	York	L	6-50	Sutton	G. Robinson	-
8.4.84	SD	Doncaster	W	38-16	Bind (2), Peacham (2), Youngman, Sanderson, Hobson	Gaitley (5)	-
10.4.84	SD	Huyton	L	10-17	McDonald, Langton	Gaitley	-
13.4.84	SD	Keighley	W	29-19	Peacham (2) K. Robinson (2), Portz	Gaitley (4, 1 dg)	437
15.4.84	SD	Cardiff C.	W	14-10	Hobson (2)	G. Robinson (2), Hardy (2 dg)	649
20.4.84	SD	Bramley	L	18-22	Peacham, Langton, K. Robinson	G. Robinson (3)	-
22.4.84	SD	Kent Invicta	W	34-12	Peacham (3), Youngman (2), K. Robinson, Hobson	Smith (3)	870
26.4.84	SD	Blackpool B.	L	18-47	McDonald, Binder, Youngman, Peacham	Gaitley	-
29.4.84	SD	Dewsbury	L	0-19	-	-	500
2.5.84	SD	Hunslet	W	25-22	Ward (2), Crowther, Peacham	Gaitley (3), Smith, Hardy (dg)	

1983-84 SECOND DIVISION TABLE

	P	W	D	L	For Dg	For Goals	For Tries	For Total	Agst Dg	Agst Goals	Agst Tries	Agst Total	PTS
Barrow	34	32	0	2	12	165	196	1126	8	48	57	332	64
Workington T	34	24	2	8	8	107	123	714	18	89	77	504	50
Hunslet	34	24	0	10	10	151	147	900	15	107	92	597	48
Halifax	34	23	2	9	22	108	121	722	13	91	86	539	48
Blackpool B	34	20	3	11	15	96	102	615	10	74	77	466	43
Swinton	34	21	0	13	20	116	128	764	11	67	73	437	42
York	34	19	2	13	7	122	123	743	14	100	89	570	40
Bramley	34	16	2	16	12	94	96	584	23	83	89	545	34
Kent Invicta	34	17	0	17	11	90	101	595	18	111	115	700	34
Huddersfield	34	15	3	16	10	79	108	600	17	96	84	545	33
Cardiff C	34	15	1	18	28	107	117	710	17	118	116	717	31
Rochdale H	34	13	3	18	25	101	81	551	11	116	106	667	29
Batley	34	13	0	21	11	77	78	477	22	108	125	738	26
Dewsbury	34	12	0	22	8	85	87	526	16	99	121	698	24
Carlisle	34	12	0	22	9	81	92	539	16	116	133	780	24
Huyton	34	9	2	23	19	66	70	431	10	105	135	760	20
Keighley	34	7	3	24	13	74	66	425	12	106	126	728	17
Doncaster	34	2	1	31	14	63	61	384	3	148	196	1083	5

4

*

1984-85

THERE was much closed-season activity in the summer of 1984. John Graham joined from Workington Town. Future Carlisle try-scoring record-holder Kevin Pape signed from Glasson Rangers ARLC. Alan Hardy signed from Castleford. Dave Smith's move from Town was formalised. George Graham resigned from the board to be replaced as chairman by Geoff Holmes. Brian Whittaker joined the board with special responsibility, along with John Risman, for the alliance team in Penrith.

The Cumbrian trickle became a flood as the season commenced, with Mark Doyle (Smiths RUFC), Chris Bowness and Alan McMullen (also ex-RU), Colin Armstrong (Broughton Red Rose ARLC) and Harry Beverley (Blackpool Borough RLFC) all joining. Steve Ferres, who went to Batley, was the most notable pre-season departure.

By November, the club had no less than twelve Cumbrian players on its books in John Risman, Alan Thompson (on loan ex-Whitehaven), Kevin Pape, John

Graham, Mark Doyle, Gary Bond, Harry Beverley, Chris Bowness, Graeme Phillips, Colin Armstrong, Alan McMullen and David Smith. Steve Brierley was temporarily back in the amateur game.

In addition to Cumbrian players, the club also recruited Cockermouth-based former Cockermouth, Seaton and Ellenborough ARLFC player Vic Semple as sponge-man and assistant physio. Vic, who was a water-bailiff in his full-time occupation, went on to stay with the club until 1995, when he was an unfortunate casualty of the enforced cutbacks at that time.

Vic went on to similar roles with Workington Town and Whitehaven, where he is still an indispensible part of the backroom staff. Vic also acted in a similar position with the Scottish national team for many years. More recently, he enjoyed the rare distinction for an Englishman of helping the Kiwi police team in New Zealand and Australia in an on-field capacity as assistant physio and sponge-man. Though now retired, Vic still resides in Cockermouth and is fondly remembered by former Carlisle directors, staff and ex-players alike for his devotion to duty and invariable good humour.

The 1984-85 season began brightly on 3rd September with a 31-15 win over Doncaster at Brunton Park. Gary Peacham scored three fine tries to confirm his promise of the previous season. The other new arrival, Kevin Pape, also opened his account with David Smith (two goals), Colin Armstrong (one goal) and Alan Hardy (one drop-goal) adding the extras. The 900 gate was considered reasonable for such lowly visitors. Next up was Keighley at Lawkholme Lane, who were shaded 21-19 with Pape and Peacham again getting over the line.

Then came a visit to newly-promoted Barrow in the first round of the Lancashire Cup. The higher division

Shipbuilders ran riot against the upstarts from North Cumbria as Les Quirk (two tries), Tony Rea (two tries), Mark Fitzgerald, Ralph McConnell and David Clough all crossed the whitewash, added to by five goals from Ian Ball. The Furness side strolled home 38-4 in front of an enviable 2,500 gate.

A 48-18 win in October against Fulham at their new Crystal Palace venue was a bitter blow for the league's other new boys, as they too were bent on rebuilding hope and prestige after a near-death experience of their own.

At this point Carlisle were really flying, with centres Peacham and Pape scoring at will and, by Christmas, were in the top half of their division, with twelve league wins from fourteen outings. In fact, the only league losses were on Boxing Day at Whitehaven in front of a near-3,000 gate and, mystifyingly, in November at Runcorn's Canal Street ground, when they lost 24-13 in front of a typically sparse Merseyside crowd of 380.

That festive defeat to Haven at the Recre sparked a slump in Carlisle's fortunes and they lost nine of their remaining fifteen games. Nonetheless, the club did finish in a very creditable fifth in a twenty-team division.

Despite the vastly improved playing form, attendances continued to disappoint after that first-year euphoria. Only 550 spectators turned out for the Easter Monday home game against Salford for example. The programme editor asked the pertinent question in his leader article: 'Where are the missing 2,500 spectators?' It was a question destined to be asked at regular intervals over the following three years at Brunton Park too, putting the lie to the boring old mantra that if only we'd stayed there instead of moving to Gillford Park in 1988, gates would have been okay.

Kevin Pape, who, along with wife Helen, is a successful shop and warehouse-owner living in a house overlooking the Solway Firth at Flimby near Maryport, remembers that season well.

'I'd recently returned from a 1982 BARLA tour of Australia and Papua New Guinea,' recalls Kevin. 'My ambition had been to sign for Workington Town but they said I wasn't fast enough. Whitehaven might have been an alternative but I always liked to be different, so when John Risman and Geoff Holmes approached me I decided on Carlisle. I think the signing-on fee was into five figures, paid over a couple of years. I played in the pre-season friendly against Workington Town, scored two tries against the team that had said I wasn't fast enough and went straight into the First Team.'

Kevin went on to a glittering ten-year career at Carlisle, playing in 320 games and scoring 186 tries.

'Towards the end of my career, Carlisle seemed to be going nowhere so I decided on a change,' he continues. 'My original thought was to join Whitehaven, but when Workington, at that time in the First Division, showed interest through Peter Walsh, their coach, I decided to pitch in my lot and show them what the lad who "wasn't fast enough" could do. I thoroughly enjoyed my couple of seasons at Workington playing at the highest level against clubs like St Helens, Leeds and Bradford. I proved to myself that I wasn't out of place in that company.'

Like a lot of players from that era, Kevin is quite scathing about the low numbers of quality players now coming through the amateur ranks in West Cumbria. He also feels that the only realistic opportunity of a Super League spot in the area was lost when Workington and Whitehaven declined to merge way back in the mid-90s. He believes that the easy money offered to footballers whose biggest injury risk is a twisted ankle from a badly-executed dive is also a factor in the decline of amateur rugby league.

Looking back on his long career, Kevin recounts the team of his era that was most memorable to him. It includes: 'Dean Carroll at scrum-half. Stevie Langton at stand-off. Gary Peacham in the other centre position and Mark Doyle on the wing. One game that stands out in my memory is when we drew away at Rochdale in the first round of the Challenge Cup in 1987 and then trounced them at Brunton Park in the replay. I got four tries in that game.' Carlisle did indeed draw 4-4 at Rochdale on 4th February of that year and then won 30-22 at Brunton Park the following week, before crashing out at Leigh, 18-6, a few days later.

Kevin played under six coaches in his career, namely John Atkinson, Alan Kellett, Roy Lester, Tommy Dawes, Cameron Bell and Paul Charlton. 'Alan Kellett, in his half-season spell, got the most out of the players,' he says now. 'Cameron Bell, as well as bringing some quite superb players to Carlisle, was a great coach. Some of the things he had us doing were unbelievable, such as the player taking a tap-penalty by kicking it over his head and behind the opposition to catch them off-guard. Another of his innovations was the flying wedge, a rugby league version of rugby union's rolling maul, but with one player holding the ball while being propelled downfield by the pack. Another of his ideas that some Super League sides have since adopted was to play a prop in the stand-off position in defence.

'Of all the players Cameron brought over, the most outstanding was Clayton Friend, but others who stick in my mind include Steve Georgallis, Kevin Denton and Hitro Okesene. And Barry Williams. Barry, in my opinion, was the best talent around in Cumbria at that time. He could have played at the very highest level if he'd so wished. An awesome talent, Barry had everything. Speed, great footwork, a superb kicking game, strength and a footballing brain to cap it off.'

When asked which of the 300-plus games he played in Carlisle colours most stick in his mind, Kevin replies: 'The derbies with Workington and Whitehaven. They were brilliant to play in.'

Happily, the amateur game continued to run strongly in 1984-85, although Aspatria, Dalston and Wigton had now joined the Cumberland League and were fielding second-string sides in the Carlisle and District.

1984-85 - CARLISLE & DISTRICT A.R.L. – FINAL PLACINGS

	P	W	D	L	F	A	Pts
Horse & Farrier	16	15	0	1	730	177	30
Morton	16	12	0	4	537	209	24
Caledonian	16	10	3	3	461	255	23
Wigton 'A'	16	8	2	6	353	372	18
Platform One	16	8	1	7	570	404	17
Dalston 'A'	16	5	2	9	347	326	12
Aspatria 'A'	16	5	2	9	362	422	12
Friars Tavern	16	2	0	14	233	746	4
Crown & Mitre Pioneers	16	2	0	14	236	918	4

Milestones in that season included:
- A loan deal with Bradford which saw Carlisle obtain the services of scrum-half Dean Carroll. This deal was recommended to Geoff Holmes by ex-Castleford player Alan Hardy, a relative of Dean's.
- The transfer to Carlisle of £25,000-listed England international Milton Huddart from Whitehaven
- The debut of Tony Peacham, brother of Gary, in March 1985
- Signing of wing man John Stockley from Blackpool Borough
- John Risman won the prestigious *Open Rugby* Courvoisier Cognac Sportsmanship Award for the month of April

Above: Don McDowall, Geoff Holmes and Dr Haworth enjoy a quiet drink together in 1984

- Gary Peacham equalled Mick Morgan's twenty-five tries in a season record that had been set in 1981-82
- Kevin Pape was an ever-present with nineteen tries to his credit
- Dean Carroll celebrated his transfer on loan from Bradford by setting a new seven-goals-in-a-match record in December's 42-8 victory at Doncaster

Border City Blues

CARLISLE – 1984-85 – SEASON SUMMARY

Chairman:	Geoff Holmes
Coach:	John Atkinson (Feb 1983-)
Records:	Attendance: 5,903 v. Workington T. (Div 2) 6 Sept, 1981
Season	Goals: 113 by S. Ferres, 1981-82
	Tries: 25 by M. Morgan, 1981-82, G. Peacham, 1984-85
	Points: 242 by S. Ferres, 1981-82
Match	Goals: 7 by D. Carroll v Doncaster, 23 Dec. 1984
	Tries No player has scored more than 3
	Points: No player has scored more than 15
	Highest Score: 47-18 v Fulham, 1984-85.
	Highest against: 68-17 v Leigh, 1983-84

	App.	Tries	Goals	D/Gls	Pts
Armstrong, Colin	6 + 4	1	5	-	- 14
Beverley, Harry	2 + 2	-	-	-	-
Binder, Tony	25	-	-	-	-
Bond, Gary	0 + 1	-	-	-	-
Bowness, Chris	14	2	-	-	8
Carroll, Dean	19	3	50	2	114
Crowther, Ian	17	-	-	-	-
Dobie, John	0 + 2	-	-	-	-
Doyle, Mark	16 + 1	4	-	-	16
Gaitley, Bob	0 + 2	-	-	-	-
Graham, John	1 + 1	1	-	-	4
Hardy, Alan	24	-	4	16	24
Huddart, Milton	9	2	-	-	8
Langton, Steve	24	7	3	-	34
Lithgow, Paul	1 + 4	-	-	-	-
Lucas, Maurice	4 + 7	1	-	-	4
McMullen, Alan	11 + 3	-	-	-	-
Miller, Sean	4	-	-	-	-

	App.	Tries	Goals	D/Gls	Pts
Pape, Kevin	31	19	-	-	76
Peacham, Gary	31	25	-	-	100
Peacham, Tony	1 + 3	-	-	-	-
Portz, Karl	29	5	-	-	20
Phillips, Graeme	0 + 5	-	-	-	-
Robinson, Graeme	22 + 3	2	6	-	20
Robinson, Kevan	25	6	-	-	24
Sanderson, John	8 + 1	1	-	-	4
Scott, Tony	11 + 3	-	-	-	-
Smith, David	16 + 5	1	13	-	30
Stockley, John	7	2	-	-	8
Sutton, Mick	22	6	-	1	25
Thomas, Mike	0 + 2	-	-	-	-
Youngman, Wally	23	8	-	-	32

TOTALS

	App.	Tries	Goals	D/Gls	Pts
32 Players		96	81	19	565

1984-85 MATCH ANALYSIS

Date	Competition	Opponent	Result	Score	Tries	Goals	Attendance
2.9.84	SD	Doncaster	W	31-15	Peacham (3), K. Robinson (2), Pape	Smith (2), Armstrong, Hardy (dg)	900
9.9.84	SD	Keighley	W	21-19	Pape, Bowness, Youngman, Peacham	Smith, G. Robinson, Hardy (dg)	-
16.9.84	LC (1)	Barrow	L	4-38	Pape	-	-
23.9.84	SD	Mansfield M.	L	14-19	Portz, G. Robinson	G. Robinson (3)	-
30.9.84	SD	Blackpool B.	W	8-6	Doyle, Peacham	-	980
6.10.84	SD	Fulham	W	47-18	Langton (2), Peacham (2), Portz, Pape, Youngman, K. Robinson	Smith (3), Langton (3), Hardy (1, 1 dg)	-
14.10.84	SD	Salford	W	19-12	Peacham, Sutton, Portz	Hardy (2, 3 dg)	-
21.10.84	SD	Rochdale H.	W	25-10	Pape (2), Langton, Peacham, Youngman	Hardy (1, 1 dg), G. Robinson	1048
28.10.84	SD	Batley	W	18-17	Portz, Doyle, Smith	Smith (3)	-
4.11.84	SD	Runcorn H.	L	13-24	Langton, Peacham	Smith (2), Hardy (dg)	-
7.11.84	JPS(P)	Bradford N.	L	8-26	Peacham	Smith (2)	1215
11.11.84	SD	Swinton	W	15-14	Pape, Peacham	Carroll (3), Hardy (dg)	1224
25.11.84	SD	Blackpool B.	W	24-16	Pape (2), Langton, Sutton	Carroll (3), G. Robinson	-

1984-85 MATCH ANALYSIS CONTINUED

Date	Competition	Opponent	Result	Score	Tries	Goals	Attendance
9.12.84	SD	Bridgend	W	28-0	Pape (2), Peacham, Doyle, Youngman	Carroll (4)	-
16.12.84	SD	Runcorn H.	W	29-10	Peacham (2), Langton, Carroll, Youngman	Carroll (4), Hardy (dg)	1200
23.12.84	SD	Doncaster	W	42-8	Peacham (2), Portz, Pape, Doyle, Youngman, Sutton	Carroll (7)	-
26.12.84	SD	Whitehaven	L	8-20	Pape	Carroll (1, Idg), Hardy (dg)	-
3.2.85	SD	Swinton	L	10-38	Peacham, Langton	Carroll	-
14.2.85	CC(1)	Hull	L	6-52	K. Robinson	Carroll	-
24.2.85	SD	Dewsbury	L	19-28	Sutton, Bowness	Carroll (5), Hardy (dg)	-
3.3.85	SD	Batley	W	18-16	Pape, Peacham, Huddart	Carroll (3)	1000
10.3.85	SD	Sheffield E.	L	11-16	Pape, Youngman	Carroll, Hardy (dg)	-
17.3.85	SD	Keighley	L	14-25	Peacham (2), Youngman	Carroll	1200
24.3.85	SD	Sheffield E.	W	32-16	Pape (2), Peacham (2), Stockley, Sanderson	Armstrong (4)	900
27.3.85	SD	Mansfield M.	W	25-8	K. Robinson (2), Carroll, Pape	Carroll (4), Hardy (dg)	750
5.4.85	SD	Whitehaven	W	5-2	-	Carroll (2), Sutton (dg)	1800
14.4.85	SD	Rochdale H.	W	14-13	Sutton, Peacham	Carroll (3)	-
17.4.85	SD	Fulham	L	10-14	Stockley, Huddart	Carroll	850
21.4.85	SD	Dewsbury	L	18-19	Lucas, Pape, Armstrong	Carroll (2), Hardy (2dg)	700
24.4.85	SD	Salford	L	17-28	Sutton, Carroll, G. Robinson	Caroll (2, 1dg)	550
28.4.85	SD	Bridgend	W	12-6	Peacham, Graham	Carroll (2)	700

1984-85 SECOND DIVISION TABLE

	P	W	D	L	For Dg	For Goals	For Tries	For Total	Agst Dg	Agst Goals	Agst Tries	Agst Total	PTS
Swinton	28	24	1	3	11	100	129	727	13	49	58	343	49
Salford	28	20	3	5	9	117	136	787	15	57	51	333	43
York	28	21	1	6	5	118	119	717	4	75	69	430	43
Dewsbury	28	21	1	6	13	91	86	539	14	57	48	320	43
Carlisle	28	19	0	9	20	81	94	558	12	73	67	426	38
Whitehaven	28	16	3	9	6	71	87	496	15	63	61	385	35
Batley	28	17	0	11	11	77	81	489	12	65	65	402	34
Fulham	28	16	1	11	7	83	87	521	10	82	88	526	33
Mansfield M	28	15	0	13	15	73	91	525	14	70	61	398	30
Blackpool B	28	15	0	13	18	66	84	486	6	64	75	434	30
Wakefield T	28	12	2	14	12	67	76	450	9	67	79	459	26
Rochdale H	28	12	2	14	8	68	73	436	8	75	77	466	26
Huddersfield B	28	12	1	15	16	68	81	476	16	80	75	476	25
Runcorn H.	28	11	1	16	24	85	67	462	20	69	95	538	23
Keighley	28	11	0	17	8	78	80	484	8	91	97	578	22
Bramley	28	9	2	17	9	67	74	439	14	81	79	492	20
Sheffield E	28	8	0	20	6	65	72	424	12	91	97	582	16
Doncaster	28	6	2	20	11	65	53	353	6	102	130	730	14
Southend I	28	4	0	24	9	49	60	347	12	103	118	690	8
Bridgend	28	1	0	27	8	53	36	258	6	128	176	966	2

Border City Blues

	P	W	D	L	For Pts	Agst Pts	Total
Hull K.R.	26	20	1	5	861	325	41
St. Helens	26	19	2	5	570	298	40
Swinton C	26	19	-	7	474	334	38
Warrington	26	18	1	7	623	384	37
Leeds	26	18	-	8	678	427	36
Bradford N	26	17	-	9	623	363	34
Wigan	26	16	2	8	569	423	34
Oldham	26	15	2	9	592	430	32
Hull	26	16	-	10	598	474	32
Salford	26	15	1	10	543	457	31
Castleford	26	15	-	11	643	375	30
Widnes	26	12	3	11	570	415	27
Hunslet	26	13	-	13	406	474	26
Huddersfield P*	24	12	1	11	419	366	25
Leigh	26	12	1	13	501	500	25
Featherstone R	26	10	2	14	391	458	22
Barrow	26	11	-	15	409	507	22
Batley	26	10	2	14	365	485	22
Dewsbury	26	9	1	16	304	550	19
York	26	8	2	16	374	502	18
Halifax	26	6	3	17	289	508	15
Workington T	26	7	-	19	245	665	14
Carlisle-Penrith	26	6	-	20	309	593	12
Wakefield T	26	5	1	20	342	725	11
Keighley	26	2	1	23	25	968	5

*Because of the odd number of member clubs, Huddersfield P. were scheduled to play only 24 matches.

5

*

1985-86

CARLISLE's close-season signings, facilitated by the shrewd judgement of John Risman, included hooker Malcolm Thomason from Broughton Red Rose ARLFC, Alan Little and Duncan Plunkett from the Carlisle and District Amateur League and GB under-19 international Brian Tunstall from Hensingham ARLC.

Dave Elliot, a talented half-back who originally played for Fylde RUFC, signed from Barrow in December 1985 at a transfer fee of £6,000. He was tired of all the chopping and changing at Barrow due to their surplus of quality scrum-half and stand-off contenders. After a couple of half-seasons at Brunton Park, where he also struggled to gain a regular place, he retired from the game to concentrate on his non-rugby working career.

Steve ('Rip') Kirkby joined Elliot in January 1986 from Barrow for a fee of £15,000 and rapidly became a crowd-pleaser - as much for his robust tackling style as for his telepathic understanding with stand-off Steve Langton. His style occasionally attracted disciplinary action from tribunals at the RFL's Chapeltown Road HQ in Leeds, but nothing as spectacular as the one in his Barrow days just before he transferred to Carlisle. Having been dismissed for some or other outrage in the traditional pre-season 'friendly' Cumbria Cup Final, he was handed a ten-match suspension. When he had the temerity to appeal against this sentence, the appeals tribunal promptly increased it to fifteen games. 'Rip' joined Carlisle immediately after this suspension. I can remember the struggle we had in getting together the funds to pay Barrow. I think it took us two years before we had paid off the last installment.

'Rip' Kirkby was worth every penny of that £15,000 in many, many ways. The crowd loved him and his no-nonsense approach. The most potent tackle in his armoury became known as 'Rip's slackener', because it invariably left its recipient with slackened limbs and lolling head. The players, especially Steve Langton, also loved him for the try-scoring chances he created. Even the opposing supporters respected his style. I can vividly remember one old guy at Rochdale being awestruck with the damage being done to his players and coming out with the immortal: 'Dus't 'a feyd 'im on raw meight, owd lad?' ['Do you feed him on raw meat?'] 'Rip' was the first in a procession of Barrow players to join the club in subsequent years.

The 1985-86 season finally got underway with an away game at Workington, in which Carlisle were beaten 32-11 in front of a healthy 1,400 Derwent Park crowd, followed by a 20-20 draw with Keighley at Lawkholme Lane, in front of a distinctly unhealthy gate of not more than 400, and then a tight 16-10 loss at home to Rochdale. A ritual 72-8 flogging by St Helens at Knowsley Road in the first round of the Lancashire Cup capped a poor opening quartet. After which, the season went from bad to worse brightened only by narrow wins over perennial strugglers Hunslet and Runcorn. By November, following a home defeat to Barrow and just one win from ten outings, the crowd were getting restless enough to start chanting 'Atkinson out'.

A stormy 'Meet the Players Forum' at the Hilltop Hotel in November upset the players to the extent that four Yorkshire-based players asked for a transfer. By the year-end, Carlisle were sitting at the bottom of the league. It wasn't just the Yorkshire lads who wanted away either. Colin Armstrong slapped in his own request. It was refused.

A January 1986 win at the bizarrely named Arena 84 (maybe that sounded better than the more traditional Fartown) against the equally bizarrely named Huddersfield Barracudas in front of just 400 unhappy West Yorkshire souls in the drizzle, and a Challenge Cup victory at home over bottom club Mansfield, did little to lift the gloom.

In the same month, newly-appointed commercial manager Sue Greenall announced to a somewhat cynical programme readership that a fund-raising target of £160,000 was to be launched. Chairman Geoff Holmes added that this sum would allow the re-recruitment of top Kiwis such as Dean Bell and Clayton Friend.

In the February, Carlisle suffered a 56-10 hammering at Oldham, the inevitable happened and Atkinson resigned, citing the split squad of Yorkshiremen and Cumbrians as the root of the club's problems.

For the record, it needs to be remembered that it was John Atkinson who stood by the club in its darkest hours, when it looked as if Carlisle might go into extinction. For over two seasons he had manfully pulled club and players together. He had been in charge for 106 games, winning 37, drawing two and losing 67. His chief difficulty was that he inherited an ageing essentially Yorkshire-based team. It was always going to be a next to impossible task to turn this into a side of locals good enough to compete in the professional ranks. To do this with such minimal funding was beyond any mere mortal.

Fortunately, Geoff Holmes's connections in Yorkshire rescued the situation. His long-term friendm, the late Alan Kellett, was persuaded to take the job on a temporary basis. Alan was adamant that his own career obligations in the stationery printing industry in Halifax could only be put on hold until the season ended. However that was just long enough to give the club the breathing space it needed.

Alan, one of the top stand-offs of his day, had done everything in the game as a player short of representing his country. After playing for Bradford Northern, Halifax and Keighley, he guided Keighley to promotion before resigning in 1980 at the same time as his friend Geoff Holmes.

Fortunately, he inherited a fairly injury-free squad that February; the only player missing being Milton Huddart who, by then, was enjoying the Australian game with Canberra Raiders.

As with many messed-up situation, any change was almost bound to be a change for the better. In this case the club got more than just an improvement. Thanks to Alan's considerable personal charisma, experienced man-management talents and deep-seated knowledge of rugby players' psyches, the season was rescued with twelve wins and a draw from the remaining sixteen games, to leave Carlisle comfortably in a mid-table position that had looked beyond their wildest dreams just three months earlier.

We all have favourite match memories from a particular season. A personal one from that year was towards the season's end at Brunton Park in a game against Whitehaven. We won by just 7-0, with the winning try coming from Tony Scott. I can still picture him getting the ball on the halfway line on the scratching shed side and then windmilling his way to the line. He was as surprised as the supporters at his long-range effort. Certainly his grin said it all.

Off the field, however, the club was still in a parlous state and chairman Geoff Holmes was fully committed to resigning by the end of the season, just three short months away. Geoff deputed his directors to go and lobby various targets as potential directors. He also made an appeal through the local paper for management help with the club. In my case, Don McDowall called my wife at home to ask if she thought that I'd be interested in joining the board. Thus it was in April 1985 that I met with Geoff Holmes in the Swallow Hilltop Hotel in Carlisle.

Geoff must have done a great selling job because, next thing, the local paper ran an article that almost deified nightclub owner Frank Lowe, farmer Robert Carter and myself as club saviours. Geoff must have been so desperate to get us all on board that he waived the need to buy £500 of shares, a requirement that had been enshrined in board minutes since 1981.

We all had a brief moment of basking in the reflected glory of a team that appeared to have turned the corner in terms of results before the grim reality of our situation began to hit home. The new board of Dr John Haworth, Brian Whittaker, Don McDowall, Robert Carter, Frank Lowe and I had all the energy, enthusiasm and optimism in the world. However as Geoff Holmes had carried out several key roles himself and been as good as his word about resigning, we were on our own with club finances, payroll, player affairs, liaison with the RFL to name but a few issues. Club records of wages etc might as well have been engraved on gold bullion bars as we'd been left so little of them.

In short, we knew virtually nothing about the real affairs of the club and therefore how to make progress. An ever-present worry was a visit from the tax authorities, or even worse the VAT-man, about whom we'd heard such harrowing tales

Frank Lowe's own financial background became invaluable at this point. Banking arrangements were changed, a pay-roll system set up, sales and purchase ledgers established and gradually the off-field financial affairs were put into some semblance of order.

An early target of our combined behind-the-scenes efforts was the various club lottery schemes. Here again we deferred to Frank Lowe's expertise and replaced all the under-performing lotteries such as The Thousand Club and the '86 Club with one simple scheme, 'The Carlisle RL Banker'. This was straightforward. Each member, and at its peak we had over 6,000 members, had his/her own card with a unique number printed on it. The card was like a cardboard version of a bank card, hence the lottery's name. Members contributed 50p per week into a draw. A random number machine then displayed the winning numbers to at least two independent witnesses. Top weekly prize was £1,000 to make the scheme competitive with the CUFC lottery. This lottery and our soon-to-be-found ability to sign players out of relative obscurity and then transfer them at a healthy profit compensated for our low gates and, against all odds, kept the club afloat for so long.

Having got the financial situation under some type of control and established a regular year-round income stream, we were able to turn our attentions to the rapidly approaching 1986-87 season and the need for an experienced coach.

I can recall debating all the potential Cumbrian contenders. The, probably unfair, conclusion we came to was that what we needed didn't exist in Carlisle and if there was anyone suitable in West Cumbria, then if they didn't already coach Workington or Whitehaven, they weren't up to much. As so often in those days when faced with that type of problem, I called an old school acquaintance, Ray French, the BBC rugby league commentator. Ray came up trumps. Within two days he had recommended two coaches to us. One was Paul Daley, an ebullient little Yorkshireman who went on to coach, amongst others, Hunslet. The other was Roy Lester, a former Leigh and Warrington player who'd cut his teeth in the southern outpost of Fulham.

The next Saturday, four of us drove out to meet them both. We met Daley in Huddersfield and Lester at the Greyhound Pub, just off the East Lancashire Road near his home in Leigh. We felt that either would have done an excellent job but Roy Lester just shaded it, as we agreed that his pioneering work at Fulham was closer to the job we had in mind at Carlisle. Another factor was that, out of a Board of six, four of us had Lancastrian origins!

We eventually agreed terms with Roy and at last allowed ourselves to anticipate the 1986-87 season with some optimism.

As far as close-season team matters were concerned, we were somewhat stymied until Roy Lester had actually joined the club. However, encouraged by Roy, we couldn't resist taking a punt on two Kiwis recommended by their agent and then checked out by a former work colleague who'd played for Featherstone 'A' team and who had then moved to New Zealand. The two were Heemi Wihongi and his compatriot Gary Leck, both from the Marist Club in Christchurch. Another draftee into the first-team squad was wing man Brian McAvoy from the local amateur ranks. Brian is now a successful painting contractor in his native Wigton.

The Carlisle and District ARL Division still existed, although several members, notably Dalston, Wigton and Aspatria, had migrated to the Cumberland League. The

Border City Blues

Horse and Farrier lads had relocated to the Pheasant pub closer to town and changed their name accordingly. Here is that season's final league table.

1985-86 CARLISLE & DISTRICT AMATEUR RUGBY LEAGUE
McEWAN-YOUNGER LEAGUE CHAMPIONSHIP

	P	W	D	L	F	A	Pts
Dalston 'A'	21	15	2	4	545	271	32
Caledonian	21	16	0	5	537	316	32
Morton	21	13	2	6	569	269	28
Pheasant	21	13	1	7	649	354	27
Platform One	21	10	1	10	515	416	21
Wigton 'A'	21	8	0	13	442	550	16
Carlisle Supp. Club	21	5	0	16	271	676	10
Penrith	21	1	0	20	290	830	2

CARLISLE – 1985-86 – SEASON SUMMARY

Ground: Brunton Park
Chairman: Don McDowall
Coach: John Atkinson (Feb 1983-Feb 1986), Alan Kellett (Feb-May 1986)
Records: Attendance: 5,903 v. Workington T. (Div 2) 6 Sept. 1981
Season Goals: 113 by S. Ferres, 1981-82
Tries: 25 by M. Morgan, 1981-82, G. Peacham, 1984-85
Points: 242 by S. Ferres, 1981-82
Match Goals: 9 by D. Carroll v Mansfield M., 16 Mar 1986
Tries: No player has scored more than 3
Points: 21 by D. Carroll v Mansfield M. 16 Mar 1986 and v. Fulham 2 May 1986
Highest Score: 47-18 v Fulham, 1984-85.
Highest against: 72-8 v. St. Helens, 1985-86

	App.	Tries	Goals	D/Gls	Pts		App.	Tries	Goals	D/Gls	Pts
Armstrong, Colin	17 + 3	-	2	1	5	O'Byrne, Mick	5	-	-	-	-
Binder, Tony	27 + 2	1	-	-	4	Pape, Kevin	38	20	-	-	80
Bishop, Gary	4	-	-	1	1	Peacham, Gary	29+1	20	-	-	80
Bond, Gary	6	-	-	-	-	Peacham, Tony	17+2	2	-	-	8
Bowness, Chris	13	5	-	-	20	Phillips, Graeme	2+4	-	-	-	-
Carroll, Dean	22	8	61	8	162	Portz, Karl	35	-	-	-	-
Crowther, Ian	4	-	-	-	-	Robinson, Graeme	13+3	-	8	-	16
Doyle, Mark	24	7	-	-	28	Robinson, Kevin	32	2	-	-	8
Elliott, David	11+2	1	1	-	6	Sanderson, Carl	3	-	-	-	-
Graham, John	2+3	-	-	-	-	Scott, Tony	8+2	2	-	-	8
Huddart, Milton	15	3	-	2	14	Skillen, Mark	2	-	-	-	-
Kirkby, Steve	15+1	4	-	-	16	Smith, David	5	2	-	-	8
Langton, Steve	28+1	10	-	-	40	Stockley, John	18	2	-	-	8
Lithgow, Paul	5+2	-	-	-	-	Sutton, Mick	13+4	-	-	1	1
Loynes, Dean	18+1	2	-	-	8	Thomas, Mick	7	1	-	-	4
Lucas, Maurice	8+3	2	-	-	8	Thomason, Malcolm	16	5	-	-	20
McAvoy, Brian	10	2	-	-	8	Tunstall, Brian	9+1	2	22	-	52
McMullen, Alan	9+11	3	-	-	12	**TOTALS**					
Miller, Craig	4	1	-	-	4	37 Players		107	94	13	629
Moll, David	0+1	-	-	-	-						

1985-86 MATCH ANALYSIS

Date	Competition	Opponent	Result	Score	Tries	Goals	Attendance
1.9.85	SD	Workington T.	L	11-32	G. Peacham, Langton	Armstrong (1, 1dg)	-
4.9.85	SD	Keighley	D	20-20	Pape, Huddart, Langton	G. Robinson (4)	-
8.9.85	SD	Rochdale H.	L	10-16	Huddart, McMullen	Armstrong	730
15.9.85	LC(1)	St. Helens	L	8-72	Langton, Pape	-	-
29.9.85	SD	Whitehaven	M	10-17	Doyle, Thomason	Tunstall	-
2.10.85	SD	Runcorn H.	W	12-2	Thomason, A. Peacham	Tunstall (2)	482
6.10.85	SD	Leigh	L	9-20	G. Peacham	Tunstall (2), Huddart (dg)	928
13.10.85	SD	Wakefield T.	L	10-36	G. Peacham	Tunstall (3)	-
27.10.85	SD	Blackpool B.	L	32-33	Tunstall, Langton, Thomason, Lucas, G. Peacham	Tunstall (6)	628
3.11.85	SD	Barrow	L	13-36	Pape, Thomas	Tunstall (2), Huddart (dg)	915
10.11.85	JPS(P)	Rochdale H.	L	6-24	Scott	Tunstall	752
13.11.85	SD	Hunslet	W	24-14	G. Peacham (3), Tunstall	Tunstall (4)	-
17.11.85	SD	Batley	L	8-16	Huddart	Tunstall, G. Robinson	734
8.12.85	SD	Bramley	L	10-24	Pape, Doyle	G. Robinson	-
15.12.85	SD	Fulham	L	13-14	Pape, Lucas	G. Robinson (2), Bishop (dg)	-

Border City Blues

1985-86 MATCH ANALYSIS CONTINUED

Date	Competition	Opponent	Result	Score	Tries	Goals	Attendance
22.12.85	SD	Leigh	L	12-58	McMullen, K. Robinson	Carroll (2)	-
26.12.85	SD	Blackpool B.	L	0-54	-	-	-
12.1.86	SD	Huddersfield B.	W	16-8	G. Peacham, Pape, Dyle, Binder	Carroll (2)	-
19.1.86	SD	Barrow	L	8-20	Binder	Carroll (2)	-
31.1.86	CC(P)	Mansfield M.	W	20-14	G. Peacham, Elliott, Langton, Doyle	Carroll (2)	482
2.2.86	SD	Doncaster	L	4-16	Pape	-	-
9.2.86	CC(1)	Oldham (at Oldham FC)	L	10-56	G. Peacham, Pape	Elliott	-
12.3.86	SD	Workington T.	W	32-20	G. Peacham (3), Langton (2), Pape	Carroll (4)	600
16.3.86	SD	Mansfield M.	W	45-13	Smith (2), Doyle (2), Kirkby, Carroll, Pape	Carroll (8, 1dg)	516
19.3.86	SD	Sheffield E.	W	15-9	Carroll, Loynes	Carroll (3, 1dg)	530
23.3.86	SD	Keighley	W	17-2	Carroll, Doyle	Carroll (3, 2dg), Sutton (dg)	-
27.3.86	SD	Runcorn H.	L	10-18	Carroll, G. Peacham	Carroll	-
6.4.86	SD	Rochdale H.	L	20-24	Thomason (2), Pape	Carroll (4)	-
11.4.86	SD	Mansfield M.	W	26-14	G. Peacham (3), Pape, McMullen	Carroll (3)	-
15.4.86	SD	Whitehaven	W	7-0	Scott	Carroll (1, 1dg)	1161
17.4.86	SD	Batley	D	8-8	Bowness	Carroll (2)	-
23.4.86	SD	Doncaster	W	32-26	Pape (3), G. Peacham (2), K. Robinson	Carroll (4)	336
27.4.86	SD	Sheffield	W	23-12	McAvoy (2), Pape, Langton	Carroll (3, 1dg)	-
-2.5.86	SD	Fulham	W	41-22	Carroll (2), Stockley (2), Pape, A. Peacham, Bowness	Carroll (6, 1dg)	-
5.5.86	SD	Bramley	W	14-10	Langton, G. Peacham, Pape	Carroll	459
7.5.86	SD	Wakefield T.	L	14-44	Bowness (2), Kirkby	Carroll	450
9.5.86	SD	Huddersfield B.	W	31-16	Kirkby (2), Bowness, Carroll, Loynes	Carroll (5, 1dg)	400
11.5.86	SD	Hunslet	W	28-8	Pape (2), Langton, Miller, Carroll	Caroll (4)	372

1985-86 SECOND DIVISION TABLE

	P	W	D	L	For Dg	For Goals	For Tries	For Total	Agst Dg	Agst Goals	Agst Tries	Agst Total	PTS
Leigh	34	33	0	1	4	166	205	1156	5	62	61	373	66
Barrow	34	27	0	7	2	131	187	1012	6	58	69	398	54
Wakefield T	34	24	1	9	10	101	117	680	3	68	74	435	49
Whitehaven	34	22	0	12	9	91	107	619	9	67	84	479	44
Rochdale H	34	21	0	13	9	125	126	763	7	73	83	485	42
Blackpool B	34	20	0	14	7	101	140	769	4	89	97	570	40
Batley	34	18	3	13	9	87	96	567	2	70	77	450	39
Bramley	34	17	1	16	4	98	102	608	9	97	115	663	35
Fulham	34	16	1	17	9	99	118	679	15	103	122	709	33
Doncaster	34	16	1	17	9	103	99	611	2	82	121	650	33
Carlisle	34	15	2	17	13	90	98	585	4	93	123	682	32
Sheffield E	34	14	1	19	6	83	86	516	11	87	108	617	29
Workington T	34	13	0	21	2	87	127	684	9	119	119	723	26
Hunslet	34	11	3	20	2	94	101	594	7	116	139	795	25
Huddersfield	34	8	4	22	8	73	97	542	11	127	144	841	20
Runcorn H	34	9	2	23	15	77	80	489	8	101	145	790	20
Keighley	34	9	2	23	7	55	71	401	14	150	151	918	20
Mansfield M	34	2	1	31	5	61	64	383	4	160	189	1080	5

Above: Powerhouse player Kevin Pape receives a trophy from former
News and Star sports reporter Andy Colquoun at Brunton Park

1985-86 SLALOM ALLIANCE TABLE

	P	W	D	L	For Pts	Agst Pts	Total
Hull	26	22	0	4	798	337	44
Castleford	26	22	0	4	701	309	44
Widnes	26	20	0	6	690	329	40
Hull KR	26	19	2	5	672	318	40
Leeds	26	20	0	6	631	279	40
Wakefield T	26	16	1	9	579	321	33
Warrington	26	15	2	9	708	479	32
Leigh	26	15	1	10	478	512	31
Barrow	26	14	2	10	583	536	30
St. Helens	26	14	1	11	588	412	29
Halifax	26	14	1	11	571	471	29
Salford	26	14	1	11	590	564	29
Wigan	26	13	2	11	546	547	28
Bradford N	26	12	2	12	454	450	26
Swinton C	26	11	1	14	465	519	23
Oldham	26	10	2	14	500	574	22
Dewsbury	26	9	2	15	381	495	20
Batley	26	9	0	17	370	582	18
Huddersfield P	26	7	0	19	398	627	14
Hunslet	26	7	0	19	340	713	14
Carlisle-Penrith	26	6	2	18	384	768	14
Whitehaven	26	6	1	19	469	683	13
Featherstone R	26	5	1	20	361	576	11
Keighley	26	0	0	26	213	1069	0

6

*

1986-87

ROY LESTER's pre-season preparations were a copybook example of moral courage. He ruthlessly pruned out those Yorkshire-based players who were unwilling to accept and adapt to the new regime of all matters team-based being centralised in Carlisle. It was the right thing to do in the medium term but it still took courage to let such experienced campaigners as Kevin Robinson leave the club, either in the pre-season or early in the new campaign.

Putting aside the annual pre-season Cumbria Cup between Workington, Whitehaven, Barrow and Carlisle (which was deemed a failure unless it resulted in a Town v Haven final at Derwent Park with a 2,000-plus gate - result and fairness of original draw immaterial - and a welcome financial distribution to all four clubs), the season opener was at York's Wigginton Road. Despite tries by Pape, Thomason and McAvoy, Carlisle were edged out 20-14 on account of superior goal-kicking skills. The near 2,000 gate that Sunday made us green with envy.

The opening home game of that season against Blackpool was infinitely worse as Lester's team of rookies were totally out-manoeuvred yet again by the tactical kicking of a Kiwi who had done the same to us on the Boxing Day of the previous season, and was to become a Carlisle favourite in later years - Peter Subritzky. The 36-5 home reverse was not the kind of result that our naive pre-season hype had predicted. Nor was the pathetically low gate of 503.

A scratchy 12-12 draw at home to a very poor Runcorn team, again in front of just 500 hopeful fans, was next up. Our sponsors on that day were DHK Springs, a Japanese company that had only months earlier settled in Carlisle to supply my employer at the time. I shudder to think of the moral blackmail used to get the company and its Japanese owners to put money into a lower division, provincial RL club.

This poor start to the season sparked the doubt process in many supporters' minds. Like fans the world over, they understood the need for change but were impatient to see results.

They had to wait. The following week at Workington saw us yet again stumble due to goal-kicking. Brian Tunstall managed four conversions from tries by Gary Bond, John Stockley, 'Rip' Kirkby and Steve Langton, but Workington ace Sid Lowden topped it with seven between the uprights. We were getting closer to that elusive first win but it wasn't to come yet.

I can recall every little detail of the next weekend when we played St Helens in the first round of the Lancashire Cup. I drove down to St Helens with my son. We were both proudly clad in Carlisle RFL jumpers - mine embroidered with my name. He was just sixteen at the time and we aimed at getting there very early so I could find a private car park to give him an illicit driving lesson. The weather that mid-

September day was simply gorgeous. We wondered how debut boy Heemi Wihongi would fare against Alex Murphy's team of all-stars. We even dared to speculate on some kind of shock result - not a Carlisle win, of course, but more like a fright for the Saints.

For the first time in my life, I went into the old changing complex at Saints behind the sticks at the Dunriding Lane end and saw the old communal tub where greats like Tom Van Vollenhoven and Vinty Karalius had washed off their mud and sweat many years before. For a few moments I was lost in memories of glory days involving boyhood heroes like Duggie Greenall and Alan Prescott. Then it was back to the director's box overlooking the paddock, from where I'd watched so many great tries in the past.

Saints were very quickly on the board with tries by Barry Ledger and Neil Holding and goals from the boot of the imperious Paul Loughlin. What the hell, we thought! They are a full division above us after all, and the receipts from a healthy 4,000 gate were to be shared with us.

Very soon the Saints players seemed to grow in stature while the Carlisle lads looked to be in miniature. St Helens tries continued to come and Saints coach Alex Murphy urged his charges to 'run at the dwarves in the middle'.

To make matters worse, with the score at about 50-0, Heemi Wihongi managed to prevent Saints' Barry Ledger scoring a try by knocking the ball from his hands as he was about to place it down. For some unfathomable reason this incensed one of the Saints directors, a local dentist, who banged on about it even as further Saints tries were being posted.

Eventually, the Carlisle lads were clutching at thin air as the Saints giants ran in a total of twenty tries and Loughlin landed sixteen goals to post a new scoring record within the professional game of 112-0.

As we made our shell-shocked way to the lounge bar, we were amazed to come across our coachload of supporters all singing 'We'll support you ever more' to the team. I was more expecting a lynch party for us directors.

The Carlisle *Evening News* the following day carried the headline 'Slaughter in the Sun'. Their rugby league reporter, Andy Colquhoun, exercised his cutting wit with the immortal words: 'Carlisle did some things well on Sunday. Their shirts were well laundered and nobody missed the team bus...'.

Strangely, or maybe thankfully, that game was barely mentioned afterwards. We all saw it as a necessary watershed as Roy Lester began to impose his own high standards and steadfast values on team matters and the club went on to have an acceptable season with seventeen wins from the following thirty games to finish in a respectable eighth position in a league of twenty clubs.

The exotically named Heemi Wihongi failed to live up to his pre-season billing, developing numerous groin strains that necessitated frequent attention by our rather attractive lady physio. He got himself dropped to the 'A' team, declined to play there and asked for his release. He was back in New Zealand by the New Year.

Another notable departure was Milton Huddart, who was sold to first division Leigh for some much-needed funds. His place was taken by Peter Subritzky, who'd kicked us to death when we played Blackpool earlier in the season. Other players on their way out included talented Yorkshire-based scrum-half Dean Carroll, who suffered a freak serious knee injury in a pre-match warm-up at Keighley.

Roy's significant signings included Don Duffy from Fulham, and Kenny Green and his brother Jimmy. Kenny, by the way, had one of the strangest pre-match rituals we had ever come across. He downed a large schooner of sherry in the dressing-room just before trotting out. Chris Wilkinson, a talented scrum-half, was signed from Fulham and Harold Henney, a veteran prop, was brought in from Runcorn.

With a view to the long-term, a very young Aussie, Garry Schubert, also made his debut as a prop and went on to play in twenty-three games that season as he commenced his long Carlisle career. Schubert, a product of Australia's NSW country football, actually started the season with Salford and joined Carlisle midway through 86-87. He later became a highly successful RL development officer within Carlisle schools, went on to a coaching career with Barrow and is presently a middle-management employee in the leisure department within Carlisle City Council.

A couple of outstanding memories of that season are the two first-team games we played at our Penrith 'A' team venue in Southend Road. The first was in the opening round of the John Player Special Cup in early December, when Carlisle entertained Keighley and won 8-2 in front of a sparse crowd of 300 on a dreadful wet and windy night. This was a shared gate. The basis of the calculation was that the gate was shared fifty-fifty after deduction of the home club's expenses, visitors' coach hire and VAT. Apparently, we broke new ground on that occasion as the costs exceeded the gate income. Keighley and us ended up sharing a loss, although there's no record of Keighley chipping in with theirs!

The next game at Southend Road in January was against Sheffield in the league, when we again won a tight fixture (17 -6) and fared a little better with a gate of 500. Those two games really exposed yet another myth touted around at that time that rugby league may have been better supported in Penrith than in Carlisle and thus ensured that all future first-team home games would be in the city.

Carlisle made the top-eight play-offs that season but were slaughtered 54-0 in the first round by league leaders

Hunslet in front of a 1,200 gate at Leeds United's Elland Road. Clearly, Hunslet had friends on Leeds City Council to have the use of such a magnificently appointed ground for all their home games in those days, although so few fans in that huge 40,000 capacity stadium did look a little incongruous.

Definitely a season of progression was the general consensus at the club, although relationships with our hosts Carlisle United remained strained as the soccer coaching staff attributed their own erratic form to our over-use of the Brunton Park pitch. Kevin Pape was once again an almost ever-present on the pitch and finished with twenty-two tries to his credit.

Coach Roy Lester told me during the drafting of this book: 'When you and the other guys met me in the Greyhound, I had very mixed feelings about Carlisle. I'd recently finished with Fulham because of all the travelling and was really looking for a Lancashire club, but as you all talked I felt that there was some excitement at Carlisle and that I could live with you guys.

'I remember meeting the players for the first time and quite frankly it felt a bit eerie. I thought that there were some excellent players there but one or two of the travellers from West Yorkshire seemed to have an agenda that wasn't totally Carlisle rugby league. One of the players, for instance, seemed far more interested in talking about the money he claimed he was owed from the previous season for a pair of boots than talking to me about gameplans etc. I went away from that first meeting a little bemused and with a sinking feeling that things were worse than I feared. Unlike at Fulham, where I knew all the characters, these guys were strangers to me.

'Eventually, we had to agree on a parting of the ways with a few of the lads who really didn't want to be there. The ones who stayed, such as Stevie Langton, the Humbersiders and the Barrow lads, were superb. The fact remained however that we needed an urgent injection of talent.

'To go through a few of the lads brought in at the start of that season: we had Don Duffy, an Aussie tackling machine who had been recommended to me at Fulham by none other than the late Jack Gibson, arguably the greatest ever Australian coach. Strangely enough, after I'd given him a billing as Jack Gibson's "Tackling Machine", the very first time he played for us he got totally cleaned out in a tackle himself. I cringed but Don quickly recovered and went on to have a great game.

'Then we had the Green brothers. Kenny was well known to me as a member of the great Leigh Championship side of 1980. I'd recruited him from Leigh for Fulham as my assistant and then brought him out of retirement to do a job at Carlisle, against his wife's wishes incidentally. We later recruited his brother Jimmy from Blackpool, and he went on to get us into the top-eight play-offs with a try against his former club in the next-to-last game of that 86-87 season.

'Another who'd been at Fulham with me was Harold Henney, a Cumbrian who we recruited from Runcorn. Here's a story about Harold from my Fulham days. We were on the coach coming home from a game and he and Don Duffy fell out over something. Harold punched Don and when I remonstrated with him and suggested that if he were to hit anyone it should be me, he obliged. So I hit him back and knocked a tooth out. We were great friends after that. When he came to Carlisle, Harold was right at the end of his career so he only played a couple of games.

'Then there was fitness fanatic John Stockley[1], a very

---

[1]Don McDowall recalls John Stockley's struggle with alliance coach Colin Porthouse's West Cumbrian dialect in the half-time pep-talk. Colin complained about the lack of support play by telling the team: 'thou's gaan up in yans!'

quick wing man from Wigan who had been with me at Fulham and who worked in one of the pubs that I later managed for Cumbria Leisure, down in Leigh. Chris Wilkinson, a Leigh-based half-back who I'd known since a lad and who we signed as an amateur for Fulham also played a few games for us in that season. He's presently working in Birchwood near Warrington.'

Asked about further recollections and any misgivings he may have felt about Carlisle's plans to move out of Brunton Park and take up residence at Gillford Park during that time, Roy replies: 'It became obvious that a move was needed when the soccer people started to make it plain that we weren't wanted there. It became a little like my time at Craven Cottage with Fulham when we had to move out to Chiswick Polytechnic's Sports Ground, near the river in London. It was a similar challenge of creating a stadium out of what was just a sports field with little or no spectator facilities. We even had to install turn-stiles and dressing-rooms etc. Gillford Park was a case of *déjà vu* for me.'

Without hesitation, Roy nominates a first-round home tie against Warrington in the John Player Special Trophy in 1987-88 as one of his most memorable matches at the club. 'We were hanging on for a draw and a lucrative rematch and were into the last minute with just twelve men after Peter Subritzky had been sent off,' he recalls. 'Brian Tunstall, who'd had a good game until that point, kicked early in the tackle count. The kick was a bad one and went straight to Warrington's Brian Johnson who raced clear before passing to David Lyon who scored under the posts to take the game 22-16. I went into where I used to get changed, locked the door and sobbed my eyes out with pure frustration. We were so close to bringing off the upset of the season.'

Meanwhile, the amateur code in the city was continuing its gradual shrinkage and the Carlisle and District ARL

Division was now down to seven teams. The Horse and Farrier lads and their long-serving chairman Ken Laverick had returned home to their spiritual roots in their original pub to the west of the city on Wigton Road.

In contrast with the gradual decline of the senior amateur league, a truly amazing thing was happening with the kids, thanks to Roy Lester's persuasiveness and vision. As current Carlisle Centurions RLFC team manager and former head of Morton school Trevor Easton recalls: 'Some people in rugby league are superb committee members. They never miss a meeting, always have some viewpoint to express and, of course, read the minutes in detail and are willing to dip their hand in their pocket for the good of the club. Every club needs them. Other people see a job, roll up their sleeves and get on with it. No messing! Elaine (Nobby) Gordon was such a person. A conversation with Roy Lester that season set her on a mission that she turned into a reality. The Carlisle Juniors were born.

'It was Elaine who approached the late Carl Steele, a local player whose playing days were behind him. And it was this dynamic duo who set up and advertised training sessions, booked the grounds and, above all, contacted others who could contribute such as Geoff Farrimond and myself. Roy Lester and members of the Carlisle board also threw in their weight. Roy arranged for Kiwi Peter Subritzky to take on a junior development role and Don McDowall ensured that his employers Carlisle City Council were aware of the real potential offered by junior development. The concept of the rugby league development officer was born and Peter was appointed to the role.

'Even in those early days, Peter was supported by the recently arrived Australian player Garry Schubert, who went on to later develop the joint Carlisle CC - Carlisle RLFC development project that took the game into local primary schools and those secondary schools that were receptive to the code. A number of very successful coaching camps were run at Carlisle's Sheepmount sports facility throughout 1986 and 1987. A high profile was achieved by enlisting the support of the game's ruling body, the RFL, who organised and funded visits to the coaching clinics by such icons of the code as Ellery Hanley and Garry Schofield.

'The primary schools proved to be very receptive to offers of rugby league coaching and soon there was an active city-wide junior school competition. Chief among the school supporters was Shaun Halfpenny, the head of a small junior school at Cummersdale, on the west side of the city. The provision of quality coaching for pupils really did help the local teachers to deliver the National Curriculum in PE.

'Unfortunately, and maybe predictably, some of the more central secondary schools were not so receptive. Excellent and sustained support was forthcoming from Morton, Harraby, Longtown and Caldew. The reluctance of the more central and longer established secondary schools to get involved was maybe due to historic ties to the Carlisle RU club which was just a few hundred yards away. Or maybe they simply looked down on the alien thirteen-a-side non-establishment game!'

1986-87 CARLISLE & DISTRICT AMATEUR RUGBY LEAGUE
DICK THOMPSON LEAGUE CHAMPIONSHIP

	P	W	D	L	Pts
Wigton	18	17	0	1	34
Crown Inn	18	15	0	3	30
Horse & Farrier	18	12	0	6	24
St. Nicholas Arms	18	8	0	10	16
C.R.L.S.C.	18	7	0	11	14
Dalston 'A'	18	4	0	14	8
Penrith	18	0	0	18	0

Border City Blues

CARLISLE – 1986-87 – SEASON SUMMARY

Ground:	Brunton Park
Colours:	Blue jerseys with red and white band, white shorts
Chairman:	Alan Tucker
Secretary:	Bob Taylor
Coach:	Alan Kellett (Feb-May 1986), Roy Lester (June 1986-)
Records:	Attendance: 5,903 v Workington T (Div 2) 6 Sept. 1981
Season	Goals: 113 by S. Ferres, 1981-82
	Tries: 25 by M. Morgan, 1981-82, G. Peacham, 1984-85
	Points: 242 by S. Ferres, 1981-82
Match	Goals: 9 by D. Carroll v Mansfield M, 16 Mar 1986
	Tries: 4 by G. Peacham v Workington ., 25 Jan, 1987
	and K. Pape v. Rochdale H, 11 Feb, 1987
	Points: 21 by D. Carroll v Mansfield M. 16 Mar 1986 and v. Fulham 2 May 1986
	Highest Score: 47-18 v Fulham, 1984-85.
	Highest against: 112-0 v. St. Helens, 1986-87

	App.	Tries	Goals	D/Gls	Pts
Armstrong, Colin	26+2	-	5	-	10
Bond, Gary	2+3	1	-	-	4
Bowness, Chris	0+1	-	-	-	-
Brierley, Steve	3+2	-	-	-	-
Carroll, Dean	8+1	-	18	2	38
Duffy, Don	29	2	-	1	9
Duncanson, Mark	0+1	-	-	-	-
Elliott, David	5	-	-	-	-
Graham, John	19+1	-	-	-	-
Green, Jimmy	1+3	1	-	-	4
Green, Ken	15+2	-	-	-	-
Henney, Harold	3	-	-	-	-
Huddart, Milton	7	1	-	2	6
Kirkby, Steve	30	12	-	-	48
Langton, Steve	35	7	-	-	28
Leck, Gary	6+2	-	-	-	-
Lithgow, Paul	16+7	3	-	-	12
Loynes, Dean	1+1	-	-	-	-
McAvoy, Brian	15+1	5	-	-	20
McMullen, Alan	3+2	-	-	-	-
Miller, Craig	2	1	-	-	4

	App.	Tries	Goals	D/Gls	Pts
Pape, Kevin	34	22	-	-	88
Peacham, Gary	21	7	-	-	28
Peacham, Tony	5	-	-	-	-
Phillips, Graeme	1+1	-	-	-	-
Portz, Karl	2+2	-	-	-	-
Rampling, Darren	1	-	-	-	-
Robinson, Kevin	3	-	-	-	-
Schubert, Garry	23	5	-	-	20
Scott, Tony	12+9	1	-	-	4
Smith, David	1+3	-	-	1	1
Smith, Joe	0+1	-	-	-	-
Stafford, Peter	0+2	-	-	-	-
Stockley, John	32	6	-	-	24
Subritzky, Peter	24+1	6	14	1	53
Thomason, Malcolm	35	6	-	-	24
Tunstall, Brian	21	-	38	-	76
Wihongi, Heemi	9	1	-	-	4
Wilkinson, Chris	5	3	-	-	12
TOTALS					
39 Players		90	75	7	517

1986-87 MATCH ANALYSIS

Date	Competition	Opponent	Result	Score	Tries	Goals	Attendance
31.8.86	SD	York	L	14-20	Pape, Thomason, McAvoy	Armstrong	-
3.9.86	SD	Blackpool B.	L	5-36	Pape	D. Smith (dg)	504
7.9.86	SD	Runcorn H.	D	12-12	Stockley, Langton	Tunstall (2)	516
10.9.86	SD	Workington T.	L	24-31	Bond, Stockley, Kirkby, Langton	Tunstall (4)	-
14.9.86	LC (1)	St Helens	L	0-112	-	-	-
21.9.86	SD	Doncaster	W	16-12	Thomason, Huddart, Miller	Tunstall (2)	-
28.9.86	SD	Keighley	L	6-16	Kirkby	Tunstall	-
5.10.86	SD	Rochdale H.	W	22-2	Lithgow (2), Pape, Wihongi	Tunstall (2), Huddart (2 dg)	518
12.10.86	SD	Sheffield E.	L	10-24	Pape (2)	Tunstall	-
19.10.86	SD	Mansfield M.	W	22-16	Kirkby (2), Langton, Stockley	Tunstall (3)	438
26.10.86	SD	Hunslet	L	8-20	Thomason	Tunstall (2)	-

86

1986-87 MATCH ANALYSIS CONTINUED

Date	Competition	Opponent	Result	Score	Tries	Goals	Attendance
2.11.86	SD	Keighley	L	16-26	Subritzky, Schubert	Tunstall (4)	507
9.11.86	SD	Huddersfield B.	W	18-10	Langton (2), Wilkinson	Tunstall (3)	481
16.11.86	Sd	Mansfield M.	W	28-16	Wilkinson (2), Subritzky, Pape	Tunstall (6)	-
23.11.86	SD	Doncaster	L	2-30	-	Tunstall	-
4.12.86	JPS (1)	Keighley (at Penrith)	W	8-2	Kirkby	Tunstall, Subritzky	300
7.12.86	JPS (2)	Widnes	L	6-36	G. Peacham	Subritzky	-
14.12.86	SD	Hunslet	W	11-8	Pape (2)	Tunstall, Subritzky (dg)	322
4.1.87	SD	Sheffield E. (at Penrith)	W	17-6	Kirkby, Duffy, Lithgow	Armstrong (2), Duffy (dg)	500
25.1.87	SD	Workington T.	W	42-6	G. Peacham (4), Pape (2), Kirkby, Subritzky	Subritzky (5)	813
4.2.87	CC(1)	Rochdale H.	D	4-4	Stockley	-	-
8.2.87	SD	Swinton	L	20-23	Kirkby (3), Thomason	Subritzky, Carroll	-
11.2.87	CC(1) Replay	Rochdale H.	W	30-22	Pape (4), Kirkby	Carroll (5)	788
15.2.87	CC(2)	Leigh	L	6-18	Pape	Carroll	-
22.2.87	SD	York	W	30-16	Pape (3), Schubert, Kirkby, Thomason	Carroll (3)	800
1.3.87	SD	Huddersfield B.	W	19-8	McAvoy, Subritzky, Pape	Carroll (3, 1dg)	-
8.3.87	SD	Rochdale H.	L	1-11	-	Carroll (dg)	-
15.3.87	SD	Runcorn H.	W	26-4	McAvoy (2), Duffy, Schubert, Pape	Carroll (3)	-
22.3.87	SD	Dewsbury	W	24-14	G. Peacham (2), Langton, Carroll (2), Subritzky (2) Subritzky	1000
5.4.87	SD	Dewsbury	W	12-6	Stockley, Schubert	Armstrong (2)	-
12.4.87	SD	Swinton	L	16-35	Subritzky, Pape, Schubert	Subritzky (2)	1200
17.4.87	SD	Whitehaven	W	16-11	Stockley, Scott, McAvoy	Subritzky (2)	3000
22.4.87	SD	Whitehaven	L	8-16	Langton	Tunstall (2)	-
22.4.87	SD	Blackpool B.	W	18-11	Thomason, Pape, J. Green	Tunstall (3)	-
26.4.87	SDP(1)	Hunslet	L	0-54	-	-	-

1986-87 SECOND DIVISION TABLE

	P	W	D	L	For Dg	For Goals	For Tries	For Total	Agst Dg	Agst Goals	Agst Tries	Agst Total	PTS
Hunslet	28	25	0	3	0	91	135	722	4	39	34	218	50
Swinton	28	23	1	4	13	104	123	713	3	52	54	323	47
Whitehaven	28	21	0	6	1	80	104	577	6	45	52	304	43
Doncaster	28	20	1	7	2	100	96	586	6	67	62	388	41
Rochdale H	28	19	1	8	7	86	85	519	11	49	65	369	39
Sheffield E	28	17	0	11	3	93	109	625	10	76	66	426	34
Bramley	28	16	0	12	3	62	70	407	12	62	76	440	32
Carlisle	28	15	1	12	7	66	81	463	6	72	74	446	31
Blackpool B	28	14	0	14	4	71	96	530	7	77	79	477	28
York	28	11	0	17	12	72	84	492	3	75	96	537	22
Runcorn H	28	10	1	17	3	54	70	391	5	82	91	533	21
Fulham	28	8	2	18	9	76	75	461	6	95	109	632	18
Batley	28	9	0	19	5	49	58	335	10	81	89	528	18
Workington T	28	9	0	19	7	69	65	405	8	92	115	652	18
Huddersfield B	28	8	0	20	10	69	77	456	5	98	118	673	16
Mansfield M	28	8	0	20	16	69	53	366	2	81	107	592	16
Dewsbury	28	8	0	20	4	56	53	328	3	86	97	563	16
Keighley	28	7	0	21	6	54	63	366	5	92	113	641	14

Border City Blues

1986-87 SLALOM LAGER ALLIANCE -SECOND DIVISION

	P	W	D	L	For Pts	Agst Pts	Total
Swinton C	26	26	0	0	838	224	52
Hunslet	26	21	1	4	645	255	43
Whitehaven	26	19	0	7	737	389	38
Bradford N	26	17	2	7	589	330	36
Oldham	26	15	0	11	605	369	30
York	26	14	1	11	510	430	29
Featherstone R	26	11	1	14	412	530	23
Workington T	26	11	0	15	418	489	22
Huddersfield P	26	10	1	15	371	569	21
Batley	26	10	1	15	310	521	21
Carlisle P	26	9	2	15	367	496	20
Bramley	26	5	1	20	237	516	11
Keighley	26	5	0	21	367	820	10
Dewsbury	26	4	0	22	244	712	8

Above: The Carlisle team poses with sponsors Daido Hayamizu Kogyo Spring Company in 1986

7
*
1987-88

THE nine-man board, by now boosted by the arrival of Dick Thompson and John Pattison, both local business colleagues of Frank Lowe, had already concluded that this would be the final season at Brunton Park, but without any clear idea as to where we would move.

The rental demands for the continued use of the soccer stadium, doubtless reasonable by football standards, were crippling the club. The constant conflicts of interest about pitch availability every time it rained and the claimed effect of wear and tear on the quality of soccer played by our hosts were another factor in the decision.

We looked at many options ranging from greenfield sites near the Garlands Hospital on the south side of Carlisle, through developing the Sheepmount athletics stadium, to building on Richardson Street park. The greenfield option fell down on planning considerations. The athletics lobby successfully killed off the Sheepmount proposal for a few years, although, with the wisdom of hindsight, the opportunity to develop this into a multi-use venue via Government grants and RFL soft loans was a golden opportunity missed. The Council's view at the time was that the city couldn't sustain two stadia with professional sports occupants. Even twenty-three years on, this still comes across as a soundbite designed to maintain status quo and keep the athletics lobby quiet at the expense of rugby league.

The Richardson Street proposal was a political non-starter due to its close proximity to a densely populated residential area and the loss of a communal leisure space that would have occurred. The Garlands option, even if we had overcome the planning objections, would have depended heavily on a housing development to make it viable and four of the directors were already heavily committed to another such residential development on the old State Management brewery site near the city centre.

Thus did Gillford Park, a roped-off area in a much larger space used for 'A' team games, come into the reckoning. It was quite simply the only choice available to us in the city if we were ever to move out of Brunton Park. The task to turn this half of a vast open field into a stadium to satisfy the RFL criteria seemed enormous; and anyway we first had the 1987-88 season whistling upon us, plus a competitive team to assemble that would see us through our final season at Brunton Park.

In truth, little additional recruitment was affordable, given the signings of the previous campaign and the upcoming costs of the Gillford Park conversion.

The nucleus of the squad was as follows: Brian Tunstall, who had joined us in 1985 from Hensingham ARLFC; Paul Lithgow, a local lad who came from The Horse and Farrier also in '85; ex-Blackpool player John Stockley; Kevin Pape, the recipient of the BNFL's Young Powerhouse of 1986-87 award; Gary Peacham, ex-Hull FC ; Brian McAvoy, a former

Wigton ARLFC player who had spent the previous season in the Alliance; Steve Langton, who had joined us in 1984; Jimmy Green, who came from Blackpool in 1986; Colin Armstrong, ex-Broughton Red Rose ARLFC, then in his third season; Malcolm Thomason, another Broughton Red Rose player in his third season; Garry Schubert, our former Australian import via Salford; Tony Scott, another Broughton Red Rose product who was a 1983 signing; Don Duffy, an Australian tackling machine; Steve Kirkby, signed from Barrow in 1983; Steve Brierley, who signed in 1983 from Dalston ARLFC; and Blackpool-based Peter Subritzky, who signed in the 1985-86 season.

The second division that season was going to be tougher than ever with top teams like Wakefield, Oldham, Barrow and Featherstone having all dropped down into our ranks.

The Carlisle Amateur League was also having a tough time and starting to crumble. A meeting in July 1987 with league representative David Freshwater revealed that there was a general loss of interest in the city. No new players were coming forward, there were admin problems due to the resignation of Jock Gordon, and BARLA were against the inclusion of Tyneside clubs into the competition. Despite this gloomy prognosis, David felt that there would still be eight teams in the competition for the 1987-88 campaign.

In the event, by the start of the season the amateur league had contracted to five clubs, with Wigton the eventual champions. In short, this was the end of the Carlisle and District Amateur League as a separate entity and, by the 1988-89, season Dalston 'A', Wigton, Horse and Farrier, Cumbria Leisure (formerly RL Supporters Club) and St Nicholas Arms had all migrated to Division Four of the Cumberland Amateur League.

After the relatively relaxed pipe-opener of the pre-season BNFL Cup, we had a real baptism of fire at Belle Vue when

**1987-88 CARLISLE & DISTRICT AMATEUR RUGBY LEAGUE
DICK THOMPSON LEAGUE**

	P	W	D	L	Pts
Wigton	12	10	0	2	20
Horse & Farrier	12	9	0	3	18
Dalston 'A'	12	5	0	7	10
St. Nicholas Arms	12	3	0	9	6
R.L. Supporters Club	12	3	0	9	6

Wakefield Trinity gave us a humiliating 56-8 rugby lesson, courtesy of Andy Mason and Mark Conway in particular. It was a beautiful late summer weekend and Kevin Harcombe was converting from all angles, as he kicked eight goals. Carlisle, missing several regulars including Pape, Peacham, Subritzky and Tunstall, and with Steve Langton sent off for a high tackle, had just two unconverted tries from Langton and Kirkby to their credit. I don't think I was the only one of the Carlisle contingent who secretly feared a repetition of the debacle at St Helens a year earlier.

The following weekend, Doncaster were the visitors and Alan Little and Alan Maclagan stepped up from alliance to first-team action in place of the injured Gary Peacham and Peter Subritzky. Both rapidly became cult figures because of their uncompromising style of play. Roy Lester, at one stage, made the very extravagant statement that MacLagan, or 'Claggy' as he was known, had a similar style to the great Vince Karalius. The striking thing about the team that weekend was that out of fifteen players in the line-up, nine were Cumbrians and only Steve Langton was from West Yorkshire. Steve Mills, formerly of Widnes and Fulham, also made his debut in that game.

Not for the first time, however, the main action was now off the pitch. It had been two years since former chairman Geoff Holmes had resigned and we were not much further forward in understanding the club's past financial affairs. We knew precisely what our assets and liabilities were since he resigned, but there were still hitherto unknown debts coming out of the woodwork. It was so bad that anyone could have claimed we owed them money from pre-1986 and we couldn't have argued otherwise. Clearly, with the club about to build a new stadium at Gillford Park and all the extra finance that entailed, there was an urgent need to get the financial affairs regularised.

After extensive, competent (and costly) legal advice, we embarked upon what was referred to as a company reformation. It's doubtful if this was its correct legal term, but that is how the solicitors described it. Basically this entailed calling a shareholders' meeting, making a statement of all known liabilities and accepting responsibility for them to go into a new company formed for such a purpose. To do this, we needed the assent of the shareholders of the old company. Happily, major shareholders like Jimmy Bendall and Andrew Jenkins, along with several others, agreed to give me their proxy vote and so the new company Carlisle Rugby League Club (1987) was born at a meeting in the

Above: Carlisle's 1987-88 squad in their final season at Brunton Park. Back Row: Raymond Edgar (kit man), Colin Porthouse (alliance coach), Steve Brierley, Colin Armstrong, Garry Schubert, Tony Scott, Alan McMullen, Dave Courtney, Brian Tunstall, Barry Kendall (physio), Vic Semple (asst. physio). Middle Row: Kenny Green (asst coach), Mark Doyle, Steve Langton, Paul Lithgow, Colin Coles, Steve Mills, Roy Lester (coach). Front: Malcolm Thomason, Kevin Pape (captain), Gary Murdock.

Pagoda nightclub in Lancaster Street one afternoon in September 1987.

At long last we knew what we were owed and to whom we owed money. The added advantage was that the only shareholders in the new club were people who cared passionately about rugby league in Carlisle and who had demonstrated that fact with action, money and commitment.

It maybe was predictable that the ink was barely dry on this new arrangement before a coach hire company from Leeds approached us claiming several thousand pounds against a bill that dated from 1984 and about which we had no knowledge. I'm unsure what the eventual outcome of this was. All I know is that we were legally able to refuse payment and that the coach proprietor took up the matter with the RFL.

We were thus a couple of months into the season with a half-decent side, a clear understanding as to our financial situation and a new venue to prepare.

Despite the wealth of enthusiastic homegrown talent, the team had a torrid start to the season with five losses, a draw and just one win, until they recorded a remarkable victory in late October in the deepest rugby league territory of Featherstone. Rovers had been relegated from Division One in 1987 and were sweeping all before them in their ultimately successful bid to get back there.

In those pre-Sky days, there was much more of a level playing field as far as sponsorship and therefore wages were concerned. As a consequence, Featherstone were able to retain their first division squad with top players like Deryck Fox, Chris Bibb, big Karl Harrison and Graham Steadman. They also had one of the wiliest coaches in the business in Peter Fox. It was therefore all the more remarkable that Carlisle defeated them on their own midden, 29-22. Both sides scored four tries, Carlisle's by Pape (2), Kirkby and Thomason. But it was Carlisle's goal-kicking that won the day, with Tunstall getting six and Peter Subritzky a drop-goal.

Featherstone's chairman Bob Ashby was also chairman of the RFL. His face was a picture as we spoiled the home team's party. We repeated the act in March at Brunton Park, when our guests included both Bob Ashby and the secretary of the RFL, David Oxley, who were in Carlisle to meet with the City Council in an initiative designed to get Carlisle CC support for the funding of Peter Subritzky as RL development officer for the city. On that occasion Carlisle won 23-18 with tries by Colin Coles (2), Langton and Mills. Barry Vickers kicked three goals and a drop-goal. Personal recollections of that day include an absolute blinder of a game from Steve Mills.

Despite our heroics against first division Warrington in the John Player Cup that Roy Lester has already recalled, and the remarkable win at Featherstone, by the year's end our season was well into the doldrums with just five wins from fourteen games. A particular low came in November, when we were beaten 16-8 by bottom club Huddersfield Barracudas at their dismal Arena 84 venue in front of 350 gloating Yorkshiremen. In those days the rugby league ground and cricket pitch shared a pavilion that served both sports, a distinctly down-market version of Headingley.

Despite our disappointing result, the afternoon was made bearable by the charm and hospitality of one of their officials, a former Olympic athlete named Tom Matthewman who competed in the 200 metres at the 1924 Paris Olympics and whose gentlemanly air was at odds with the run-down surroundings.

With the on-field action completed, a board meeting discussed several options. Ellenborough ARLFC product Gary Murdock, who had been making steady progress in our

'A' team, was brought through into the first team in place of Jimmy Green. Gary went on to have a good career with Carlisle before he began a coaching career in the amateur ranks in the mid-nineties. He returned to Carlisle in 2003 to coach the newly-formed Carlisle Centurions and took us to the final of the Harry Jepson Trophy at Wilderspool. Colin Coles, a wing man from Glasson Rangers ARLFC, was also signed at that time and soon made the first team.

An issue that was to become a long-running saga with Whitehaven over top amateur Martin Oglanby kicked off too. This was a strange affair. One of our directors felt that Martin had pledged his future to Carlisle but Whitehaven chairman David Wigham was adamant he was their man. As far as I can recall, there was no contract in writing to tie the bemused player to either club and, in any event, he wanted to stay as an amateur. It became a real bone of contention between the clubs and he eventually joined Workington!

Late in 1987 another odd episode took place that would have far-reaching consequences on player recruitment. Colin Deans, the iconic Scottish rugby union hooker from Hawick with fifty-two caps to his credit, had recently retired from the international game. Director Frank Lowe quickly spotted an opportunity. He wondered if Colin, a likeable, sincere and fit-looking 32-year-old, might be tempted to throw in his lot with us as a player and fitness coach.

As a result several of us had dinner with Colin one evening in a pleasant hotel on the outskirts of Hawick; the Mansfield House Hotel if I remember correctly. The upshot being that Colin decided to pursue a developmental role in the fifteen-a-side code at Hawick, so it all came to nought. However, the die was cast for future recruitment incursions north of the border.

Closer to home, recruitment from rugby union saw us sign Barry Vickers from Netherhall RU in Maryport. Barry quickly established himself as a rock-solid full-back and a reliable sharp-shooter who took over the kicking role from Brian Tunstall. Barry's signature was treated with urgency as we were tipped off by one of our scouts (the late Eric Smith of Dalston) that Workington Town were to contact him after the festive season.

Not all the news was positive, though. Carlisle United continued to press for repayment of £60,000, this being the balance of their original investment in rugby league in 1981. This obligation was eventually discharged with a negotiated one-off payment of £26,000 in 1988.

Carlisle and Whitehaven met in the preliminary round of the Challenge Cup when a decent 1,800 crowd saw us draw, 8-8, at Brunton Park. Carlisle's scorers were Paul Lithgow with a try and Brian Tunstall with two goals. The replay was played at the Recre the following Wednesday in front of an even better 2,700 crowd. Carlisle completely outplayed Haven to win 22-8 with tries by Armstrong, Mills, Pape and Coles.

There then followed a depressingly long run of defeats until early spring 1988. It was then that, with another otherwise mediocre season coming to a close, Carlisle again rediscovered their form and once more set the board the challenge of funding winning pay for six straight wins on the trot. Welcome as the wins were, they could hardly have come at a worse time. There was no longer anything to play for and we were looking to save every penny to fund the switch to Gillford Park the following season. Nevertheless, a gate of over 2,000 for our last ever regular game at Brunton Park, which we lost 34-16 to Oldham, provided a welcome boost to our meagre war chest.

That war chest and our directors' generosity were going to get a real test over the summer months as our protracted negotiations with the British Rail Property Board, the

Carlisle City Council planning deptartment, the Rugby
Football League and the committee of the Railway Club at
Gillford Park were coming to a conclusion.

After a minor diversion when we deemed the land just to
the immediate south east of Gillford Park to be a better
option, only for the Council who owned it to block our
interest, the enormity of what needed to be done in just four
months began to hit us.

Our target was to completely enclose the playing area
with a four-foot ranch-type wooden fence, enclose the
stadium with an eight-foot high corrugated steel fence, and
build a new block to contain the referee's changing room
and first-aid room. We also had to renovate the existing
changing-room and build a 500-seater stand.

We acquired a used industrial cabin to serve as our
headquarters and to house our new groundsman/kit-
man/player confidante and anything else we could ask him
to do, Raymond Edgar. Raymond and his trusty sidekick,
commercial manager Steve Lithgow, became the heart and
soul of the club and kept us all sane throughout the difficult
times ahead.

Personal memories of that summer are that it was one of
the wettest on record and that we all virtually lived at
Gillford Park to get the ground ready. We were all quite fit in
those days and those without practical skills quite happily
laboured to the numerous builders, plumbers, electricians,
scaffolders, surveyor etc, either in a paid capacity or as
volunteers conscripted to build the ground.

One such volunteer was a local councillor and the wife of
Carlisle MP, Eric Martlew. Elsie Martlew and her husband
were long-term supporters of the club (husband Eric
continued a tradition originally started by Vernon Addison,
former managing editor of the local paper, by donating a
bottle of scotch to any player who scored three or more tries

in a match). Elsie, more than most, understood the machinations of local government upon which the club was heavily dependent for future development, and she had amply demonstrated her business acumen in a separate project elsewhere in the city. Elsie was quite happy to get her own hands (and face!) dirty by creosoting the fence along with the rest of us.

The following season we had no hesitation in inviting Elsie to join us on the club's board, where she kept us all straight and legal. She may have pondered the wisdom of the move later the following season when we visited Barrow on Boxing Day, but that's another story.

The Health and Safety executive would have had a coronary had they witnessed our goings on, as we willingly assumed tasks for which we were totally untrained. One of my own most cringe-worthy memories is of losing control of a dumper-truck laden with concrete blocks and pinning Frank Low against a wall. Happily the machine stalled with Frank still in one piece.

I still smile at the memory of Doc Haworth, too, face as black as the ace of spades, with cigar in mouth, wheeling endless barrow-loads of ashes to make the standing area around the perimeter of the ground.

It was during these works that Raymond Edgar began to emerge as a leading light behind the scenes in club affairs. Raymond, via his friendship with Steve Lithgow, had joined the club as alliance team kit-man at Brunton Park. Because of his talent in getting jobs done on a shoe-string, his love of the club and the trust he earned of players and directors alike, he became totally indispensible and assumed the official roles of groundsman, kit-man and eventually lottery manager. Unofficially, he just about ran the club during the frequent business-related absences of the directors.

Raymond maintains his love of rugby league in Carlisle

Above: Dick Thompson, Mally Cooper, Alan Gilbertson, Elaine Gordon and Raymond Edgar take a tea-break whilst helping with the building of Gillford Park

and attends many of the Centurions' home games. He is quite adamant that the RFL should have treated Carlisle far better and given them support equivalent to that afforded to Celtic Crusaders, for example. Like many, he feels that Carlisle's eventual demise can be traced back to the forced move from city centre Brunton Park to the distinctly unglamorous Gillford Park. In fact, he revealed his early forebodings during the preparation of this book, when he recalled the aggressive and hostile attitude that one or two of the Railway Club committee adopted as soon as we had signed the agreement to play there.

Raymond was, and still is, an astute judge of rugby players. It is a quality respected by the players themselves, who are still regular callers at his house or at the busy

Carlisle Market cards and gift shop that he and his family now run. He has instant recall of the club's highlights and can clearly recount such cameo occasions as Castleford coach John Joyner's utter despair in 1995, when little home-spun Carlisle Border Raiders dumped them out of the Regal Trophy. Rugby league in Carlisle owes a lot to Raymond's patience, fortitude, hard work, common sense and loyalty, and I am not alone in the value I place on his friendship.

A vivid recollection of my own of that era is of director Robert Carter, his pal Eddie Wharton and myself stripping out the flooring of an upper floor of the Old Carlisle State Brewery one Sunday morning. The exercise involved Eddie and I ripping out 8ft x 4ft plywood sheets and dropping them out of an upstairs hoist-opening to the ground below, where Robert waited to load them into his cattle wagon. Any that failed to pass this 'drop test' were slit into two-foot wide strips to form the platform of the scaffolding terracing.

By far the biggest challenge was the stand that still serves purpose on the halfway line. Of enormous help in this was a guy called George Russell, a clerk of works in his normal paid employment. George did most of the marking out for us, he supervised the foundation work, advised us on rectification work that was needed and generally kept us legal.

We almost - but not quite - finished the work in time for the first home game in September.

Border City Blues

CARLISLE – 1987-88 – SEASON SUMMARY

Chairman: Alan Tucker
Secretary: Robert Carter
Coach: Roy Lester (June 1986-)
Records: Attendance: 5,903 v. Workington T. (Div 2) 6 Sept. 1981
Season Goals: 113 by S. Ferres, 1981-82
Tries: 25 by M. Morgan, 1981-82, G. Peacham, 1984-85
Points: 242 by S. Ferres, 1981-82
Match Goals: 9 by D. Carroll v Mansfield M, 16 Mar 1986
Tries: 4 by G. Peacham v. Workington T, 25 Jan, 1987
and K. Pape v Rochdale H, 11 Feb, 1987
Points: 21 by D. Carroll v Mansfield M 16 Mar 1986 and v Fulham 2 May 1986
Highest Score: 47-18 v Fulham, 1984-85.
Highest against: 112-0 v St. Helens, 1986-87

	App.	Tries	Goals	D/Gls	Pts		App.	Tries	Goals	D/Gls	Pts
Armstrong, Colin	29+1	2	6	1	21	Mills, Steve	32	12	-	-	48
Bond, Gary	0+1	-	-	-	-	Murdock, Gary	21	2	-	-	8
Bowness, Chris	8	-	-	-	-	Murdock, Paul	0+6	-	-	-	-
Brierley, Steve	13+3	-	-	-	-	Pape, Kevin	31	22	-	-	88
Coles, Colin	27	4	-	-	16	Peacham, Gary	1	-	-	-	-
Courty, Dave	5+4	-	-	-	-	Schubert, Garry	33	2	-	-	8
Doyle, Mark	27	5	-	-	20	Scott, Tony	15+9	1	-	-	4
Duffy, Don	9	-	-	-	-	Stockley, John	1	-	-	-	-
Green, Jimmy	12	-	-	-	-	Subritzky, Peter	12	2	-	3	11
Green, Kenny	1	-	-	-	-	Thomason, Malcolm	25	2	-	-	8
Kirkby, Steve	21+1	2	-	-	8	Tunstall, Brian	20	-	54	2	110
Langton, Steve	30	11	-	-	44	Vickers, Barry	9	-	24	2	50
Lithgow, Paul	9+1	1	-	-	4	Whitchurch, Duncan	2+2	-	-	-	-
Little, Alan	6+1	-	-	-	-						
Maclagan, Alan	1+3	-	-	-	-	**TOTALS**					
McAvoy, Brian	3+1	1	-	-	4	30 Players		69	84	8	452
McMullen, Alan	26+1	-	-	-	-						

1987-88 MATCH ANALYSIS

Date	Competition	Opponent	Result	Score	Tries	Goals	Attendance
30.8.87	SD	Wakefield T.	L	8-56	Kirkby, Langton	-	-
6.9.87	SD	Doncaster	D	18-18	Schubert, Langton, Doyle	Tunstall (3)	709
9.9.87	SD	Keighley	W	26-12	Langton, Pape, Mills	Tunstall (7)	497
13.9.87	LC(1)	Whitehaven	L	12-28	Armstrong, Pape	Tunstall (2)	-
20.9.87	SD	Workington T.	L	12-24	Pape, McAvoy	Tunstall (2)	816
27.9.87	SD	Rochdale H.	L	5-20	Pape	Subritzky (dg)	-
9.10.87	SD	Springfield B.	L	9-12	Subritzky	Tunstall (2), Subritzky (dg)	-
25.10.87	SD	Featherstone R.	W	29-22	Pape (2), Kirkby, Thomason	Tunstall (6), Subritzky (dg)	-
8.11.87	SD	Huddersfield B.	L	8-16	Pape (2)	-	-
15.11.87	JPS(1)	Warrington	L	16-22	Pape, Langton	Tunstall (4)	1055
22.11.87	SD	Bramley	W	20-6	Langton, Pape, Mills	Tunstall (4)	400
29.11.87	SD	Workington T.	L	2-14	-	Tunstall	-
6.12.87	SD	Runcorn H.	W	13-11	Pape	Tunstall (4, 1 dg)	507
20.12.87	SD	Sheffield E.	W	14-12	Mills (2)	Tunstall (3)	559
1.1.88	SD	Whitehaven	W	6-4	Mills	Tunstall	-
10.1.88	SD	Springfield B.	W	29-0	Scott, G. Murdock, Schubert, Thomason	Tunstall (6, 1 dg)	639

1987-88 MATCH ANALYSIS CONTINUED

Date	Competition	Opponent	Result	Score	Tries	Goals	Attendance
17.1.88	CC(P)	Whitehaven	D	8-8	Lithgow	Tunstall (2)	1867
20.1.88	CC(P) Replay	Whitehaven	W	22-8	Armstrong, Mills, Pape, Coles	Tunstall (3)	-
24.1.88	SD	Sheffield E.	L	10-12	Langton, Mills	Tunstall	-
31.1.88	CC(1)	Hull K.R.	L	6-14	-	Tunstall (3)	-
14.2.88	SD	Oldham	L	4-26	Pape	-	-
21.2.88	SD	Doncaster	W	16-6	Pape, Subritzky	Armstrong (4)	-
28.2.88	SD	Wakefield T.	L	8-22	Mills, Pape	-	920
2.3.88	SD	Bramley	L	13-23	Pape, Doyle	Armstrong (2, 1 dg)	-
9.3.88	SD	Barrow	L	2-10	-	Vickers	586
13.3.88	SD	Rochdale H.	L	10-11	Pape (2)	Vickers	459
20.3.88	SD	Keighley	W	14-10	Pape, Langton	Vickers (3)	-
23.3.88	SD	Huddersfield B.	W	22-12	Doyle (2), Coles, Pape	Vickers (3)	446
27.3.88	SD	Featherstone R.	W	23-18	Coles (2), Langton, Mills	Vickers (3, 1 dg)	849
1.4.88	SD	Barrow	W	17-16	G. Murdock, Mills	Vickers (4, 1 dg)	-
5.4.88	SD	Whitehaven	W	16-7	Langton, Doyle	Vickers (4)	1132
10.4.88	SD	Runcorn H.	W	18-10	Langton, Mills, Pape	Vickers (3)	-
17.4.88	SD	Oldham	L	16-34	Pape, Langton, Mills	Vickers (2)	2049

1987-88 SECOND DIVISION TABLE

	P	W	D	L	For Dg	Goals	Tries	Total	Agst Dg	Goals	Tries	Total	PTS
Oldham	28	23	1	4	3	116	134	771	5	59	53	335	47
Featherstone R.	28	21	2	5	10	107	122	712	7	57	58	353	44
Wakefield T.	28	20	1	7	0	103	115	666	5	49	53	315	41
Springfield B.	28	18	0	10	4	74	74	448	12	60	56	356	36
Sheffield E.	28	16	1	11	4	67	88	490	7	67	72	429	33
York	28	15	1	12	14	86	93	558	6	82	89	526	31
Mansfield M.	28	15	1	12	7	68	74	439	4	56	74	412	31
Keighley	28	15	0	13	5	78	84	497	2	75	69	428	30
Barrow	28	14	2	12	4	61	64	382	5	72	62	397	30
Workington T.	28	15	0	13	14	65	59	380	5	70	74	441	30
Carlisle	28	14	1	13	8	70	60	388	6	76	72	446	29
Runcorn H.	28	14	0	14	10	63	71	420	3	79	77	469	28
Whitehaven	28	10	1	17	7	63	71	417	6	67	78	452	21
Bramley	28	10	1	17	4	70	64	400	6	89	104	600	21
Dewsbury	28	10	0	18	5	66	70	417	5	73	92	519	20
Doncaster	28	9	2	17	2	72	65	406	6	85	84	512	20
Fulham	28	10	0	18	4	63	63	382	9	85	95	559	20
Rochdale H.	28	10	0	18	8	53	52	322	8	69	92	514	20
Huddersfield B.	28	7	1	20	3	52	69	383	3	81	108	597	15
Batley	28	6	1	21	9	46	51	305	11	94	81	523	13

1987-88 SLALOM LAGER ALLIANCE -SECOND DIVISION

	P	W	D	L	For Pts	Agst Pts	Total
Whitehaven	26	18	2	6	612	356	38
Carlisle	26	18	2	6	544	331	38
Blackpool S	26	18	1	7	560	379	37
Bradford N	26	16	2	8	506	396	34
Oldham	26	15	3	8	622	487	33
Wakefield T	26	15	1	10	538	374	31
Featherstone R	26	15	1	10	512	422	31
Batley	26	14	1	11	412	446	29
Barrow	26	13	2	11	641	449	28
Dewsbury	26	11	0	15	371	465	22
Huddersfield P	26	9	3	14	408	639	21
Rochdale H	26	10	0	16	481	465	20
Workington T	26	8	0	18	422	468	16
Doncaster	26	6	1	19	355	682	13
Bramley	26	6	1	19	355	698	13
York	26	5	2	19	313	595	12

8

*

1988-89

CARLISLE's 1988-89 season opened at the vast mausoleum that was Station Road, Swinton. The faded trappings of past glories remained. The big old stand was still there. The affable club directors offered great liquid hospitality in a grand old board room that had the biggest one-piece decorated carpet I've ever seen - with the Swinton crest woven into the middle of it. It was as if nothing had changed in thirty years. Even the great Alan Buckley, the finest centre of his day, still popped in for a friendly drink or two. The Swinton directors' tipple of choice, incidentally, was a very large whisky in a glass of milk.

After all the pre-season hype - with Roy predicting this as Carlisle's year - we lost. Not heavily, but 28-20, to a vastly experienced team containing such stars as Paul Topping, Steve Snape, Gary Ainsworth and, the master himself, former Great Britain international John Woods.

On the next weekend, 4th September saw the first ever senior game played at the new Gillford Park, against Batley.

Yet the match was still in doubt right up to the Thursday, as we still needed to finish off the spectator facilities.

In the event, the game went ahead without any covered accommodation. The matchday programme was a single photocopied sheet prepared the day before, and the PA system was a mic and couple of speakers borrowed from the Railway Club concert room. This equipment, used with the permission of the club steward, had to be returned before the committee arrived for the evening bingo ritual.

It must have been quite an amusing sight for our visitors. The home directors, instead of wearing the blazers, shirts, ties and slacks that were almost obligatory in those days, were to a man clad in old jeans etc and hammered away in the stand at every lull in play, as we fixed the rudimentary bench-seating in place.

The game itself was merely a diversion. For the record, Carlisle drew 17-17, with Colin Coles and Garry Schubert getting the tries. Barry Vickers (four goals) and 'Rip' Kirkby (drop-goal) were the other scorers. Despite the novelty value of labouring directors and a new ground, the crowd was a disappointing 675.

We won the next three games, away at Workington 11-10, and at home to Chorley 17-7 and Huddersfield 40-1. New signing Barry Vickers played a major part, collecting fifteen goals in a three-game tally.

Carlisle then entered a bit of a slump with just one win (a shaky 30-10 home victory over basement club Runcorn) from six games, lightened only by the signing that October of two charismatic and capable Australians in Darryl Pitt (who went on to a lengthy career with London Broncos) and Tony Catton. Then we were into problems of a totally different kind.

There was a major cock-up in communication between the British Rail Property Board and our landlords, the

Railway Club. The detail is obscure but the Property Board, with whom we were obliged to negotiate, had agreed a concession in rental for the first year of our occupancy but omitted to tell the Railway Club, whose somewhat bombastic treasurer saw fit to make a public announcement to the local press that the rugby club was in default and were henceforth banned from the ground! Happily, wiser council prevailed. Still on file is the joint press statement that we made with the eminently sensible Railway Club secretary to the effect that it was all a misunderstanding and it was business as usual.

Sadly, these 'misunderstandings' with the Railway Club committee continued to blight our time at Gillford Park and erupted at depressingly frequent intervals. I think the truth of the matter is that, in those days, the Railway Club did reasonably well as a members' drinking club and the rugby was seen as an unwelcome intrusion with unsympathetic priorities into the social world of one or two of the men who ran the club's affairs. I suspected that there was also a political element as the aforementioned former Carlisle City Labour councillor and one-time Mayor who was the club treasurer resented the blatant capitalist leanings of some of the rugby management.

An uneasy relationship with Cumbria police over the costs to the club of the attendance of police officers at Gillford Park also came to the fore. The exact financial numbers are now unimportant but we were being billed several hundreds of pounds each home game for a couple of bobbies who probably saw attendance at the games as a perk of the job. The club took legal advice with regard to its obligations in this respect and, after being appropriately briefed as to our rights as outlined in case law 'Harris v Sheffield United', organised a meeting with the assistant chief constable at the Cumbria police HQ, near Penrith. This later developed into a saga that lasted over a couple of seasons, but with an ultimately satisfactory conclusion as the charges stopped after a period of deliberation. Maybe the police eventually realised that there was no need for their presence and you can't get blood from a stone!

The next problem was not so easily resolved. Roy Lester, who had earlier in the year accepted a senior management position in Lancashire with Frank Lowe's Cumbria Leisure Ltd, dropped a bombshell by suddenly resigning. It was perfectly understandable that he should find a stressful job in Carlisle too much on top of his Lancashire commitments but the timing was dreadful. We were just two months into the season with a team that he had assembled from contacts loyal to him.

To his credit, the late Alan Kellett, our former coach, helped out along with 'A' team coach Colin Porthouse, but both had other commitments so it was never going to be more than a one or two-week fix. We ran an advertisement in the *Rugby Leaguer* and got the usual miscellany of applications from unknown provincial Australian coaches, and wannabe coaches from other sports.

It was the late Ivor Kelland, former player and coach at Barrow and rugby league commentator for BBC Radio Cumbria, who recommended former Barrow coach Tommy Dawes to us. Tommy, a top long-serving full-back for Barrow in the Sixties had been the saviour of his club in the 1983-84 season and coached them to a Lancashire Cup win against all the odds and then the Second Division Championship by a mile. Tommy's reputation went ahead of him and, after meeting a couple of us in the Lakes Court Hotel by Carlisle railway station, he was appointed Carlisle coach in December 1988 on a contract that ran until the end of the 1989-90 season.

Tommy was a very likeable guy. He was an

uncomplicated and honest character who wore his heart on his sleeve and, in those days when many of us smoked, was rarely to be seen without a cigarette in his mouth. He was instrumental in the signing of two very influential players that season from Barrow in big Dave Kendal (actually Dave was already signed but staying away and Tommy acted as mediator and brought him back) and Steve Rea, a very skilled half-back. One particular memory of Steve was at Chiswick, where he scored an unbelievable try from broken play in an impossible position deep in his own half, beating just about the entire Fulham team.[1]

I should have asked Tommy Dawes for his opinion about a strange incident at the Barrow club after our Boxing Day game there. Having easily beaten them 28-6 at Gillford Park, we had high hopes for the return game at Craven Park. It wasn't to be; we lost 15-10 in a dour game, with Malcolm Thomason our sole try scorer. Afterwards, as was customary, we all made our way to the Barrow boardroom, in those days a tiny cupboard of a room under the old wooden stand, for the usual cuppa etc and post-match formalities. It was then that proceedings took a most bizarre turn.

Barrow's book of boardroom etiquette, probably written with a quill pen in the 1900s, stated that women were not allowed in the inner sanctum. Unbelievably, their chairman invoked this rule and the bluff but affable Bob Brady, their long-time benefactor, director and club stalwart was delegated to tell Elsie Martlew, Carlisle club director, that

---

[1]Dave and Steve were until recently both still very much involved in the game in South Lakeland. Dave, who has a successful roofing business was, until late 2007, a director at Barrow RLFC and Steve had a role with youth rugby at the same club until family commitments rescheduled his priorities. Tommy Dawes, meanwhile, has long since retired from the game and has happily adapted to a golfing life at his local Walney Golf Club. He retains happy memories of his season-and-a-half at Carlisle and says he was shocked at the decision to merge with Barrow in 1998.

she would have to wait outside. To say that we were dumbfounded would be a gross understatement.

Fortunately, Elsie and the rest of us just took at as an excuse to leave early and avoid the traditional excruciating victory speech that we knew would be forthcoming. It could have become a diplomatic incident if Elsie hadn't simply treated it as just an amusing consequence of Barrow RLFC's isolation in a time-warp at the end of the A590.

Many, many years later in the by-then totally emancipated Barrow boardroom, I teased Bob Brady about the incident. He remembered it vividly, feigned embarrassment and put the blame squarely on the shoulders of his chairman, Bill Pears.

As 1988 drew to a close, the club received an unconditional cash offer of £25,000 from Hull KR for the transfer of the long-serving Colin (Buck) Armstrong. We weren't aware of their interest until that approach but to a cash-strapped club like Carlisle it was a fairytale ending to the year. Colin had been a loyal player for us but we could no more stand in the way of him playing at a higher level than we could sneeze at twenty-five grand.

The year 1989 thus opened with cash in the bank and a new feeling of well-being. This immediately translated into results on the pitch. We marked New Years Day with a narrow 9-8 victory in the home derby against Whitehaven and followed this up with five further wins on the trot, including a 52-10 hammering of Fulham at Gillford Park, to give us our longest winning streak for some while.

That February we progressed to a lucrative second round Challenge Cup tie with Leeds at Headingley, following a club record 58-1 victory over Mansfield Marksmen at the Harvey Hadden Sports Stadium, at which Barry Vickers set a new club goals-in-a-match record with nine through the uprights.

That Headingley clash attracted a shared gate of 9,500 and, although Carlisle were beaten 24-4 through tries from household names like Andrew Ettingshausen, John Bentley, Phil Ford and Ray Ashton (who later coached Workington Town), the solitary 'Rip' Kirkby try sent us all into raptures. Tommy Dawes also berated Furness-born referee Colin Steele for disallowing a Carlisle try in the dying moments.

The cash situation, already unaccustomedly healthy, further improved when we at last received a £20,000 grant from Carlisle City Council, application for which had been started a year previously. This enabled us, with a lot of self-help, to install proper concrete terracing with a sheet-steel roof on the north side of the ground.

By February 1989, the residual Yorkshire-based players Gary Peacham, Dean Carroll and Steve Langton, all still in their mid-twenties, were deemed not to be part of the club's future and were transfer-listed at ludicrously ambitious fees of £25,000, £42,000 and £50,000. In those days, there was a feeling within the game that if, as so often happened, a player was signed without an agreement with the selling club, then the transfer tribunal, whose onerous task it was to set an appropriate fee, would be swayed by a sky-high asking price.

Predictably, then, it was some while before the Yorkshire-based players were actually transferred to other clubs and, in any case, at a fraction of the asking price. In modern day employment law, what we did then would have probably been construed as illegal and 'in restraint of trade' as it restricted those lads' further employment as professional rugby league players. But there again, just a few years later, the entire lifetime contract system employed in both soccer and rugby league was found in the European Court of Justice to be illegal, as the Bosman Case became a watershed in British sport.

Above: The Carlisle Junior Rugby League squad pictured in 1989. Back row: Cll'r Cyril Webber, Alan Tucker, Garry Schubert, Trevor Eston, Kevin Pape, Elaine "Nobby" Gordon, Tommy Dawes, Harry Pinner.
Middle Row: Johnathan Farrimond, Mark Johnston, Spencer Sharpley, Tony Kirkwood, Chris Easton, Paul Blaylock, Gary Dixon, unknown, unknown, Craig Stalker. Front Row: Craig Barwick, unknown, unknown, Lee Marsden, Mike Marsden, Kieron Richardson, Andrew Penny, Martin Stalker, Danny McCluskey

A much more positive action that season with long-term implications was the appointment of Garry Schubert as schools development officer. Garry replaced Peter Subritzky in a post that was initially funded by the club and Carlisle City Council alone but which, after a frustrating delay, was eventually contributed to by the RFL.

Garry very quickly earned the respect of everyone, as the wealth of unsolicited testimonials received from the staff and pupils of secondary and junior schools across the city amply demonstrated. In fact, the current Carlisle Centurions RLFC side, which now plays in the summer conference, is heavily dependent on youngsters who learned the game in the late-Eighties and early-Nineties as a result of the efforts of Garry, his band of willing volunteers and the staff at the participating schools.

Trevor Easton, now a mainstay of Carlisle Centurions, recalls those early days with Garry Schubert and company.

'A Carlisle under-11s team played the West Cumbria League squad in their run-up to the curtain-raiser for the 1988 Wembley Challenge Cup final,' he recalls. 'Carlisle went down 12 points to 30 but it was clear that the juniors had arrived. The late Carl Steele continued to develop the grass roots and that resulted in the formation of the Carlisle Junior Rugby League Club and an application to enter the established West Cumbria Youth League at under-12s. Carl did well to attract support from other coaches, including local teacher Trevor Easton, Royal Mail worker Mike Richardson and Wiganer Geoff Farrimond.

'Carlisle's 1988-89 under-12s squad included a number of players who remained in the game beyond their teenage years. Mike Marsden went on to join the county under-14s squad and, along with his brother Lee, was a regular with the St Nicholas Arms, later Carlisle Saints, at open age. Mike was also went on to be a regular with Carlisle Centurions in their inaugural season in 2003 under coach Gary Murdock and, the following season, stepped in to coach the squad when Buck Armstrong withdrew from the post.

'Also in the initial under-12s squad were Shaun Marshall, who like Mike, went on to join the county representative squad, and Chris Easton, who made his mark, a few years later, with the all-conquering Leeds University Rugby League Club of 1995-96.

'Most notable, however, was Anna Gordon, the first girl to be registered as a player with the Cumbria League. Unfortunately the League Rules prevented her, or any other female, from continuing beyond the age of 12.

'In 1988 another female player, Vikki Young, was fielded in a curtain-raiser at Sheffield Eagles. Carlisle won 32-0 and Vikki played a full part, making several penetrating runs from her position on the right wing. She had to wait another five years before the Carlisle women's team was formed and competed, over three seasons, against the likes of Barrow, Wigton and St Helens in the women's league.'

The amateur clubs from the previous season's Carlisle and District Amateur League (Wigton, Dalston 'A', Cumbria Leisure, Horse and Farrier and St Nicholas Arms) were meanwhile making unspectacular progress in Division Four of the Cumberland Amateur Rugby League. Andrew Hodgkinson of St Nicholas Arms ARLFC was appointed BARLA representative for Carlisle clubs.

1988-89 CUMBERLAND AMATEUR RUGBY LEAGUE

Division Two

	P	W	D	L	F	A	Pts
Distington	16	14	1	1	366	116	29
Flimby	15	13	0	2	355	150	26
Westfield Hotel	16	10	0	6	271	161	20
Dalston	16	10	0	6	276	176	20
Great Clifton	14	7	2	5	189	195	16
Glasson Rangers 'A'	15	5	1	9	176	315	11
St. Bees	16	5	0	11	260	328	10
Wath Brow Hornets 'A'	16	3	0	13	130	275	6
Maryport	16	1	0	15	173	388	2

Division Four

	P	W	D	L	F	A	Pts
Broughton Moor	21	20	0	1	794	179	40
Cockermouth	21	18	0	3	616	234	36
Wigton	22	15	0	7	490	327	30
Crown and Anchor	22	14	1	7	488	298	29
Dalston 'A'	22	14	0	8	406	297	28
Cumbria Leisure	22	12	0	10	333	251	24
Lowca 'A'	20	9	1	10	319	207	19
Horse and Farrier	22	7	0	15	267	466	14
St Nicholas Arms	21	6	0	15	224	472	12

Along with flying high in the second division of the Cumberland League, city club Dalston was also branching out into Ladies rugby league. The advent of this and its subsequent travails is recalled by Elaine McCullough, one of the players who was involved from the start of the venture.

'The birth of ladies rugby league in Carlisle came about

in 1989,' says Elaine. 'An advertisement was placed in the local newspaper by Dalston ARLFC, enquiring if there were any ladies in the Carlisle area interested in playing the game. Following this meeting, there were sufficient of us to form a team. Some had no previous experience and saw it as a means of keeping fit. Others were wives and girlfriends of players, already familiar with the code and jumping at the chance to give the game a try.

'We all agreed, however, that this was the most physical and demanding sport we had ever played. Many recall now how they were so sore and stiff after training and matches; one even remembering how her children had to roll her out of bed the next morning. She was unable to move a single muscle! The women did not escape their fair share of serious injuries either, such as dislocated fingers, damaged knee ligaments and even broken bones. Our first coach was Elaine Gordon; others included the late Carl Steele, Trevor Easton, Paul Woods, Stephen Cox and Mike Rayson.

'The womens team trained at various venues including Harraby school and gym, Gillford Park, Morton school, and even the Lower Viaduct car park, using the lights there to see on dark evenings. Matches were usually held at Gillford Park and Morton school.

'Our baptism to the code was the first friendly against Rochdale Ladies, played in torrential rain. By the end of the game, the teams were unrecognisable. This might have deterred us from continuing – but we were made of sterner stuff, despite being well beaten.

'Initially, all our games were friendlies and not in a league structure. But then we joined the Ladies League and played against sides mainly in the north west, including Barrow, Lancaster University, Rochdale, Warrington and Wigan, along with the likes of Stanningley, Sheffield, Halifax and Hull. There wasn't a great deal of success, but the enjoyment factor outweighed the results. We also competed in seven-a-side tournaments during the summer months.'

The womens team even played a curtain-raiser to a Carlisle Border Raiders match, against Wigan Ladies at Gillford Park, as Elaine remembers. 'We attracted attention from the local media, Border Television, who came to a training session to interview the players about their involvement in this unusual ladies sport,' she says.

'The team used The St Nicholas Arms pub in London Road as its base, and aftermatch hospitality was held there, which also provided a friendly social aspect. Indeed, the team was even named Carlisle Codys after the landlord of the St Nick, Mr Pat Cody. He was a huge support to the girls, not only providing a base, but also allowing them to use his minibus for away fixtures. However, the venues we visited were not always so desirable. Wigan's facilities then were a far cry from the DW Stadium. The ladies' changing facilities were in a toilet cubicle with no door or toilet seat!

'Funding was difficult too. The ladies paid subs each week to help pay for post-match refreshments and fuel to away matches. Strips were initially borrowed from other male teams and eventually the side received its own strip by way of sponsorship from S&K Chadwick. The girls also purchased their own team tracksuit, purple and navy blue, which looked extremely professional. However, it was to be a lack of funding that brought the ladies' game to a close some years later, unable as it was to sustain the income required. Rather than end their playing careers, some ladies switched codes and joined Carlisle RUFC, at Warwick Road. They were a well-established rugby club who could provide support for the ladies game and are still going strong today.'

The junior game, meanwhile, was developing apace in schools as well as at the club, under the leadership of Garry Schubert, who successfully combined a playing role with that of a full-time employee of the City Council in a position jointly funded by them and the RFL.

By dint of personality, backed up with a lot of cold-calling, Garry successfully got many of the junior schools to make his coaching assistance part of the sporting curriculum. As briefly referred to by Trevor Easton earlier, the secondary schools were a tougher nut to crack but rugby league became accepted as an extra-curricular activity at Morton, Harraby, Cardinal Newman, Lochinvar and Caldew schools. Indeed Garry recalls that the then-head of Lochinvar school, current Centurions management committee member Malcolm Jackson, enjoyed the sessions so much that he actually played alongside his Year 10 pupils, giving and receiving no quarter in the tackles.

Now working in the sports and leisure department at Carlisle City Council, Garry recalls that time well. 'I played rugby league as a kid in a small town about three hours north of Sydney, he says. 'When I graduated to the senior side, the two coaches, Brian Atherton and Eddie Woods, both of whom were originally from Widnes, suggested that I might enjoy a spell in England. Arrangements were made for me to join Salford under their coach, Kevin Ashcroft. After I'd been six months at Salford, a conversation between Kevin and his old mate Roy Lester at Carlisle saw me heading north after a couple of trials at Blackpool. I saw Carlisle as a far better option because Blackpool seemed to be in a permanent state of flux with their training venues.

'I remember arriving in Carlisle on New Years Day 1987. My first digs were a tiny flat on the top floor of the old supporters club. I was then moved to a flat in the Legends nightclub and from there to Oswald Street, off London Road.

'Carlisle was a totally different city in those days. It was heavily industrialised and gave me my first experience of snow. A strong memory is that the city life seemed to be a succession of gloomy winter days followed by long cold dark nights.

'As far as schools development was concerned, the fact that most of the junior school heads were male was a great help. They saw rugby league as being a sport with which they could empathise and a great character development tool. Some of the teachers who helped me were Mr Rutter from Rob't Ferguson, Mr Baker from Kingmoor, Shaun Halfpenny from Cummersdale, Trevor Easton from Morton, Malcolm Jackson from Lochinvar, George Perkins from Harraby, and Brian Glencross from Cardinal Newman. I was also given great support by fans Jean Pharaoh and Elaine Gordon. The late Carl Steele was a former player who took a major role in coaching.

'I take great satisfaction from the fact that some of the youngsters who came through the system went on to play professionally. Players such as the Stalker twins, who signed for Workington, and Jonathan Farrimond, who became a BARLA international and played pro for the former Carlisle Border Raiders. Sadly, the early-Nineties recession dried up the available funding for rugby league and when I was reassigned to other duties by Carlisle City Council, the schools development programme came to an end. I'm glad to see, though, that the RFL have managed to restore the programme for 2010. History is repeating itself and we are now looking to recruit a schools development officer once again.

'On the field, I really enjoyed my rugby with Carlisle,' continues Garry. 'The blood and thunder derbies were great to play in, as was the occasional cup game when we took on opposition from a higher league. I was very happy at Carlisle but was ready for a change when the opportunity came to join Workington in August 1991 under coach Dean Williams. I then enjoyed five good years there under Peter

Walsh. But when Peter left to rejoin Illawarra in Australia and new coach Ross O'Reilly brought in new players, it reduced my opportunities for first-team rugby so, at the age of 30, I joined Barrow as player-coach. Sadly, my growing responsibilities in the leisure department created a conflict for my time and I left after just one season.'

Garry went on to marry Christine, the girl he met in his early days at Carlisle Border Raiders, and they now have a daughter, Rebecca, who is a student in linguistics at York University.

Other practical and welcome helpers who emerged that season, and who were to stay loyal to the club to the very end, included Councillor Cyril Weber who lived just a mile away from the stadium. Cyril, chairman of the City Council's leisure committee, went on to become a fixture as our matchday announcer. He also established, with his wife Rosemary, a thriving souvenir shop which sold replica kit, club badges and Carlisle RLFC mugs. His son, Gareth, was also a great supporter, acting in the early days as ballboy and scoreboard operator before playing in the academy under-21s side in later years.

Border City Blues

CARLISLE – 1988-89 – SEASON SUMMARY

Chairman:	Alan Tucker
Secretary:	Robert Carter
Coach:	Roy Lester (June 1986-Nov 1988), Tommy Dawes Dec 1988-)
Records:	Attendance: 5,903 v. Workington T. (Div 2) 6 Sept. 1981
Season	Goals: 113 by S. Ferres, 1981-82
	Tries: 25 by M. Morgan, 1981-82, G. Peacham, 1984-85
	Points: 242 by S. Ferres, 1981-82
Match	Goals: 9 by D. Carroll v Mansfield M,
	16 Mar 1986; B. Vickers v Mansfield M, 29 Jan, 1989
	Tries: 4 by G. Peacham v. Workington T., 25 Jan, 1987
	and K. Pape v. Rochdale H., 11 Feb, 1987
	Points: 22 by B. Vickers v. Mansfield M., 29th Jan, 1989
	Highest Score: 58-1 v. Mansfield., 1988-89
	Highest against: 112-0 v. St. Helens, 1986-87

	App.	Tries	Goals	D/Gls	Pts
Armstrong, Colin	16+2	2	-	2	10
Bowness, Chris	1+3	-	-	-	-
Brierley, Steve	20+7	2	-	-	8
Carroll, Dean	3+3	1	-	-	4
Catton, Tony	11+3	2	-	1	9
Coles, Colin	18+1	8	5	-	42
Courty, Dave	1+1	-	-	-	-
Doyle, Mark	30	9	-	-	36
Ferguson, Gary	1	-	-	-	-
Graham, John	1+2	-	-	-	-
Kendall, Dave	21+3	3	-	-	12
Kirkby, Steve	24+1	6	-	1	25
Langton, Steve	16	6	-	-	24
Lithgow, Paul	2	-	-	-	-
Little, Alan	2+1	-	-	-	-
McAvoy, Brian	15+2	5	-	-	20
McMullen, Alan	3	-	-	-	-
Murdock, Gary	33	10	-	-	40
Murdock, Paul	0+4	-	-	-	-

	App.	Tries	Goals	D/Gls	Pts
Pape, Kevin	33	14	-	-	56
Peacham, Gary	2	-	-	-	-
Pitt, Darryl	19+1	7	-	-	28
Pollard, Damian	4+3	-	-	-	-
Rea, Steve	5+1	5	-	-	20
Richardson, Dave	3	2	-	-	8
Robinson, Paul	9+2	-	-	-	-
Schubert, Garry	31	2	-	-	8
Scott, Ian	0+2	-	-	-	-
Scott, Tony	33	4	-	-	16
Stafford, Peter	5+3	1	8	-	20
Thomason, Bryan	0+1	-	-	-	-
Thomason, Malcolm	32	8	-	-	32
Tunstall, Brian	1+2	-	-	-	-
Vickers, Barry	28	1	99	3	205
Wilkes, Mark	6+1	-	-	-	-
TOTALS		98	112	7	623
35 Players					

1988-89 MATCH ANALYSIS

Date	Competition	Opponent	Result	Score	Tries	Goals	Attendance
28.8.88	SD	Swinton	L	20-28	Coles, Langton, Armstrong	Vickers (3, 2dg)	-
4.9.88	SD	Batley	D	17-17	Coles, Schubert	Vickers (4), Kirkby (dg)	675
11.9.88	SD	Workington T.	W	11-10	Langton	Vickers (3), Armstrong (dg)	-
18.9.88	LC(1)	Chorley B.	W	17-7	Langton, Doyle	Vickers (4), Armstrong (dg)	645
25.9.88	SD	Huddersfield	W	40-1	Pape (2), Langton, Doyle, Thomason, Murdock	Vickers (8)	701
28.9.88	LC(2)	Warrington	L	18-34	Thomason, Brierley	Vickers (3), Stafford (2)	-
2.10.88	SD	Leigh	L	10-12	Langton	Stafford (3)	890
9.10.88	SD	Doncaster	L	6-24	McAvoy	Stafford	812
16.10.88	SD	Keighley	L	12-26	Carroll, Murdock	Stafford (2)	-
23.10.88	SD	Runcorn H.	W	30-10	Pape, Kirkby, McAvoy, Pitt	Vickers (7)	523
30.10.88	SD	Barrow	L	6-28	Langton	Vickers	785
6.11.88	SD	Batley	W	13-6	McAvoy, Armstrong	Vickers (2, 1dg)	-
13.11.88	JPS(1)	Wakefield T.	L	14-34	McAvoy, Pitt	Vickers (3)	-
20.11.88	SD	Chorley B.	L	4-18	-	Vickers (2)	-

1988-89 MATCH ANALYSIS

Date	Competition	Opponent	Result	Score	Tries	Goals	Attendance
4.12.88	SD	Dewsbury	W	26-15	Murdock, Pitt, Pape, Doyle	Vickers (5)	395
11.12.88	SD	Leigh	L	6-24	Pape	Vickers	-
18.12.88	SD	Swinton	L	6-28	Pitt	Vickers	563
26.12.88	SD	Barrow	L	10-15	Thomason	Vickers (3)	-
1.1.89	SD	Whitehaven	W	9-8	Thomason	Vickers (2), Catton (dg)	902
8.1.89	SD	Fulham	W	52-10	Pape (2), Richardson (2), McAvoy, Doyle, Thomason, Kirkby, Murdock	Vickers (8)	512
15.1.89	SD	Huddersfield	W	14-7	Thomason, Scott, Murdock	Vickers	-
22.1.89	SD	Rochdale H.	W	44-12	Murdock (2), Doyle, Catton, Stafford, Kirkby, Pape	Vickers (8)	635
29.1.89	CC(1)	Mansfield M.	W	58-1	Coles (3), Doyle (2), Scott, Pape, Pitt, Vickers, Thompson	Vickers (9)	663
5.2.89	SD	Keighley	W	20-4	Kendall (2), Pitt	Vickers (4)	850
12.2.89	CC(2)	Leeds	L	4-24	Kirkby	-	-
26.2.89	SD	Chorley B.	L	8-17	Pape	Vickers (2)	650
5.3.89	SD	Runcorn H.	W	48-4	Kirkby (2), Doyle (2), Schubert, Pitt, Kendall, Scott, Pape, Catton	Vickers (4)	-
12.3.89	SD	Dewsbury	L	4-14	-	Vickers (2)	-
27.3.89	SD	Whitehaven	L	14-30	Pape, Rea	Vickers (3)	-
2.4.89	SD	Fulham	W	26-22	Pape (2), Murdock, Brierley, Rea	Coles (3)	-
5.4.89	SD	Doncaster	L	6-15	Thomason	Vickers	-
9.4.89	SD	Workington T.	W	24-18	Coles (2), Rea, Murdock, Scott	Coles (2)	600
16.4.89	SD	Rochdale H.	W	26-18	Rea (2), Murdock, Coles	Vickers (5)	-

1988-89 SECOND DIVISION TABLE

	P	W	D	L	For Dg	Goals	Tries	Total	Agst Dg	Goals	Tries	Total	PTS
Leigh	28	26	0	2	3	127	167	925	6	64	51	338	52
Barrow	28	21	1	6	4	107	127	726	4	47	57	326	43
Sheffield E	28	19	1	8	11	103	113	669	12	55	60	362	39
York	28	17	1	10	11	89	99	585	11	62	62	383	35
Swinton	28	16	2	10	5	88	110	621	12	75	80	482	34
Doncaster	28	17	0	11	7	104	96	599	8	78	75	464	34
Whitehaven	28	15	2	11	10	82	87	522	8	61	62	378	32
Keighley	28	16	0	12	3	92	91	551	7	81	89	525	32
Rochdale H	28	15	0	13	1	107	110	655	3	107	115	677	30
Bramley	28	14	1	13	6	89	104	600	12	85	83	514	29
Carlisle	28	14	1	13	6	91	81	512	7	71	73	441	29
Batley	28	13	3	12	27	63	77	461	10	59	72	416	29
Dewsbury	28	13	0	15	12	93	80	518	8	101	104	626	26
Hunslet	28	12	1	15	11	67	82	473	10	89	88	540	25
Fulham	28	10	0	18	10	77	75	464	8	95	113	650	20
Chorley B	28	9	1	18	8	60	70	408	7	93	85	533	19
Workington T	28	9	1	18	7	63	58	365	9	80	95	549	19
Huddersfield	28	9	1	18	10	55	70	400	9	91	106	615	19
Mansfield M	28	4	1	23	6	55	48	308	7	107	137	769	9
Runcorn H	28	2	1	25	4	32	39	224	4	143	177	998	5

1988-89 SLALOM LAGER ALLIANCE - FIRST DIVISION

	P	W	D	L	For Pts	Agst Pts	Total
Wigan	26	18	1	7	708	359	37
Castleford	26	17	2	7	659	421	36
St Helens	26	16	1	9	626	514	33
Leeds	26	16	0	10	651	453	32
Hull K.R	26	15	1	10	553	477	31
Widnes	26	13	1	12	590	531	27
Salford	26	13	1	12	539	475	27
Hull	26	12	3	11	483	445	27
Halifax	26	11	1	14	418	497	23
Warrington W	26	11	0	15	540	570	22
Swinton C	26	9	2	15	424	636	20
Hunslet	26	9	0	17	437	632	18
Carlisle	26	8	1	17	400	536	17
Whitehaven	26	6	2	18	316	798	14

Above: Carlisle coach Tommy Dawes,
on the microphone in 1989

9

*

1989-90

DURING the summer of 1989 the improvement work at Gillford Park continued despite the ongoing squabbles with a tiny minority of the committee at the Railway Club. These fall-outs were so debilitating that several members of the Carlisle RL board were keen for the rugby club to walk away and take any other option, anywhere.

In the close-season, Frank Lowe heard that Harry Pinner, the former GB and St Helens captain who'd been playing for Bradford Northern, was looking to change clubs. Pinner had always been a personal favourite, especially for his leadership of both Saints and the GB team in the 1985 series against New Zealand. The 25-8 victory over the Kiwis when Garry Schofield ran in four tries at Central Park remains indelibly etched in the memory.

Upon gaining the support of the board, Frank and I went to Harry Pinner's home, a delightful olde worlde cottage near Warrington, to agree terms prior to a substantial offer to Bradford. By July 1989 our bid was accepted and Harry became a Carlisle player, just in time for a couple of pre-season friendlies. Tommy Dawes thought he had died and gone to heaven to have such a skilled, experienced and high-profile player at his disposal.

Harry was a knowledgeable and entertaining conversationalist with a deep fund of funny anecdotes from his extensive international career, one of which entailed a fellow international falling out with the electronic voice at a New Zealand hole-in-the-wall cash dispensing machine.

I remember one conversation with him when he was decrying the obsolescence of good ball-handling forwards in favour of powerful straight runners whose main role was to tire the opposition tacklers, die with the ball and then effect the quickest play-the-ball possible. Harry's term for such players was 'sheep's heads and battering-rams'. A sheep's head and battering-ram Harry most certainly was not. He was a delightfully gifted ball player with the heart of a lion. In the few months that Harry graced a Carlisle jumper, his sublime skills and strength in the tackle had us in raptures.

No one, however, foresaw the events of the next couple of months. Harry became very unhappy with his lot, was quite critical of some of his fellow players and after just ten games said that he was going to retire. The player whose contract had just cost us twenty-five grand from Bradford, plus his own considerable personal terms, was going to pack it all in and take up an assistant coaching role at Wigan.

Immediately, we took legal advice, served papers and ended up with an equitable settlement in compensation for the money expended to date. Whether the settlement was paid by Harry Pinner or an involved third party I'm unsure. Suffice to say, justice was done.

With the wisdom of hindsight, Harry, who'd graced the world stage, was never going to settle for lower division rugby league with a club 120 miles away from his home and

Above: Harry Pinner, leading his Carlisle team-mates out against Runcorn

with players who were so far below his own capabilities. Both he and we at Carlisle were naive to think otherwise.

That close-season was a hive of activity at Carlisle RLFC. Straight after the Harry Pinner signing, we'd had an approach from a Brian Fox in the Newcastle area. Brian was anxious to get involved. He'd had some involvement with the burgeoning amateur game in the North East and was keen to invest in Carlisle. To cut a long story short, he eventually made a substantial contribution to club funds and joined the board as 'Our Man in the North East'.

From the few in-depth conversations I had with Brian, I understood that he'd made quite a lot of money out of recycling scrap plastic, primarily off-cuts from a local factory that made disposable nappies and waterproof trainer pants. He confided that his early start in business actually came from buying out-of-date scampi direct from boat operators at the quay and selling them to Chinese restaurants in his native North East. Sadly, Brian passed away after a brief illness before any of us had really got to know him. A real character taken away in his prime.

Brian introduced us to a very fast winger from Newcastle named Gerry Nicholson. Brian, not one for understatement, claimed he was as fast as Martin Offiah. It was a claim that saw the lad immediately christened Geordie Offiah by Raymond Edgar. The name stuck.

Gerry went on to play half a season with Carlisle and was undoubtedly fast, but he and his young wife and child never really settled into life away from the North East. He suffered a series of injuries and returned to the North East amateur game. Last we saw of him he'd carved out a career in sports physiotherapy in Gateshead.

We engaged a future assistant coach, Dave Robley, a PE teacher from Aspatria, to carry out sprint-training with our players, which was a first for us. On 14th July, we received an approach from an unknown Kiwi called Bradley Hepi, who was anxious to come and play for us. We duly signed him in the St Helens clubhouse after an 'A' team game the following month, when the menacing Emosi Koloto and Joe Grima from Widnes appeared as if by magic, like a pair of pantomime villains, to ensure their boy got fair terms.

After the usual Cumbrian Cup pre-season friendly competition, we opened with a hammering of Runcorn by 54-14, in which Rea, Pape and new boy Eddie Southwell scored a brace apiece. We were then turned over 30-22 at Workington before the big one against Widnes at Brunton Park.

The decision to use Brunton Park for this Lancashire Cup first-round tie attracted a lot of debate inside and outside the club. Some supporters castigated us for spending £1,700 to stage a game at the ground we had been forced to leave just two seasons earlier. The financial reality however was that we could only accommodate 2,000 supporters at Gillford

Park and we expected 4,000. The extra spectators were worth around £8,000, half of which was admittedly due to go to Widnes, as it was to be a shared gate.

We actually got a gate a bit higher than our expectations and 4,500 supporters were able to marvel at the skills of such as Jonathan Davies, Martin Offiah, Alan Tait, Brimah Kebbie, Paul Moriarty and company. In fact they were literally the best team in the world as, later that season, they won the World Club Challenge 30-18 against Canberra Raiders at Old Trafford, in front of 30,000 ecstatic observers.

Prior to the game I asked Harry Pinner about our likely tactics to contain such superstars. His reply has stuck in my mind. 'Alan,' Harry said. 'We've got to get amongst um and just mither um off their game.' The 46-6 result in Widnes's favour - Carlisle try by Harry Pinner - was never in doubt, and our supporters enjoyed standing shoulder to shoulder and sharing rounds of drinks with the famous Chemics players in the supporters club bar in Botchergate afterwards. Surely, a social scene impossible to imagine in any other professional team sport.

The rest of 1989 was a bit of a disaster on the field despite the arrival of two Kiwis in the already-signed Brad Hepi and then Hitro Okesene. Both would have a major impact on the game, in Carlisle and elsewhere.

After the Widnes loss, we recorded eight more defeats on the run before a quite remarkable game at Gillford Park against Halifax. Halifax, who had just a couple of seasons earlier, in April 1987, beaten Saints 19-18 in the Challenge Cup final at Wembley, had since suffered a brush with insolvency and been relegated. They were still a very potent side and one of the pacesetters in the second division.

Whatever came over the team on that late November Sunday, we only wished they could reproduce at will. The Kiwis, Hepi and Okesene, had absolute blinders. Hitro

Okesene in particular put in consecutive thunderous but fair tackles against two separate members of the Halifax pack that left them both sidelined. Steve Rea at stand-off revelled in the spaces left by the battered and bruised Halifax forwards and ran in three tries in a stirring 30-20 victory.

Sadly, it was a flash in the pan. By the year-end we'd won just four out of fifteen games and had little option other than to sever Tommy Dawes's contract. This was an extremely tough decision as Tommy's wife had passed away that season and undoubtedly and understandably this was affecting his coaching, but Tommy, being the man he is, respected that decision and we parted on good terms.

Still, we closed the season with a great 24-4 win at home to Whitehaven, a game in which local lad Alan Little began his bid for a regular first-team place with two fine tries. Wins against our West Cumbrian rivals always airbrushed previous bad form.

Fortunately for Carlisle, there was a coaching option that awaited our call in New Zealand. It was Dean Bell's Carlisle-based father-in-law, Tom Parker, who alerted us to the availability of Dean's dad, Cameron Bell. Cameron had coached at the highest level in New Zealand, including the Auckland side that beat the British in 1988 and the cream of Australia in 1989. Dean was still a cult figure in Carlisle as well as in the UK game in general, so we had no hesitation in making a conference call to Cameron, agreeing personal terms and arranging flights and local accommodation for him and his wife Janice. Their dog Tammy went into quarantine to be reunited with her owners a few months later.

Cameron couldn't arrive until 18th February, the day we were due to play Keighley at Gillford Park. His presence at Heathrow however must have had some sort of subliminal impact, as we halted another string of depressing defeats

Above: Cameron Bell gets down to some paperwork in the office

(this time six since Boxing Day) with an emphatic 38 -9 win over the Yorkshiremen.

One of the first things Cameron picked up on about our players' attitude to the game was their obsession with on-field grooming. He certainly made the local TV headlines when he announced a matchday ban on shaving and male deodorants. The logic was that the last thing you wanted an opposition player to notice about you after a rib-crushing tackle was your fragrance and soft skin. This was just a gimmick, though, as he started to reform serious bad habits and attitudes.

It would be over-charitable to claim an immediate transformation of results - the stark statistics are that, after his arrival, the club won just four of their remaining nine fixtures. The attendances reflected this poor form with an average of just 449 attending the games in the second half of the season. Our seventeenth position out of a league of twenty-one teams was our worst since 1982-83.

And at the end of that season, yet another row developed with the police. During one of our games at Gillford Park we'd engaged one of the policemen in a conversation. He had been quite innocently asked if he was pleased to get four hours overtime, plus a travelling allowance to attend our games (this was what the police were charging us for each bobby in attendance). He was quick to point out that he and his mate got just two hours overtime and no travel allowance. Our letter was waiting on the chief constable's desk the following morning. After over a month without a reply, we wrote again and offered to take the story to the press. The reply was almost instantaneous and was as big a load of blather and bureaucratic nonsense as we had ever read. We were slowly winning this battle.

Despite all this hassle, better times lay ahead, with the Carlisle juniors going on to win their first silverware when the club was honoured as the Junior Rugby League Club of the Season in 1990-91. A fitting tribute to the ongoing efforts of Garry Schubert and his volunteers.

Professionally, the close-season that year was one of the busiest yet when Cameron Bell managed to persuade David Oxley, the secretary general of the RFL, that Carlisle was a special case as a development club and ought to be allowed virtually unlimited numbers of New Zealand and South Sea Island imports. Carlisle was not the most popular team in Cumbria and there were frequent jealous comments from other clubs. Looking back on it, it's hard to blame them. At the peak, Carlisle must have resembled a suburb of Auckland. We were a magnet for all New Zealanders north of the M62.

An immediate priority that summer was to agree and formalise the recruitment of Clayton Friend from North Sydney. Clayton was still a legend in Carlisle after his exploits in the 1982-83 campaign. Since then, he had done nothing but enhance that reputation by playing in the full New Zealand national side and through his exploits in the senior Australian competition with North Sydney. The club ended up paying a fairly nominal fee to Norths for him and so he travelled to Carlisle for the new season.

Other New Zealand players recruited in that initial off-season signing spree included: Paul Earsman, who'd played in Auckland; Nigel White, who was already here and had played for both Workington and Whitehaven; Brad Hepi, who'd played for Carlisle since the previous year; Karl Findlay, who was already here and who had played some RU for Highland; Hitro Okesene, who by now was an old Carlisle hand; and Mark Perry, who had been in the UK since November 1989 and living in London. Others signed early in the season included Greg Rowe from New Plymouth and Nahu Timoko.

They didn't all hit the headlines of course. Paul Earsman and Mark Perry rarely made the first team and Nahu Timoko played just a handful of games.

Certainly Gillford Park looked as if a delegation from the United Nations had descended and frequent barbecues, especially of the 'hangi' variety, where the meat was cooked underground, became commonplace. We all learned new words and one that sticks in the mind was 'puha', a variety of soft thistle that Cameron and the other New Zealanders used to collect from around the ground and use as a vegetable. We were also reminded of a good few old Anglo Saxon words too when Mally Cooper's Weimarana, a hound called Oscar, ate the entire five kg of burgers we had just bought and set down for a post-training barbecue.

We really pushed the boat out in that off-season and organised a seven-a-side fun day at Gillford Park. The total prize money was large enough (£2,800) to attract a good attendance with teams of top stars from St Helens, Salford, Widnes, Rochdale, Sheffield, Barrow and Whitehaven to join our own lads. It was a great and memorable day out with some superb rugby played, but it made quite a loss so the idea was never repeated.

Another Cameron Bell-inspired idea that summer was a name change to Carlisle Border Raiders. 'Raiders' was intended to be an anglicisation of the old Borders word 'Reivers' and was a bit of a poke at orthodoxy, to reflect our growing habit of raiding players from Borders rugby union clubs. The new nickname created a bit of a stir at the RFL at Chapeltown Road (this was well before Super League when such American Football-type names became all the rage) and I still have on file a somewhat tetchy exchange of letters with David Oxley on the subject. From memory, he never knowingly referred to us as Carlisle Border Raiders for the rest of his time in office.

A much more prosaic memory of that summer is of Don McDowall's and my attempts at building a ramp for disabled access to the grandstand. This had become a real issue with the Council planning department, and rightly so. It was a part of the planning consent conditions, so we just had to bite the bullet and get it done. The directions we'd received from others in the know were simple. We just had to form a fifteen-metre ramp to scale a height of about one-and-a-half metres by compacting rubble with a 'whacker-plate' in readiness for a skilled builder to face it off with concrete and safety rails. We struggled in vain for a day-and-a-half to make it look like the foundations of a ramp. The damn 'whacker-plate' just had a mind of its own and took off downhill every time we used it.

We'd just about packed the job in as an impossible task when experienced builder and future director Mally Cooper appeared on the scene to share his concreting skills. Don and I cringed with embarrassment as, single-handedly, Mally manoeuvred the damn machine to do in half-an-hour what we'd worked in vain for a day-and-a-half to achieve.

1989-90 CUMBERLAND AMATEUR RUGBY LEAGUE

Division Two

	P	W	D	L	F	A	Pts
Distington	16	14	1	1	366	116	29
Flimby	16	14	0	2	355	150	28
Westfield Hotel	16	10	0	6	271	161	20
Dalston	16	10	0	6	276	176	20
Great Clifton	16	8	2	6	189	197	18
Glasson Rangers 'A'	15	5	1	10	176	315	11
St. Bees	16	5	0	11	215	373	10
Wath Brow Hornets 'A'	16	3	0	13	130	275	6
Maryport	16	1	0	15	173	388	2

Division Three

	P	W	D	L	F	A	Pts
Ellenborough 'A'	16	13	1	2	562	170	27
Corkickle	16	12	2	2	532	235	26
Egremont 'A'	16	11	0	5	297	198	22
Aspatria	16	10	1	5	254	186	21
Hensingham 'A'	16	9	1	6	345	193	19
Westfield Welfare	16	6	1	9	274	378	13
Frizington 'A'	16	4	0	12	280	646	8
Seaton 'A'	16	3	0	13	246	446	6
Flimby 'A'	16	1	0	15	110	448	2

Division Four

	P	W	D	L	F	A	Pts
Broughton Moor	22	20	1	1	794	179	41
Cockermouth	22	18	0	4	632	278	36
Wigton	22	15	0	7	490	327	30
Crown and Anchor	22	14	1	7	488	308	29
Dalston 'A'	22	14	0	8	400	291	28
Cumbria Leisure	22	12	0	10	333	251	24
Lowca 'A'	22	10	2	10	363	223	22
Horse and Farrier	22	7	0	15	267	466	14
Maryport 'A'	22	6	0	16	252	397	12
St. Nicholas Arms	22	6	0	16	244	500	12
Penrith	22	6	0	16	260	560	12
Distington 'A'	22	2	0	20	162	905	4

Border City Blues

CARLISLE – 1989-90 – SEASON SUMMARY

Chairman: Alan Tucker
Secretary: Robert Taylor
Coach: Tommy Dawes (Dec 1988-Jan 1990), Cameron Bell (Feb 1990-)
Records: Attendance: 5,903 v. Workington T. (Div 2) 6 Sept. 1981
Season Goals: 113 by S. Ferres, 1981-82
Tries: 25 by M. Morgan, 1981-82, G. Peacham, 1984-85
Points: 242 by S. Ferres, 1981-82
Match Goals: 10 by B. Vickers at Nottingham C., 11 Mar 1990
Tries: 4 by G. Peacham v. Workington T., 25 Jan, 1987
and K. Pape v. Rochdale H., 11 Feb, 1987
Points: 24 by B. Vickers v. Nottingham C., 11 Mar 1990
Highest Score: 60-0 v. Nottingham C., 1989-90
Highest against: 112-0 v. St. Helens, 1986-87

	App.	Tries	Goals	D/Gls	Pts		App.	Tries	Goals	D/Gls	Pts
Armstrong, Ian	0+1	-	-	-	-	Okesene, Hitro	16+2	3	-	-	12
Bowness, Chris	3+2	-	-	-	-	Pape, Kevin	27	16	-	-	64
Brierley, Steve	30	2	-	-	8	Pinner, Harry	10	1	-	-	4
Coles, Colin	22	7	1	-	30	Pollard, Damian	5+5	1	-	-	4
Cubiss, George	1	-	1	-	2	Rea, Steve	20+1	8	-	-	32
Doyle, Mark	16	3	7	-	26	Robinson, Paul	5+7	-	-	-	-
Graham, John	2+2	-	-	-	-	Schubert, Garry	26	2	-	-	8
Hepi, Brad	25	3	-	-	12	Scott, Ian	0+4	-	-	-	-
Kavanagh, Michael	7+4	3	1	-	14	Scott, Tony	20+4	2	-	-	8
Kendall, Dave	15+2	2	-	-	8	Southwell, Eddie	12+4	5	-	-	20
Kohlass, Darren	2	-	-	-	-	Thomason, Malcolm	31	7	-	-	28
Lithgow, Paul	9+2	3	-	-	12	Tunstall, Brian	0+1	-	1	-	2
Little, Alan	9+2	4	-	-	16	Vickers, Barry	25	4	72	1	161
MacLagan, Alan	0+1	-	-	-	-	Whitchurch, Duncan	2	-	-	-	-
McNichol, Tony	19+2	9	-	-	36	Williams, Barry	6	-	-	-	-
Murdock, Gary	24+1	2	-	-	8						
Murdock, Paul	1+2	-	-	-	-	**TOTALS**					
Nicholson, Gerry	12+3	3	-	-	12	33 Players		90	83	1	527

1989-90 MATCH ANALYSIS

Date	Competition	Opponent	Result	Score	Tries	Goals	Attendance
3.9.89	SD	Runcorn H.	W	54-14	Rae (2), Pape (2), Southwell (2), Thomason, Doyle, Kendall, Brierley	Vickers (7)	707
10.9.89	SD	Workington T	L	22-30	Lithgow (2), Pape, Southwell	Vickers (3)	-
17.9.89	LC(1)	Widnes (at Carlisle FC)	L	6-46	Pinner	Vickers	4329
1.10.89	SD	Fulham	L	6-50	-	Vickers (3)	-
8.10.89	SD	Workington T.	L	12-14	Doyle, Hepi	Vickers (2)	768
15.10.89	SD	Swinton	L	14-26	Rea, Kendall, Thomason	Doyle	-
22.10.89	SD	Oldham	L	10-32	Southwell	Vickers (3)	1059
29.10.89	SD	Hunslet	L	12-26	Pollard, McNichol	Doyle (2)	-
5.11.89	SD	Dewsbury	L	12-20	Nicholson, Thomason	Doyle (2)	-
12.11.89	SD	Ryedale-York	L	12-22	McNichol, Pape	Doyle (2)	446
19.11.89	SD	Keighley	L	22-30	McNichol (2), Coles, Pape	Vickers (3)	-
26.11.89	SD	Halifax	W	30-20	Rea (3), Pape, Coles	Vickers (5)	1102
3.12.89	RT(1)	Dewsbury	L	4-14	Vickers	-	-
17.12.89	SD	Nottingham C.	W	15-14	Pape, McNichol	Vickers (3, 1dg)	360

134

1989-90 MATCH ANALYSIS

Date	Competition	Opponent	Result	Score	Tries	Goals	Attendance
26.12.89	SD	Runcorn H.	W	18-9	Okesene, Kavanagh, Brierley	Vickers (3)	-
29.12.89	SD	Trafford B.	L	12-36	Thomason, Vickers	Vickers (2)	-
1.1.90	SD	Whitehaven	L	12-24	Pape, Coles	Vickers, Kavanagh	-
7.1.90	D	Swinton	L	10-28	Doyle, Rea	Cubiss	425
14.1.90	SD	Ryedale-York	L	14-52	Thomason (2), McNichol	Turnstall	-
21.1.90	SD	Bramley	L	18-21	Okesene, Nicholson, Bea, Little	Vickers	419
30.1.90	CC(1)	Rochdale H.	L	6-38	Thomason	Coles	-
18.2.90	SD	Keighley	W	38-9	Pape (3), Coles, McNichol, Scott, Murdock	Vickers (5)	354
25.2.90	SD	Halifax	L	4-32	Pape	-	-
4.3.90	SD	Dewsbury	L	12-22	Vickers, Schubert	Vickers (2)	520
11.3.90	SD	Nottingham C	W	60-0	Pape (2), Hepi (2), Schubert, Lithgow, Murdock, Okesene, Vickers, Nicholson	Vickers (10)	-
18.3.90	SD	Hunslet	L	2-4	-	Vickers	495
25.3.90	SD	Bramley	W	24-18	Pape (2), Coles, Scott	Vickers (4)	-
1.4.90	SD	Fulham	L	2-14	-	Vickers	492
4.4.90	SD	Trafford B.	W	24-6	Little, Southwell, Kavanagh	Vickers (6)	355
8.4.90	SD	Oldham	L	16-48	Coles, Kavanagh, McNichol	Vickers (2)	-
16.4.90	SD	Whitehaven	W	24-4	Little (2), McNichol, Coles	Vickers (4)	530

1989-90 SECOND DIVISION TABLE

	P	W	D	L	For Dg	Goals	Tries	Total	Agst Dg	Goals	Tries	Total	PTS
Hull K.R.	28	25	0	3	2	168	191	1102	2	32	31	190	50
Rochdale H	28	24	0	4	3	147	170	977	2	74	68	422	48
Oldham	28	24	0	4	3	128	155	879	3	51	55	325	48
Ryedale-York	28	20	1	7	3	97	114	653	4	65	51	338	41
Halifax	28	20	0	8	5	106	131	741	4	66	56	360	40
Swinton	28	20	0	8	7	89	122	673	13	64	66	405	40
Dewsbury	28	19	1	8	13	81	82	503	7	54	74	411	39
Fulham	28	16	2	10	2	75	86	496	2	81	81	488	34
Doncaster	28	15	2	11	7	67	98	533	7	66	65	399	32
Trafford B	28	15	0	13	11	80	95	551	5	87	93	551	30
Huddersfield	28	14	0	14	7	77	77	469	2	81	81	488	34
Batley	28	13	0	15	6	68	81	466	6	68	84	478	26
Bramley	28	11	0	17	13	74	63	413	7	90	109	623	22
Hunslet	28	10	0	18	6	63	66	396	6	104	124	710	20
Chorley	28	10	0	18	9	67	64	399	6	94	106	618	20
Whitehaven	28	10	0	18	6	63	66	396	6	104	124	710	20
Carlisle	28	9	0	19	1	81	87	511	7	83	113	625	18
Workington T	28	6	0	22	9	53	49	311	10	105	122	708	12
Keighley	28	6	0	22	8	66	74	436	11	121	146	837	12
Nottingham C	28	4	0	24	5	57	51	323	8	146	183	1032	8
Runcorn H	28	0	0	28	4	35	36	218	7	134	165	935	0

Border City Blues

1989-90 SLALOM LAGER ALLIANCE - FIRST DIVISION

	P	W	D	L	For Pts	Agst Pts	Total
Hull	28	23	1	4	847	325	47
Leeds	28	22	1	5	826	422	45
Castleford	28	18	0	10	763	561	36
Hull KR	28	17	0	11	600	420	34
St. Helens	28	16	0	12	671	582	32
Wigan	28	16	0	12	644	562	32
Oldham	28	15	1	12	586	495	31
Warrington W	28	15	1	12	652	669	31
Halifax	28	13	0	15	517	630	26
Featherstone R	28	11	0	17	635	636	22
Widnes	28	11	0	17	450	685	22
Salford	28	9	2	17	623	600	20
Swinton C	28	10	0	18	441	802	20
Hunslet	28	7	0	21	425	780	14
Carlisle	28	4	0	24	449	960	8

10

*

1990-91

THIS was going to be a really crucial season. The clubs had voted to progress to a three-division structure for 1991-92 so, unless we were to be condemned to life with the Runcorns and Trafford Boroughs, we had to finish in the top eight by the following April.

Happily, it got off to a great start with our new-look team firing on all cylinders to hammer derby rivals Workington 38-18 in the Lancashire Cup in front of an encouraging 1,100 crowd. We went out in the next round to first division Warrington in front of 1,400 supporters, but could now concentrate on the main issue: the league.

The team was really going well at this stage, no more so than our Kiwi imports - minus Brad Hepi, whose permanent release was being obstructed by the NZRL authorities and who didn't start until the season was several weeks old.

The Kiwi form brought the best out of our local lads too; especially Kevin Pape, who scored seven tries in the first five games. Gates also improved with an average of 1,000 a game as we won ten of our fourteen league games by Christmas. Particularly impressive was Clayton Friend who, apart from his cousin Dean Bell, was, in my opinion, the best player ever to pull on a Carlisle shirt. The lad was superbly fit and had every skill in the game, including a watertight defence in his usual midfield sweeper role. Clayton was sensational and we all overlooked his occasional indulgences with strange herbal-smelling hand-rolled cigarettes.

Clayton was totally unperturbed by the prospect of playing away from our own midden too. A 13-8 victory at rivals Workington in early October was especially pleasing. He was on top form on that occasion and made the match-winning try for Brad Hepi.[1] Even more impressive was Clayton's form against Barrow a fortnight later at home when he scored a brace in our 44-26 win to position us firmly at the top of the table.

Successive losses against Leigh at Hilton Park and then Wakefield at home in front of a bumper 1,500 crowd brought us back down to earth, before we were back on the winning trail with narrow victories against Chorley, Dewsbury and Leigh. The best was yet to come at Batley just before Christmas.

This was the era of British Aerospace's brief flirtation with live rugby league broadcasting and their cameras were at Batley's sloping Mount Pleasant. The late Keith Macklin dressed in a Father Christmas hat was sat just behind us doing the commentary. It must have been one of the classic BAe live games as Carlisle, led by Hitro Okesene with two tries, ran riot in a 38-9 Yuletide extravaganza of open rugby.

After a couple of losses over the festive period, the season

---

[1]That was the inaugural night of Town's brand new £75,000 floodlights, funded with cash raised by public subscription. Superb as they were, our green-eyed alter-egos were gratified when they temporarily failed ten minutes into the second half!

fell away slightly with eight defeats from fifteen games. One of these losses saw Carlisle exit the Challenge Cup in the preliminary round at home to Workington. This was an epic battle that we lost 9-8 at a packed Gillford Park. The recorded attendance that day was 1,911 supporters, but the true gate was probably more as the bumper crowd tested our security measures and I witnessed several dozen coming through the ballboy gate at the far end of the ground before we could get a steward over there. The local authority, along with the fire service, had earlier pronounced our maximum capacity as being 3,600. I've no idea how that was calculated, but having been in that little ground with 2,000 in attendance I must conclude that they'd blundered somewhere along the route.

Certainly our own calculation using the formula prescribed in the sports ground planning rules those days was considerably less, at about 2,300. We kept quiet about the discrepancy and put it down to the combined police and fire authorities' lack of a good traditional maths education.

Looking dispassionately at the attendance figures nineteen years after the event, the fall off in gates after that Workington cup tie is still a bitter disappointment. Apart from a 1,200 gate for Workington at home in early April, crowds had melted away to a few hundred. As in the very early days, the citizens of Carlisle were only willing to support the club in numbers when they were winning every game by a large margin.

We had gambled that our team of international all-stars would pay for themselves via increased gate income. We needed an average gate of 1,500 supporters to break even, but we actually achieved just 945. Our average up to and including the cup defeat was 1,100. The average after it was 667. There's nothing quite as fickle as a Cumbrian rugby league supporter.

Despite the reduction in gates and the state of our

overdraft we had nevertheless achieved our prime objective. We finished in eighth place and guaranteed our place in the new second division for 1991-92 season. Nor had we lost all our future major derby games; Whitehaven had missed the cut but Workington had qualified.

We had also strengthened our back-room operations by appointing a promotions manager in Marion Jones, a personable Carlisle woman with a background in media advertisement sales who was to get our sponsorships organised. Marion has for a number of years been the licensee of the Joiners Arms, a friendly and traditional pub near the city centre.

In late 1990, we became embroiled in a most bizarre row with Carlisle United over what we saw as innovative marketing. We announced to the press that any season ticket holders at the soccer club would, as a one-off to encourage them to try the oval-ball game, be admitted free to the next Border Raiders home match. From the squeals of outraged indignation at the soccer club just across the city you'd have thought we'd ordered the death of their first-born. To this day I don't understand their problem. The soccer was played on Saturdays and we played on Sundays, so it wasn't a question of either soccer or rugby. Cameron Bell was as dumbfounded as the rest of us at this strange British reaction to inventive promotion.

Cameron himself recalls his impressions of Carlisle and its rugby team all those years ago. 'I was shocked at the casual attitude to training,' he says. 'The standard of rugby was quite poor compared with what I'd been used to back home in Auckland. For my first training session at the Sheepmount there were just fifteen players. I asked Keith [Keith Davis, Carlisle's alliance team coach] where the rest were, as I'd normally expect at least twenty players training for a first-team place. When he told me that the turnout was quite good by normal standards and it represented the players training for both the first team AND the alliance team I was astonished.

'We were doing fitness training in the gym down there and I discovered that Barry Williams (who, incidentally, I got to know as one of the most talented players I'd ever trained anywhere) could not manage twenty press-ups! That gave me some idea of the scale of the task. When I got to know Barry better, he told me that he'd been picked to go on tour down under with The British Amateur Rugby League team but had turned it down. Other players confirmed this to me and it just blew my head off that a lad could be picked to tour for his country and then just decline.

'Another shock to the system was when I travelled on the bus with Keith and the alliance team to a game at Leeds. We joined the bus at Penrith and there were only four players aboard. Keith didn't bat an eyelid as we set off and picked up players en route. We still only had twelve when we arrived at Headingley, but Leeds loaned us a couple and we got the game played. We only narrowly lost too! It was all a real culture shock.'

Even so, there were some exceptionally talented players amongst the local lads, as Cameron was to discover. 'Apart from Barry Williams,' he says, 'there were the two Scottish players Colin Paxton, before he had a serious horse-riding accident, and George Graham, the former Stirling County rugby union prop who, after leaving Carlisle, joined Newcastle Falcons and gained several full Scottish RU caps. Steve Brierley was something special too and Kevin Pape was Carlisle's "Prince of Centres" without a doubt.

'Something that was quite new to me was the two or three-hour bus trip to away games. In Auckland, all the clubs we played were within a short drive of each other. I really enjoyed those trips, though, as a good way of seeing other parts of England. My wife, Janice, travelled on the supporters' bus and she felt the same way. Marvellous.

'Away from rugby, a part of English social life that we both found strange was your habit of both men and women dressing up in their good clothes to go to the pub.

'I have very little contact with rugby these days. I live about an hour-and-a-half to the south east of Auckland and there's no rugby here. It's a dairy farming area. Just thinking about the NZ players we had over there then: Kevin Denton I saw about five years ago and we talked all night about Carlisle. Mike Dorreen I saw on TV recently, when he was parading with other Warriors veterans at Stacey Jones's farewell party. Brad Hepi is director of coaching at one of the London RU clubs. Ken McIntosh is coaching in Auckland and I see him quite often. Mark Perry married an English girl and he came to see me during my time at Barrow. Greg Rowe is working on the oil rigs off New Plymouth and Karl Findlay married a Carlisle girl. They live west of Auckland.

'I see my nephew Clayton Friend quite often. He's as fit today as when he played. He's got a decorating business in Auckland and employs five or six men, while his wife still works as a nurse. And of course I see my son, Dean, and his family.'

The 1990-91 season, despite the prominence of overseas players, was also marked by the signing of another of our growing contingent of Scottish players. Phil Manning, a wingman with Ayr, had excelled in the early season Selkirk Sevens and was soon snapped up to start his apprenticeship in the league code.

Closer to home, we were all acutely aware of the plight of Whitehaven player Gary Charlton. Gary had been dismissed from the field for a shocking tackle during a cup tie between Whitehaven and Castleford in December 1989, and had subsequently received a *sine die* suspension from the disciplinary tribunal at the RFL. Whitehaven, maybe caught up in the sanctimonious mood of the moment, added to the lad's misery by severing the 22-year-old's contract and declining any support for him.

In November 1990, we started the ball rolling to get Gary reinstated as a player and then onto Carlisle's books. We finally achieved this on 1st December 1990 after he had effectively served a thirty-match ban as a Whitehaven player.[2] Gary repaid Carlisle by serving the club for many years to come, until the merger with Barrow in 1998. Even then he followed the merged club and continued to play at Barrow for a year after a brief return to Whitehaven. As the writing of this book got underway, his appointment as joint-head coach with Martin Oglanby at Workington Town RLFC had just been announced. Gary has inherited all his dad Paul's attributes of courage, inner-strength and stamina.

It was in the coming off-season that the club got cabin-mania! Maybe this malaise was triggered by one of our directors, Robert Carter, who had a good connection for the supply of these industrial boxes. We began with three small ones that were mounted on low support walls and linked with a sort of landing. These were refurbished with acrylic perspex-sheet covered picture windows and fitted out with a fridge for drinks, half a dozen chairs and a long low table. Voila! Private hospitality boxes.

We then acquired two quite large cabins which were mounted one on top of the other. The ground floor one was the rugby office while the upper one was for sponsors' use and labelled, rather grandly, as the hospitality suite. The stability of this construction was questionable and few would venture onto the upper floor in a full-blooded north

---

[2]Note, a similar *sine die* suspension dished out to Leigh player Jason Donahue had been commuted to just twelve games after his club stood by him.

Border City Blues

Cumbrian gale. Indeed, Marion Jones, our commercial manager vacated the lower floor during one - admittedly apocalyptic - storm, stating that she felt that, like Dorothy in *The Wizard of Oz*, she was going to be blown, cabin and all, to the Land of Oz.

1990-91 CUMBERLAND AMATEUR RUGBY LEAGUE

Division Two

	P	W	D	L	F	A	Pts
Dalston	20	17	0	3	358	162	34
Great Clifton	20	14	1	5	547	308	29
Ellenborough 'A'	20	12	1	7	397	296	25
Corkickle	20	12	1	7	361	268	25
Broughton Red Rose	20	11	2	7	396	235	24
Westfield Hotel	20	11	1	8	277	253	23
Wath Brow Hornets 'A'	20	9	3	8	396	336	21
St. Bees	20	9	1	10	231	333	19
Maryport	20	5	0	15	250	471	10
Glasson Rangers 'A'	20	3	0	17	168	513	6
Kells 'A'	20	2	0	18	224	430	4

Division Three

	P	W	D	L	F	A	Pts
Egremont 'A'	20	18	0	2	544	147	36
Wigton	20	17	0	3	549	164	34
Hensingham 'A'	20	15	0	5	581	185	30
Cockermouth	20	14	0	6	449	223	28
Broughton Moor	20	11	1	8	439	369	23
Seaton Rangers 'A'	20	10	0	10	372	340	20
Aspatria	20	7	2	11	362	348	16
Frizington 'A'	20	7	0	13	295	502	14
Dalston 'A'	20	5	1	14	140	633	11
Westfield Welfare	20	3	0	17	170	499	6
Flimby 'A'	20	1	0	19	130	621	2

Division Four

	P	W	D	L	F	A	Pts
Lowca 'A'	20	18	0	2	494	167	36
Dearham	20	14	1	5	424	268	29
Broughton Red Rose 'A'	20	14	0	6	497	323	28
Horse and Farrier	20	11	0	9	355	307	22
Penrith	20	10	1	9	454	405	21
Linton Holme	20	9	0	11	412	467	18
Distington 'A'	20	9	0	11	333	440	18
St. Nicholas Arms	20	8	0	12	366	379	16
Maryport 'A'	20	8	0	12	361	271	16
Cockermouth 'A'	20	7	0	13	263	437	14
Great Clifton 'A'	20	1	0	19	264	757	2

CARLISLE – 1990-91 – SEASON SUMMARY

Chairman:	Alan Tucker
Secretary:	Elsie Martlew
Coach:	Cameron Bell (Feb 1990-)
Records:	Attendance: 5,903 v. Workington T. (Div 2) 6 Sept. 1981
Season	Goals: 113 by S. Ferres, 1981-82
	Tries: 25 by M. Morgan, 1981-82, G. Peacham, 1984-85
	Points: 242 by S. Ferres, 1981-82
Match	Goals: 10 by B. Vickers at Nottingham C., 11 Mar 1990
	Tries: 4 by G. Peacham v. Workington T., 25 Jan, 1987
	and K. Pape v. Rochdale H., 11 Feb, 1987
	Points: 24 by B. Vickers v. Nottingham C., 11 Mar 1990
	Highest Score: 60-0 v. Nottingham C., 1989-90
	Highest against: 112-0 v. St. Helens, 1986-87

	App.	Tries	Goals	D/Gls	Pts		App.	Tries	Goals	D/Gls	Pts
Armstrong, Ian	3	-	-	-	-	Manning, Phil	10+2	1	-	-	4
Brierley, Steve	33	2	-	-	8	Murdock, Gary	1+5	-	-	-	-
Catton, Tony	1+1	-	-	-	-	Okesene, Hitro	18+1	10	-	-	40
Charlton, Gary	18+1	3	-	-	12	Pape, Kevin	31	19	-	-	76
Coles, Colin	15+3	10	-	-	40	Perry, Mark	0+1	-	-	-	-
Cowgill, Dave	0+1	1	-	-	4	Pollard, Damian	3	1	-	-	4
Davies, Lee	0+2	-	-	-	-	Robinson, Paul	5+5	-	-	-	-
Denton, Kevin	15+1	3	-	-	12	Rowe, Greig	17	8	-	1	33
Dorreen, Mike	5	2	-	-	8	Schubert, Garry	32	3	-	-	12
Doyle, Mark	15+3	7	2	-	32	Scott, Tony	24+6	1	-	-	4
Friend, Clayton	31	5	-	3	23	Seagar, Stuart	0+1	-	-	-	-
Hepi, Brad	23	10	-	-	40	Southwell, Eddie	12+1	3	-	-	12
Hewer, Gary	0+1	-	-	-	-	Thomason, Malcolm	30	8	-	-	32
Kavanagh, Michael	11+2	3	-	-	12	Timoko, Nahu	8	2	-	-	8
Kendall, Dave	7	-	-	-	-	Vickers, Barry	27+2	1	87	0	178
Little, Alan	6+3	1	-	-	4	White, Nigel	3	1	-	-	4
Lunt, Peter	0+1	-	-	-	-	Williams, Barry	21+7	7	27	4	86
McIntosh, Ken	1	-	-	-	-						
Maclagan, Alan	2+6	-	-	-	-	**TOTALS**					
McNichol, Tony	1+2	-	-	-	-	37 Players		112	116	8	688

1990-91 MATCH ANALYSIS

Date	Competition	Opponent	Result	Score	Tries	Goals	Attendance
26.8.90	LC(1)	Workington T.	W	38-18	Pape (2), Kavanagh, Denton, Doyle, Rowe	Williams (5), Doyle (2)	1104
2.9.90	LC(2)	Warrington	L	7-28	-	Williams (2), Vickers, Rowe (dg)	1596
9.9.90	SD	Chorley	W	5016	Pape (2), Coles (2), Okesene (2), Denton, Schubert, Pollard	Vickers (6), Williams	785
16.9.90	SD	Dewsbury	W	24-13	Okesene (2), Coles, Southwell, Pape	Williams (2)	-
23.9.90	SD	Runcorn H.	W	44-13	Pape (2), Okesene (2), Rowe (2), Friend, Scott	Vickers (6)	839
30.9.90	SD	Bramley	W	44-15	Coles (2), Williams, Thomason, Hepi, Friend, Doyle, Rowe	Vickers (4), Williams (2)	847
5.10.90	SD	Workington T.	W	13-8	Hepi	Vickers (4), Friend (dg)	-

Border City Blues

1990-91 MATCH ANALYSIS CONTINUED

Date	Competition	Opponent	Result	Score	Tries	Goals	Attendance
14.10.90	SD	Rydale-York	D	17-17	Hepi, Dorreen, Coles	Vickers (2), Williams (dg)	1150
21.10.90	SD	Swinton	L	10-22	Pape, Cowgill	Vickers	-
4.11.90	SD	Barrow	W	44-26	Friend (2), Coles, Pape, Schubert, Kavanagh, Okesene	Vickers (8)	906
11.11.90	SD	Leigh	L	16-24	Coles, Hepi	Vickers (4)	-
18.11.90	RT(P)	Wakefield T.	L	10-28	Hepi, Doyle	Williams	1479
25.11.90	SD	Chorley	W	12-8	Pape, Timoko	Vickers (2)	-
9.12.90	SD	Dewsbury	W	12-10	Williams, Kavanagh	Vickers (2)	573
16.12.90	SD	Leigh	W	19-16	Thomason, Pape	Vickers (5), Friend (dg)	963
23.12.90	SD	Batley	W	38-9	Okesene (2), Pape, Williams, Timoko, Coles, Brierley	-	-
26.12.90	SD	Barrow	L	4-34	Thomason	-	-
30.12.90	SD	Whitehaven	L	10-14	Pape, Dorreen	Williams	1004
20.1.91	SD	Keighley	W	30-4	Brierley, Pape, Williams, Little, Denton	Williams (5)	-
27.1.91	CC(P)	Workington T.	L	8-9	Williams	Williams, Vickers	1911
3.2.91	SD	Runcorn H.	D	12-12	Coles, Pape	Vickers (2)	-
17.2.91	SD	Swinton	L	11-32	White, Pape	Williams (1, 1dg)	673
24.2.91	SD	Batley	L	13-19	Thomason, Rowe	Vickers (2), Williams (dg)	480
3.3.91	SD	Ryedale-York	L	12-18	Pape, Thomason	Vickers (2)	-
10.3.91	SD	Keighley	W	32-18	Hepi, Rowe, Okesene, Thomason	Vickers (8)	495
17.3.91	SD	Doncaster	L	7-14	Manning	Williams, Friend (dg)	-
24.3.91	SD	Trafford B.	W	52-14	Doyle (3), Hepi (2), Rowe, Pape, Williams, Friend	Vickers (8)	-
1.4.91	SD	Workington T.	L	5-12	-	Vickers (2), Williams (dg)	1210
4.4.91	SD	Trafford B.	W	28-0	Vickers, Southwell, Doyle, Charlton, Schubert	Williams (4)	415
7.4.91	SD	Bramley	L	12-17	Hepi, Charlton	Williams, Vickers	-
10.4.91	SD	Doncaster	W	24-8	Charlton, Hepi, Rowe	Vickers (6)	590
14.4.91	SD	Whitehaven	W	18-12	Pape, Thomason, Southwell	Vickers (3)	-
21.4.91	SDP(1)	Salford	L	12-26	Williams, Thomason	Vickers (2)	-

1990-91 SECOND DIVISION TABLE

	P	W	D	L	For Dg	For Goals	For Tries	For Total	Agst Dg	Agst Goals	Agst Tries	Agst Total	PTS
Salford	28	26	1	1	12	130	146	856	3	38	35	219	53
Halifax	28	24	0	4	1	116	177	941	3	54	50	311	48
Swinton	28	21	2	5	13	75	90	523	6	56	63	370	44
Ryedale-York	28	20	2	6	7	90	93	559	12	53	44	294	42
Leigh	28	18	1	9	6	104	121	698	12	64	58	372	37
Workington T	28	18	1	9	19	73	83	497	11	56	50	323	37
Fulham	28	17	2	9	2	82	71	450	10	64	50	338	36
Carlisle	28	16	2	10	7	101	101	613	13	58	74	425	34
Doncaster	28	16	0	12	11	76	86	507	10	66	73	434	32
Hunslet	28	13	2	13	9	79	88	519	6	74	71	438	28
Huddersfield	28	13	1	14	5	78	83	493	11	73	80	477	27
Whitehaven	28	13	0	15	6	67	68	412	8	92	100	592	26
Keighley	28	12	0	16	4	68	79	456	6	97	97	588	24
Dewsbury	28	10	1	17	14	60	69	410	7	62	81	455	21
Trafford B	28	10	0	18	6	79	86	508	12	99	102	618	20
Batley	28	10	0	18	7	49	58	337	6	64	83	466	20
Barrow	28	8	2	18	5	71	67	415	5	104	123	705	18
Chorley	28	7	1	20	10	63	63	388	7	107	125	721	15
Bramley	28	7	1	20	9	69	58	379	2	116	123	726	15
Runcorn H	28	3	1	24	5	61	56	351	7	108	139	779	7
Nottingham C.	28	2	0	26	6	51	44	284	7	137	166	945	4

1990-91 SLALOM LAGER ALLIANCE - SECOND DIVISION

	P	W	D	L	For Pts	Agst Pts	Total
Bradford N	24	20	0	4	900	354	40
Workington T	24	18	1	5	517	411	37
Rochdale H	24	17	1	6	521	355	35
Carlisle	24	15	3	6	632	311	33
Hunslet	24	16	1	7	572	445	33
Dewsbury	24	14	2	8	490	389	30
Sheffield E	24	14	0	10	636	489	28
Batley	24	13	1	10	481	399	27
Swinton C	24	12	2	10	534	463	26
Doncaster	24	11	1	12	405	377	23
Ryedale-York	24	9	0	15	460	453	18
Huddersfield	24	9	0	15	507	555	18
Barrow	24	9	0	15	361	562	18
Fulham	24	9	0	15	352	568	18
Keighley	24	7	1	16	448	636	15
Bramley	24	7	0	17	332	734	14
Trafford B	24	6	0	18	395	596	12
Whitehaven	24	3	1	20	257	703	7

11

*

1991-92

THERE was much coming and going before a ball had been kicked in the 1991-92 campaign.

We had signed Rob Ackerman, the former Welsh RU international, from Leeds, where he had been plying his trade after a long career with Whitehaven that lasted until midway through the 1989-90 season. 'Rip' Kirkby had returned to the club from a horrific fractured leg but, sadly, never went back into first team action. Chris Bowness returned after a long spell back in the amateur game with Hensingham and Paul Lithgow returned after a season or two's soccer action.

A Scottish 'B' international who played for both the army and Stirling County, George Graham approached us for a trial. He excelled in training to the point that we went to his army HQ in Penicuik, just outside Edinburgh, to sign him immediately. As already described, George went on to have a long and illustrious career with Carlisle before joining Rob Andrew's Newcastle Falcons in 1995, when rugby union finally embraced open professionalism. He then went on to achieve his ambition of gaining several full Scottish international caps. He currently coaches rugby union. Two of his sons play both rugby codes in Carlisle and regularly appear for Carlisle Centurions RLFC.

George remembers signing for Carlisle quite clearly. 'I'd always watched rugby league on TV and enjoyed it,' he says. 'In fact, in 1988, well before I joined Carlisle, I'd been approached by a couple of scouts from Hull KR, so the seeds of playing league were already planted when Phil Manning (Carlisle winger, originally from Ayr RU) suggested I give it a try. I attended a training session with Cameron Bell and gave it my best. I must have impressed because the next thing I knew, we were at my house in Penicuik discussing terms. After we'd shaken hands on everything I took a phonecall from George Fairbairn (Hull KR's iconic former player - himself a Borders Scotsman - who was at that time the club's coach). George had heard on the grapevine about me signing for Carlisle and offered to match anything they offered. I explained that I'd given my word and would be joining the Cumbrians.

'I had a lot to learn about the intensity and set-plays of the league game and the discipline of the line marking. My first game was in the alliance team where I scored five tries. My debut first team game was at Sheffield. I remember getting injured and Scotty [Carlisle's long-serving forward Tony Scott] telling me not to be so soft as I wasn't still playing rugby union!'

Carlisle had also signed a talented Aboriginal half-back named Wayne Alberts who was due to arrive pre-season but whose paperwork had been cocked up. He actually arrived at Manchester Airport at 6am on a Saturday morning, two weeks before schedule. I was in bed when I took a phonecall from an immigration official telling me that he had arrived.

However, his paperwork said he was here on a tourist visa but his suitcase was full of rugby kit. In short, he had the wrong work permit.

To cut a long story short, we funded him to take a cheap off-peak holiday to Portugal for ten days so that we could progress a work permit to allow him entry (these things were still quite informal in those days). Sadly, Wayne went on frequent 'walkabouts' and, after a few games, returned home. That was a shame because he was a fearless and immensely strong little player who rapidly became a crowd pleaser. The rigours of a cold wet and windy Cumbrian winter must have been too much for him.

Another overseas signing that summer was Steve Georgallis from Eastern Suburbs, in Sydney. Steve was a class act who stayed with us a couple of seasons before returning to the NRL.

Gone the other way but still in Cumbria was Garry Schubert, whose new club Workington took advantage of the recently introduced contract system to sign him and take their chances at a transfer tribunal that would determine the fee, if any, to be paid to Carlisle.

There had been a degree of rationalisation of our Kiwi contingent with Mark Perry, Kevin Denton, Mike Dorreen, Greg Rowe and Nahu Timoko having all departed at various points over the previous months.

We'd strengthened our coaching staff with the recruitment of Gary Charlton's dad, Paul, and Dave Robley as alliance team coach and assistant coach respectively. Paul Charlton was something of a hero, of course, in West Cumbria as a former GB fullback and coach of Workington Town in the 1970s. Dave Robley, a school teacher who had been working with Carlisle, mainly in a sprint-conditioning capacity, was more used to the fifteen-a-side code at Aspatria.

On the commercial front we'd secured, in ICL, a leading

multinational in IT hardware and software with 21,000 employees worldwide, the most prestigious (and lucrative) sponsor the club had ever had. Basically, the seeds of this sponsorship stemmed from ICL's desire for a major presence in Cumbrian local government. ICL clearly felt that sponsorship of the city's professional rugby league club would sweeten the negotiations yet to come with both city and county councils, a thought that was shamelessly touted to their area manager over a good few drinks at the conveniently timed Mayor's black-tie dinner.

An innovation that summer was the addition of a further member of the fair sex to our organisation to join director Elsie Martlew and commercial manager Marion Jones. We'd been contacted by a former Chorley director, Miriam Lewis, to see if we could use her assistance.

We interviewed Miriam, were impressed by her ambitions for the club and her knowledge of rugby league affairs at our level, and appointed her in a general management capacity. Both Frank Lowe (our RL Council rep) and I were spending increasing amounts of time away from Carlisle. The other directors were all heavily committed to their own businesses and we felt that the club needed some professional know-how in our absence. One of Miriam's initial tasks was to get the 'Banker' lottery and its 6,000 members onto a computer database.

The three small cabins we'd bought and installed during the off-season were fully fitted and furnished and rechristened as 'VIP boxes, available for hire at £90 per game inclusive of match entry, programme, refreshments and soft drinks; alcoholic drinks at cost and capable of seating seven people in centrally-heated comfort.' That 'central heating', by the way, was courtesy of some small salvaged electric blow heaters, whose use we discouraged on the grounds of a strong smell of burning rubber.

Above: Kevin Pape receives the pre-season BNFL Cumbria Cup at Gillford Park in 1991

Our pre-season friendly Cumbria Cup competition had gone well as we successfully defended the trophy for a third time and we were looking forward to our life in the new second division along with Sheffield, Leigh, Oldham, London Crusaders, Rochdale Hornets, Ryedale York and our neighbours, Workington Town.

Our first league game was on the Bank Holiday Monday at Rochdale's Spotland ground that they shared with the town's soccer club. This was a nothing sort of game. It ended in an 18-18 draw with Kevin Pape, Steve Brierley and Gary Charlton crossing for tries and Barry Vickers kicking three goals. The vast Spotland stadium looked empty but records show there were 1,200 present.

The opening home game was a real cracker against Sheffield. We won 23-12 with tries from Hepi and Friend, and Barry Williams's sharp-shooting was responsible for seven goals. Steve Georgallis, who became such a favourite at Gillford Park, must have sat that one out.

The following weekend we went to third division Whitehaven (oh, how we enjoyed referring to them like that) in the first round of the Lancashire Cup and slaughtered them 44-12 with Brierley (2), Georgallis, Charlton, Williams, Friend and Lithgow scoring tries and Vickers kicking six goals.

An away loss to Leigh at Hilton Park in front of nearly 3,000 supporters followed before we went to Workington midweek for the second round of the Lancashire Cup. Workington were really motoring. They'd signed Joe Faimalo from Eastern Suburbs and Garry Schubert, Alan McMullen and Mark Wilkes from us and, in ex Carlisle via Hull KR Colin Armstrong, Martin Oglanby, Peter Riley, Mark Roskell and Steve Wear had the lion's share of the West Cumbrian talent. They were really up for the game.

The Town floodlights didn't fail and nearly 4,000 fans were treated to a classic encounter that Carlisle won 11-2 courtesy of a Friend try, two Vickers goals and three drop-goals from an on-form Barry Williams.

Three days later we entertained Workington in the league in front of 1,700 ecstatic supporters at Gillford Park and ran out comfortable 39-10 winners courtesy of tries by Lithgow (2), Friend (2), Thomason, Williams, Murdock and Georgallis. Vickers was off-form that Sunday and converted just three with Williams chiming in with a drop-goal.

Our Lancashire Cup semi-final at Rochdale on 10th October saw Carlisle sitting proudly in second place in the league and Barry Vickers boasting the longest unbroken scoring run in the game, with fourteen since 24th March. In his fifteenth, he kicked just one penalty as we were outplayed 19-6 by an experienced Rochdale side containing players of the calibre of Australian Brett Clark, plus Matt Calland, Phil Fox and Colin Whitfield.

The next major Cup competition to come our way that

season was the Regal Trophy. We'd progressed through to the second round courtesy of a fairly routine victory at home over Highfield, a reincarnation of Runcorn who by now had migrated to the Hoghton Road ground of St Helens Town FC, just in the shadow of the huge cooling towers of Bold power station.[1]

The second round was Widnes at home at the end of November. Happily for our supporters, Brunton Park wasn't an available option so we settled for Gillford Park with some additional temporary scaffold-based terracing in case we got lucky with a bumper gate. Sadly, Widnes, despite still having Jonathan Davies, Alan Tait, Paul Moriarty, Esene Faimalo and David Hulme in their line-up, were no longer the all-conquering drawcard of old and the temporary terracing remained an unloved and unused white elephant. Just under 2,000 turned up to see Alan Tait (two tries), Esene Faimalo, Mark Sarsfield, Darren Wright and Jonathan Davies cross the line, with Davies kicking just three goals. Carlisle, certainly not outclassed, responded with tries from Okesene, Vickers and Georgallis, with Vickers and Williams kicking a goal each to leave the Merseysiders to progress to the next round, 30-16.

Widnes then went on to win in the final by beating Leeds by 24-0 at Wigan's Central Park the following January, so we felt we'd acquitted ourselves well on that late November day at homely old Gillford Park.

The newly-erected upstairs sponsors' lounge was treated to some pretty auspicious company that afternoon too, as

---

[1] St Helens is my home town and Saints remain my number one love after Carlisle, but the way they treated Highfield was a disgrace. The local paper, the *St Helens Reporter*, seemed to close ranks with the Saints against them and the publicity they received was non-existent. They were never in competition for gates as they played on alternate weekends, attracted two or three hundred at the most to their games and deserved better from a rugby league town.

Jonathan Davies and company, plus a cast of dozens of sponsors, well-wishers and autograph hunters, crammed inside.

Another memorable game, if only because of the epic return car journey, came just a couple of days before Christmas when we played Ross Strudwick's newly-named London Crusaders (formerly Fulham) at the vast Crystal Palace National Sports Stadium. We were narrowly beaten 12-8 with Rob Ackerman scoring our solitary try and Barry Williams kicking two goals.

Apart from the twelve-hour return trip (which colleague Mally Cooper slept through both ways), the other abiding memory is of wonderment that London could pay their way in that huge, hideous and soulless place with gates of around 300 brave souls, when we could not at basic old Gillford Park with gates of around twice that number. Little did we realise that Fulham/London were habitually insolvent and alleged to have experienced more company reincarnations than you could shake a stick at. It now seems that the RFL, in their desire to have a team in the capital, were happy to condone such irregularities.

For us, that was almost as good as it got that season as, despite beating Workington four times in the league and once in the Regal Trophy, they knocked us out in the preliminary round of the Challenge Cup 11-4 at Derwent Park in front of 2,700 ecstatic 'Marras'. To make it worse, Garry Schubert, newly signed from Carlisle, scored their solitary try with other points coming from the boots of Wear (three goals) and Marwood. Carlisle's points came from two penalties by Barry Williams. How we envied Town that year as they went on to have three consecutive money-spinning home games in the cup before bowing out to Hull at Derwent Park in front of over 5,000 supporters.

Despite playing some excellent rugby that second half of

the season, crowds tailed off as the tedium factor of playing four games against the same seven clubs became evident. In fact, our last two home games against Rochdale and York attracted less than 500 supporters apiece.

The best was saved for last however as we gained ample revenge at Workington for that Challenge Cup defeat. I still have a picture in my mind of Derwent Park that Easter Monday as we put them to the sword, 40-12. It was a Barry Williams showpiece as he scored two fine tries and kicked six goals in a seven-try romp that he shared with Knox, Pape, White, Thomason and Friend. The dispirited Workington fans in that 1,500 crowd howled with a mixture of anger and frustration as he held up three fingers to indicate their relegation to the third division while on his way to a second try.

Carlisle, on the other hand, had guaranteed survival by finishing sixth in that eight-team league.

Despite the boredom of playing the same teams four times and the conviction that the game would revert to just two divisions after the following season, there were many things to look back on with pride that close-season. We had achieved a long-held ambition of recruiting several players from over the border. George Graham (Stirling County), Colin Paxton, Grant Harris and Derek Armstrong (Hawick RU) had all joined us and some higher profile targets were in our sight. Also from Hawick, conditioner-sponge man and good friend to the club, Jimmy McFarlane - aka 'Wee Jimmy' - also joined us. Both Barry Williams and Rob Ackerman were selected that season to play for Wales.

Off the field, our hardy band of fanatical supporters had started an hilariously irreverent fanzine called *Get them Onside Ref*. The few copies of that scurrilous publication that remain still make me smile with their light-hearted skits at other clubs' icons. For example, Ray Ashton, Workington

Above: Carlisle's Barry Williams launches a clearing kick

Town's ex-Leeds and GB player-coach was always referred to as Ray Ashbin. Another piece claimed that Whitehaven's popular side stand had featured in *Bridge over the River Kwai* as a prisoner of war hut and that "If Town get promoted this season they'll come back down again; all the players have money on it".

Despite all the work we'd done at Gillford Park, for the third time in five years thoughts once again turned to the council-owned Sheepmount Athletics Stadium.

I still have a bound document, dated 9th April 1992, containing an application outline to the Trustees of the Foundation for Sport and Arts, asking for their support in building a centre of excellence for rugby league at the Sheepmount. The document contains letters of support from, amongst others, the RFL's David Oxley, director of leisure services on Carlisle council Euan Cartwright, Ian McCartney the MP for Makerfield, and Eric Martlew MP, our own local member.

The project would have upgraded the Sheepmount to

full athletics stadium status, thereby providing a venue for major athletics meetings, as well as a rugby league ground with facilities for soccer, hockey and lacrosse. The total cost would have been around £1.3 million.

In the end, the Foundation awarded us a £150,000 grant which made no sense whatsoever in the context of the Sheepmount proposal. Rather than decline this money we eventually agreed to ask that it be applied towards a new stand and changing accommodation at Gillford Park. Every nerve and fibre in our bodies was aching to move away and secure our future and here we were, in effect being granted a large sum of public funds payable in 1994, to stay there. There was even then a rarely spoken feeling within the club that, if Gillford Park represented our professional future in the game, our days were numbered.

On a more positive note, the Juniors graduated to the under-16s competition before being gradually absorbed into the St Nicholas Arms open age comp and the Border Raiders academy side in subsequent seasons. Trevor Easton offers the following reminiscences on the subject.

'A fledgling under-16s squad was fielded the previous season against Hensingham, in preparation for full West Cumbria League competition in 1991-92,' Trevor writes. 'This gave an opportunity to young players to develop their skills for the local amateur scene. The under-16s ladder gave the opportunity for Jonno Farrimond, Brian Underwood, Martin and Craig Stalker, Anthony Carr, Tony Kirkwood and Spenser Sharpley and many others, to step into the open age arena with confidence.

'Jonno Farrimond was selected for the BARLA under-19s tour of New Zealand and the Pacific in 1994 and he played in three of the Tests. He was named man of the match in the second. Jonno also played two Tests against France in the BARLA GB shirt. He went on to join Carlisle Border Raiders and Barrow, where a serious shoulder injury cut short a very promising career.

'Other graduates of the Juniors who went on to become professionals include Brian Underwood with Carlisle, and Craig and Martin Stalker, who joined Workington Town. It was natural that the Border Raiders would turn to the Juniors when they formed their first Carlisle academy squad. In addition to Farrimond and Underwood, the lads who graduated to the big boys included Mike Dodds, the current captain of the Centurions, Andrew Dalton, Jamie McTear, Gareth Milburn, Terry Glencross, Spencer Sharpley, Mike Marsden and Richard Massey, who caught the eye with John Moore's university in student rugby league. The transfer of the players to the academy meant that the plan to enter an under-18s squad into the West Cumbria League had to be abandoned.

'Were it not for Elaine Gordon there would be very few local players who were given - and took - the opportunity to develop their love and skills in rugby league. Neither the Carlisle academy, the Carlisle Saints or the Centurions would have had access to such a pool of quality players.'

Trevor recalls how, as a coach, one of his most memorable moments was when Cameron Bell phoned him to see if there was a young player who could 'come off the bench' in an 'A' team game at Gillford Park. A robust and skilful 16-year-old back-rower from Morton, Kevin Blaylock, stepped forward. 'The smile on his face as he sat in the dug-out was only exceeded by the size of the grin when he was put on to play the biggest ten minutes of his life,' says Trevor. 'He didn't stop talking about it for weeks, nor did he take a backward step in those ten minutes of glory!'

Border City Blues

1991-92 CUMBERLAND AMATEUR RUGBY LEAGUE

Division One

	P	W	D	L	F	A	Pts
Ellenborough	18	14	0	4	455	191	28
Hensingham	18	12	2	4	458	180	26
Frizington	18	12	1	5	292	263	25
Kells	18	11	0	7	412	242	22
Glasson Rangers	18	10	2	6	367	272	22
Wath Brow Hornets	18	10	2	6	290	273	22
Lowca	18	7	1	10	310	369	15
Dalston	18	6	0	12	250	349	12
Flimby	18	3	0	15	188	390	6
Great Clifton	18	1	0	17	177	670	2

Division Two

	P	W	D	L	F	A	Pts
Seaton Rangers	20	15	1	4	503	254	31
Maryport	20	15	1	4	385	216	31
Egremont 'A'	20	14	2	4	384	235	30
Corkickle	20	13	2	5	420	294	28
Westfield Hotel	20	13	1	6	412	300	27
Ellenborough 'A'	20	9	4	7	370	327	22
Distington	20	8	0	12	260	327	16
Broughton Red Rose	20	6	0	14	247	329	12
Wigton	20	5	0	15	248	467	10
Wath Brow Hornets 'A'	20	3	1	16	197	461	7
St Bees	20	3	0	17	179	395	6

Division Three

	P	W	D	L	F	A	Pts
Cockermouth	22	21	0	1	714	118	42
Dearham	22	17	1	4	526	239	35
Broughton Moor	22	17	1	4	583	303	35
Hensingham 'A'	22	14	4	4	563	201	32
Kells 'A'	22	14	0	8	508	403	28
Aspatria	22	11	2	9	425	395	24
Frizington 'A'	22	8	1	13	386	639	17
Seaton Rangers 'A'	22	8	0	14	254	504	16
Lowca 'A'	22	5	1	16	224	230	11
Westfield Welfare	22	5	0	17	248	786	10
Glasson Rangers 'A'	22	4	0	18	214	383	8
Dalston 'A'	22	3	0	19	171	615	6

Division Four

	P	W	D	L	F	A	Pts
Horse and Farrier	20	15	0	5	533	232	30
Cockermouth 'A'	20	13	0	7	308	315	26
Maryport 'A'	20	12	0	8	426	288	24
Great Clifton 'A'	20	11	2	7	445	375	24
Linton Holme	20	11	1	8	463	364	23
Penrith	20	10	2	8	353	228	22
St Nicholas Arms	20	10	0	10	430	395	20
Wigton 'A'	20	7	1	12	356	509	15
Corkickle 'A'	20	6	2	12	270	486	14
Distington 'A'	20	6	0	14	187	320	12
Flimby 'A'	20	5	0	15	220	479	10

CARLISLE – 1991-92 – SEASON SUMMARY

Chairman:	Alan Tucker
Secretary:	Miriam Lewis
Coach:	Cameron Bell (Feb 1990-)
Records - Match:	Goals: 10 by Barry Vickers at Nottingham C., 11 Mar 1990
	Tries: 4 by G. Peacham v. Workington T., 25 Jan, 1987
	and K. Pape v. Rochdale H., 11 Feb, 1987
	Points: 24 by B. Vickers v. Nottingham C., 11 Mar 1990
Season	Goals: 113 by S. Ferres, 1981-82
	Tries: 25 by M. Morgan, 1981-82, G. Peacham, 1984-85
	Points: 242 by S. Ferres, 1981-82
Career	Goals: 352 by Barry Vickers, 1988-
	Tries: 141 by Kevin Pape, 1984-
	Points: 733 by Barry Vickers, 1988-
	Highest Score: 60-0 v. Nottingham C., 1989-90
	Highest against: 112-0 v. St. Helens, 1986-87
Attendance:	5,903 v. Workington T. (Div 2) 6 Sept. 1981 at Brunton Park
	1,874 v. Widnes (Regal Trophy), 24 Nov 1991 at Gillford Park

	App.	Tries	Goals	D/Gls	Pts		App.	Tries	Goals	D/Gls	Pts
Ackerman, Rob	31	4	-	-	16	Knox, Simon	10+3	3	-	-	12
Alberts, Wayne	5+1	1	-	-	4	Lithgow, Paul	12+3	4	-	-	16
Armstrong, Ian	17+5	-	-	-	-	Lunt, Peter	0+1	-	-	-	-
Armstrong, Malcolm	3	-	-	-	-	Manning, Phil	3	1	-	-	4
Black, James	2	-	-	-	-	Murdock, Gary	18+9	2	-	-	8
Bowness, Chris	0+1	-	-	-	-	Okesene, Hitro	31	4	3	-	22
Brierley, Steve	31+1	3	-	-	12	Pape, Kevin	27	9	-	-	36
Charlton, Gary	22	5	-	-	20	Paxton, Colin	8+1	-	-	-	-
Doyle, Mark	0+1	-	-	-	-	Pollard, Damian	7+1	3	-	-	12
Findlay, Carl	10+4	2	-	-	8	Robinson, Paul	6+9	-	-	-	-
Friend, Clayton	30	17	2	3	75	Scott, Tony	9+9	-	-	-	-
Georgallis, Steve	18	8	-	-	32	Southwell, Eddie	3+1	-	-	-	-
Graham, George	21+1	3	1	1	15	Thomason, Malcolm	25+3	2	-	-	8
Harris, Grant	8	6	-	-	24	Vickers, Barry	24+1	3	63	1	139
Hepi, Brad	27	10	-	-	40	White, Nigel	1	1	-	-	4
Johnston, Robert	1+1	-	-	-	-	Williams, Barry	25+2	10	18	8	84
Kavanagh, Mike	7+5	2	-	-	8	**TOTALS**					
						33 Players		103	87	13	599

1991-92 MATCH ANALYSIS

Date	Competition	Opponent	Result	Score	Tries	Goals	Attendance
2.9.91	SD	Rochdale H.	D	18-18	Pape, Charlton, Brierley	Vickers (3)	-
8.9.91	SD	Sheffield E.	W	23-12	Hepi, Friend	Vickers (7), Willams (dg)	850
15.9.91	LC(1)	Whitehaven	W	44-12	Brierley (2), Georgallis, Charlton, Williams, Friend, Lithgow, Murdock	Vickers (6)	-
22.9.91	SD	Leigh	L	22-32	Ackerman (2), Okesene, Hepi	Vickers (3)	-
26.9.91	LC(2)	Workington T.	W	11-2	Friend	Vickers (2), Willams (3dg)	-
29.9.91	SD	Workington T.	W	39-10	Lithgow (2), Friend (2), Thomason, Williams, Murdock, Georgallis	Vickers (3), Williams (dg)	1700
6.10.91	SD	Rydale-York	W	26-6	Vickers, Georgallis, Pollard, Friend, Hepi	Vickers (3)	-
10.10.91	LC(SF)	Rochdale H.	L	6-19	Pollard	Vickers	-

161

Border City Blues

1991-92 MATCH ANALYSIS CONTINUED

Date	Competition	Opponent	Result	Score	Tries	Goals	Attendance
13.10.91	SD	London C.	W	12-4	Friend, Pape	Vickers (2)	696
20.10.91	SD	Oldham	L	10-30	Okesene	Vickers (3)	1185
6.11.91	SD	Sheffield E.	L	6-12	Georgallis	Vickers	-
10.11.91	SD	Leigh	L	12-16	Hepi, Williams	Vickers (2)	825
17.11.91	RT(1)	Highfield	W	28-10	Vickers, Lithgow, Georgallis, Williams, Hepi	Vickers (4)	-
24.11.91	RT(2)	Widnes	L	16-30	Okesene, Vickers, Georgallis	Vickers, Williams	1874
1.12.91	SD	Workington T.	W	17-11	Friend, Pollard	Vickers (4), Friend (dg)	-
8.12.91	SD	Rydale-York	W	28-10	Williams (3), Manning, Georgallis	Vickers (4)	598
22.12.91	SD	London C.	L	8-12	Ackerman	Williams (2)	-
26.12.91	SD	Workington T.	W	25-6	Pape, Georgallis, Alberts, Graham	Vickers (4), Williams (dg)	1098
5.1.92	SD	Oldham	L	4-14	Pape	-	-
13.1.92	CC(P)	Workington T.	L	4-11	-	Williams (2)	-
19.1.92	SD	Sheffield E.	L	22-25	Friend (2), Ackerman, Okesene	Williams (3)	610
2.2.92	SD	Leigh	L	18-19	Charlton (2), Pape	Vickers (3)	-
9.2.92	SD	Rochdale H.	L	0-5	-	-	615
16.2.92	SD	Ryedale-York	L	1-22	-	Friend (dg)	-
23.2.92	SD	London C.	W	28-24	Hepi (3), Kavanagh (2)	Vickers (4)	495
1.3.92	SD	Rochdale H.	L	14-44	Pape (2), Friend	Vickers	-
8.3.92	SD	Oldham	L	17-20	Harris (2), Friend	Vickers (1, 1dg), Friend	-
15.3.92	SD	Leigh	W	19-11	Findlay (2), Hepi	Okesene (2), Vickers, Graham (dg)	867
22.3.92	SD	London C.	L	15-20	Friend (2), Harris	Graham	-
29.3.92	SD	Oldham	L	10-23	Graham, Hepi	Williams	849
5.4.92	SD	Sheffield E.	L	14-32	Friend (2), Harris	Graham	-
12.4.92	SD	Rochdale H.	W	20-8	Knox (2), Pape, Harris	Friend, Williams (2dg)	468
17.4.92	SD	Ryedale-York	W	22-8	Williams, Charlton, Harris, Graham	Williams (3)	482
20.4.92	SD	Workington T.	W	40-12	Williams (2), Knox, White, Pape, Thomason, Friend	Williams (6)	-

1991-92 SECOND DIVISION TABLE

| | P | W | D | L | For | | | | Agst | | | | |
					Dg	Goals	Tries	Total	Dg	Goals	Tries	Total	PTS
Sheffield E	28	21	1	6	10	121	141	816	10	61	66	396	43
Leigh	28	21	0	7	17	92	104	617	9	62	67	401	42
Oldham	28	18	2	8	6	84	96	558	5	72	68	421	38
London C	28	14	0	14	0	74	70	428	5	75	82	483	28
Rochdale H	28	12	2	14	5	87	110	619	11	73	83	489	26
Carlisle	28	12	1	15	10	70	85	490	6	72	79	466	25
Ryedale-York	28	5	2	21	8	53	56	338	3	115	129	749	12
Workington T	28	4	2	22	8	63	44	310	15	114	132	771	10

1991-92 YOUNGER'S ALLIANCE - SECOND DIVISION WEST

| | P | W | D | L | For | Agst | |
					Pts	Pts	Total
Rochdale H	18	15	0	3	637	292	30
Salford	18	13	1	4	662	242	27
Leigh	18	12	0	6	493	320	24
Huddersfield	18	10	0	8	472	313	20
Swinton C	18	9	0	9	433	385	18
Carlisle	18	9	0	9	428	392	18
Barrow	18	9	0	9	401	368	18
Keighley C	18	7	1	10	322	428	15
Whitehaven	18	5	0	13	305	644	10
Chorley B	18	0	0	18	133	902	0

12

*

1992-93

AS soon as the 1991-92 season was over, we resumed our cross-border recruitment drive. A target for quite a while had been Gary Armstrong, the great Scottish rugby union international scrum-half with fifty caps to his credit and whose club team was Jedforest. Despite several meetings at the Moss Paul Hotel on the A7 near Langholm at which we discussed a lucrative deal for him, he decided to stay in the fifteen-a-side code. He was a self-employed HGV driver at the time and I suspect he feared his full-time occupation would have been at risk had he swapped codes.

Gary mentioned his discussions with the Border Raiders in his biography several years later. He stated that his own solicitor had advised against the Carlisle venture as the money on offer was disproportionate to Carlisle's total income. This in fact was totally true. A further reality though was that any contract money to be paid to him was to come from a lucrative commercial sponsorship already agreed in principle had he joined.

Border City Blues

Colin Paxton, arguably the most talented of our group of Hawick players, had suffered a serious leg fracture during the previous season whilst engaged in that curious Borders ritual, the Riding of the Marches. He trained hard to get playing again, but although he achieved this objective a season or two later, I can't help but think that the injury had destroyed either his confidence or his motivation, as he never seemed to deliver his full potential on the field.

There were other targets in the Borders in that period but in truth it was extremely difficult to make progress because they placed too high a price on their services, probably based on hearsay as to what higher division clubs than us were offering. Certainly, wherever we went, scouts from Wigan, Leeds and Hull KR in particular had preceded us.

We had numerous discussions with Carlisle RU club aimed at a joint development there. These discussions were to crop up with monotonous regularity but, at best, we were viewed by the union outfit as a route to a bigger sports and arts foundation grant. Just as we were wedded to the thirteen-a-side code, they were equally immovable about their own priorities, which didn't really include a professional rugby league club.

Not for the first time, we considered checking out the possibilities of moving back to Brunton Park and we had several meetings with Carlisle United's Andrew Jenkins and a couple of his board members. Shortly after these meetings, United's new saviour, Michael Knighton, appeared at the club and we were obliged to listen to fanciful visions of five star hotels, butterfly farms, football museums and the like. We made our excuses and left.

When our new season finally resumed in August, it was thus with bitter disappointment that we were still at Gillford Park and with no prospect of a move on the horizon. It was as if fate was binding us and the Gillford Park Railway Club together. Whichever way we turned was a blocked avenue. Both we and the Railway Club were stuck in an unhappy marriage.

Very early in the season, we were hit with four separate and ostensibly unrelated board resignations. Bob Taylor resigned to spend more time on his newly-established planning consultancy business. Elsie Martlew resigned in protest over an issue of management responsibilities. Don McDowall left due to a conflict of interest with his council work and Doc Haworth resigned as he'd always intended to do after ten years on the board. Doc's resignation had little practical impact as he continued to work even harder for the welfare of Carlisle rugby league and its players and even gave himself the additional task of commentator on the match videos.

Local builder and long-term supporter of the club, Mally Cooper, and mine host at the St Nicholas Arms, Pat Cody, joined as directors. Both Mally and Pat were long-term supporters and had given a great deal of practical help in the past. Pat's pub was the headquarters of Carlisle Saints ARLFC and Pat was its major sponsor.

Otherwise, with the country as a whole in the grip of a recession, we were all at a very low ebb. So too at RFL HQ at Chapeltown Road, Leeds, where David Oxley had retired as boss and his replacement, Maurice Lindsay, had few options other than to cut costs by declaring redundant about a third of the staff.

Clubs sought to cut back too. Trafford Borough were to return to the Fylde as Blackpool Gladiators, while the other half of the original Blackpool double act, Chorley, were to move from Victory Park to Horwich FC's ground. Swinton, whose response to the economic realities of the time and their own administration order had been to sell their Station Road ground for housing, had taken on a five-year tenancy at Bury FC's Gigg Lane. Scarborough Pirates had folded after just one season and there were leaks coming from the RFL that Blackpool, Chorley and Nottingham were to be culled at the season's end to pave the way for two divisions of sixteen teams each.

The pick of Carlisle's incoming players that season were: Kevin Fox from Salford, Troy Clarke from Australia, Willie Richardson on loan from Whitehaven, Dave Smith and Steve Georgallis (on four-month contracts each from the NRL) and Kevin Bethwaite from Aspatria RU. I signed the latter on the last day of 1992; rumour had it that Workington chairman Tom Mitchell had lined Kevin up for early in the new year.

Regrettably, we had to face financial reality and release Clayton Friend to our neighbours, Whitehaven. We simply could not afford his considerable playing terms any longer. I suppose that what happened to us was not so unusual, as almost every one of our budget projections came unstuck. There were no lucrative cup games, very few travelling supporters with the teams we played, no derby games and no big transfer deals to bail us out. The end of Georgallis and Smith's short-term contracts at the year-end came as financial relief.

We didn't do too well off the field either. General manager Miriam Lewis listened to the wrong supporters in response to a question as to how the programme could be improved. They told her something that didn't need folding to fit in their pockets would be a step forward. The result was a strangely narrowed booklet; about half the width of our regular programme; but with the same number of pages and at the same price. It was totally unloved by supporters and advertisers alike. The only person who mourned its passing was its proposer, a programme contributor who had his own column, 'The Raiding Party'.

The playing season was as bad as they come. We won

only six league games throughout the entire campaign and finished seventh out of a league of eight. With Barrow, Workington and Whitehaven all languishing in the lower division, there was absolutely nothing to whet the Carlisle public's interest. Gates were a disaster with only the visits of Oldham and Featherstone providing anything approaching a decent attendance and never into four figures.

Neither was there any relief in the cup competitions. We were knocked out by fifty-odd points at Widnes in the first round of the Lancashire Cup. It was in that game that Malcolm Thomason was knocked cold. We took him to nearby Whiston hospital, from which he discharged himself after three hours without treatment demanding I get him back to Maryport. I can still hear the immortal words: '...ah's gaan yam, marra.'

We scraped a win at Bramley in the first round of the Regal Trophy in front of just 500 supporters (our share of that gate barely covered our transport costs) and were then hammered, again by fifty-odd points at Castleford in the next round.

We fared even worse in the first round of the Challenge Cup as cannon fodder to Halifax, who enjoyed a 66-12 romp at our expense at Thrum Hall.

The only bright spot in that desperate season was our solitary win away from home at Gigg Lane, when our future player-coach, Hugh Waddell, by then 34 years of age and playing on loan from Sheffield, had a blinder for Swinton. The saving grace was that, unlike in previous bad seasons, we didn't close it by having to pay winning bonuses out of non-existent gate takings when there was nothing left to play for.

Amongst the departures at the end of that season was our general manager, Miriam Lewis, who was leaving the area to get married. The last time I spoke to her was in 1998

Above: Carlisle's George Graham scatters the opposition defence

when she was working in a PR capacity with a multinational construction corporation engaged in building a new super-gaol in Liverpool. I think her two years at Carlisle after being with another struggling club, Chorley Borough RLFC for a few years, had sickened her off rugby league for life.

There were very few club directors in that second division who were sorry to see the end of the three-division experiment after the 1992-93 season. To play the same clubs four times may have worked in Scottish football, but it was a disaster in English rugby league.

1992-93 CUMBERLAND AMATEUR RUGBY LEAGUE

Division One

	P	W	D	L	F	A	Pts
Ellenborough	18	16	0	2	655	209	32
Hensingham	18	14	0	4	491	159	28
Wath Brow Hornets	18	12	0	6	349	212	24
Kells	18	12	0	6	337	227	24
Seaton Rangers	18	8	1	9	305	416	17
Frizington	18	7	2	9	321	373	16
Lowca	18	7	0	11	254	388	14
Maryport	18	6	1	11	225	384	13
Glasson Rangers	18	4	1	13	218	377	9
Dalston	18	1	1	16	176	596	3

1992-93 CUMBERLAND AMATEUR RUGBY LEAGUE CONTINUED

Division Two

	P	W	D	L	F	A	Pts
Broughton Red Rose	16	13	0	3	366	165	26
Great Clifton	16	11	2	3	270	194	24
Westfield Hotel	16	9	2	5	427	236	20
Flimby	16	9	2	5	368	272	20
Egremont	16	10	0	6	312	260	20
Cockermouth	16	8	1	7	281	264	17
Corkickle	16	3	2	11	242	278	8
Distington	16	2	1	13	191	526	5
Wigton	16	2	0	14	222	484	4

Division Three

	P	W	D	L	F	A	Pts
Broughton Moor	14	12	0	2	392	156	24
Linton Holme	14	12	0	2	360	216	24
Dearham	14	10	1	3	333	125	21
Westfield Welfare	14	7	2	5	286	215	16
St. Bees	14	6	0	8	223	198	12
St. Nicholas Arms	14	5	0	9	200	347	10
Aspatria	14	2	1	11	174	330	5
Penrith	14	0	0	14	100	481	0

1992-93 CUMBERLAND AMATEUR RUGBY LEAGUE ALLIANCE

Division One

	P	W	D	L	F	A	Pts
Hensingham 'A'	18	16	0	2	322	113	32
Ellenborough 'A'	18	15	0	3	445	205	30
Kells 'A'	18	13	1	4	345	191	27
Wath Brow Hornets 'A'	18	12	1	5	364	175	25
Seaton Rangers 'A'	18	9	0	9	223	326	18
Glasson Rangers 'A'	18	7	0	11	348	291	14
Frizington 'A'	18	6	0	12	214	364	12
Lowca 'A'	18	5	0	13	220	390	10
Dalston 'A'	18	3	0	15	102	181	6
Cockermouth 'A'	18	3	0	15	168	515	6

Division Two

	P	W	D	L	F	A	Pts
Great Clifton 'A'	14	12	0	2	362	146	24
Broughton Red Rose 'A'	14	11	0	3	234	134	22
Westfield Hotel 'A'	14	9	0	5	335	170	18
Maryport 'A'	14	9	0	5	261	210	18
Distington 'A'	14	5	0	9	258	213	10
Flimby 'A'	14	4	0	10	143	415	8
Dearham 'A'	14	3	0	11	192	294	6
Wigton 'A'	14	3	0	11	168	371	6

Border City Blues

CARLISLE – 1992-93 – SEASON SUMMARY

Chairman:	Alan Tucker
Coach:	Cameron Bell (Feb 1990-)
Records:	
Match	Goals: 10 by Barry Vickers at Nottingham C., 11 Mar 1990
	Tries: 4 by G. Peacham v. Workington T., 25 Jan, 1987
	and K. Pape v. Rochdale H., 11 Feb, 1987
	Points: 24 by B. Vickers v. Nottingham C., 11 Mar 1990
Season	Goals: 113 by S. Ferres, 1981-82
	Tries: 25 by M. Morgan, 1981-82, G. Peacham, 1984-85
	Points: 242 by S. Ferres, 1981-82
Career	Goals: 352 by Barry Vickers, 1988-92
	Tries: 160 by Kevin Pape, 1984-
	Points: 733 by Barry Vickers, 1988-92
	Highest Score: 60-0 v. Nottingham C., 1989-90
	Highest against: 112-0 v. St. Helens, 1986-87
Attendance:	5,903 v. Workington T. (Div 2) 6 Sept. 1981 at Brunton Park
	1,874 v. Widnes (Regal Trophy), 24 Nov 1991 at Gillford Park

	App.	Tries	Goals	D/Gls	Pts		App.	Tries	Goals	D/Gls	Pts
Archer, Darren	1	-	-	-	-	Murdock, Gary	21+1	4	-	-	16
Armstrong, Derek	10+2	-	-	-	-	Murdock, Paul	0+4	-	-	-	-
Armstrong, Ian	23+1	-	-	-	-	Pape, Kevin	29	19	-	-	76
Bethwaite, Kevin	13+2	4	25	-	66	Richardson, Willie	7+1	1	5	-	14
Brierley, Steve	19+2	1	-	-	4	Robinson, Paul	4+3	-	-	-	-
Burns, William	0+2	-	-	-	-	Rossen, Geoff	1	-	-	-	-
Charlton, Gary	26	2	-	-	8	Roy, Jeff	2	1	-	-	4
Clarke, Troy	12	2	13	-	34	Scott, Tony	22+3	-	-	-	-
Doyle, Mark	1+1	1	-	-	4	Smith, David	7+1	4	17	-	50
Fox, Kevin	29	5	-	-	20	Southwell, Eddie	10+8	1	-	-	4
Friend, Clayton	2	-	-	-	-	Spee, Milt Van Der	0+1	-	-	-	-
Gaffney, Mike	0+1	-	-	-	-	Tait, Alan	0+1	-	-	-	-
Georgallis, Steve	15	9	-	-	36	Thomas, Phil	0+2	-	-	-	-
Graham, George	21	4	-	-	16	Thomason, Malcolm	31	2	-	-	8
Harris, Grant	15+3	-	-	-	-	Vannett, Paul	5	-	-	-	-
Hibberd, Craig	17+1	4	2	2	22	Wassell, Colin	7	-	-	-	-
Iti, Brett	5	3	-	-	12	Wilkinson, Les	0+4	-	-	-	-
Kavanagh, Mike	1+1	1	-	-	4	Williams, Barry	6+5	7	3	-	34
Knox, Simon	32	8	-	-	32						
Lunt, Peter	10+4	-	-	-	-	**TOTALS**					
Manning, Phil	7+5	4	7	-	30	40 Players		87	72	2	494
Montford, Craig	5+3	-	-	-	-						

1992-93 MATCH ANALYSIS

Date	Competition	Opponent	Result	Score	Tries	Goals	Attendance
30.8.92	SD	Bramley	W	18-10	Kavanagh, Doyle, Pape	Manning (2), Williams	502
6.9.92	SD	Oldham	L	14-38	Williams (2), Pape	Manning	-
13.9.92	LC(1)	Widnes	L	8-52	Pape, Williams	-	-
20.9.92	SD	London C.	L	14-46	Manning, Williams	Manning (2), Williams	493
27.9.92	SD	Featherstone R.	L	10-30	Pape, Georgallis	Williams	-
4.10.92	SD	Rochdale H.	W	24-12	Williams, Knox, Graham, Fox	Smith (3), Clarke	508
15.10.92	SD	Huddersfield	W	24-4	Georgallis (2), Knox, Smith	Smith (4)	-
1.11.92	SD	London C.	D	18-18	Charlton, Pape, Graham	Smith (3)	-
8.11.92	RT(1)	Bramley	W	16-12	Smith, Georgallis, Pape	Smith (2)	-

1992-93 MATCH ANALYSIS CONTINUED

Date	Competition	Opponent	Result	Score	Tries	Goals	Attendance
15.11.92	SD	Oldham	L	20-25	Pape, Georgallis, Fox, Smith	Smith, Clarke	983
22.11.92	SD	Bramley	D	18-18	Smith, Thomason, Georgallis, Pape	Smith	-
29.11.92	SD	Featherstone R.	L	14-38	G. Murdock, Thomason	Smith (3)	1068
6.12.92	RT(2)	Castleford	L	0-54	-	-	-
13.12.92	SD	Rochdale H.	L	18-26	Knox (2), Georgallis	Clarke (3)	-
10.1.93	SD	Rochdale H.	W	16-12	Richardson, Bethwaite, Pape	Clarke (2)	508
14.1.93	SD	Huddersfield	L	24-36	Clarke (2), Hibberd, Georgallis, Pape	Clarke (2)	-
17.1.93	SD	Oldham	L	21-32	Pape (2), Georgallis	Bethwaite (2), Manning (2), Hibberd (dg)	885
20.1.93	SD	Bramley	L	2-6	-	Hibberd	-
24.1.93	SD	Huddersfield	L	12-28	Graham, Hibberd	Clarke (2)	763
31.1.93	CC(1)	Halifax	L	16-66	Fox, Pape, Roy	Clarke (2)	-
7.2.93	SD	London C.	L	14-28	Graham, Knox	Bethwaite (3)	301
14.2.93	SD	Swinton	W	26-22	G. Murdock (3), Fox, Willaims	Bethwaite (3)	340
21.2.93	SD	Oldham	L	16-56	Iti (2)	Bethwaite (4)	-
28.2.93	SD	Featherstone R.	L	10-26	Bethwaite, Iti	Bethwaite	-
7.3.93	SD	Bramley	L	8-11	Knox	Richardson (2)	502
14.3.93	SD	Swinton	W	19-18	Knox (2), Pape	Richardson (3), Hibberd (dg)	-
21.3.93	SD	Huddersfield	L	16-29	Brierley, Pape, Williams	Bethwaite (2)	640
28.3.93	SD	London C.	L	8-30	Pape	Bethwaite (2)	-
4.4.93	SD	Featherstone R.	D	30-30	Hibberd (2), Manning (2), Southwell	Bethwaite (4), Hibberd	913
9.4.93	SD	Swinton	L	12-23	Bethwaite, Manning	Bethwaite (2)	-
12.4.93	SD	Swinton	L	16-19	Pape (2), Charlton, Fox	-	521
18.4.93	SD	Rochdale H.	L	12-50	Bethwaite, Pape	Bethwaite (2)	-

1992-93 SECOND DIVISION TABLE

	P	W	D	L	For Dg	Goals	Tries	Total	Agst Dg	Goals	Tries	Total	PTS
Featherstone R	28	24	1	3	0	128	185	996	2	55	60	352	49
Oldham	28	20	1	7	5	122	126	753	3	76	87	503	41
Huddersfield	28	15	0	13	9	82	98	565	4	82	95	548	30
Rochdale H	28	14	0	14	4	91	109	622	3	90	106	607	28
London C	28	12	2	14	2	76	95	534	6	82	98	562	26
Swinton	28	10	0	18	5	58	72	409	4	82	117	636	20
Carlisle	28	6	3	19	2	68	79	454	5	100	129	721	15
Bramley	28	7	1	20	4	46	58	328	4	104	130	732	15

1992-93 YOUNGER'S ALLIANCE - SECOND DIVISION

	P	W	D	L	For Pts	Agst Pts	Total
Salford	22	19	0	3	827	270	38
Ryedale-York	22	18	1	3	751	316	37
Workington T	22	14	0	8	556	462	28
Dewsbury	22	13	2	7	510	311	28
Leigh	22	13	1	8	560	358	27
Sheffield E	22	13	1	8	477	443	27
Oldham	22	11	0	11	615	510	22
Swinton	22	10	1	11	501	573	21
Bramley	22	10	0	12	408	512	20
Hemel Hempstead	22	9	1	12	401	593	19
Keighley C	22	8	3	11	426	619	19
Hunslet	22	8	0	14	479	546	16
Huddersfield	22	8	0	14	362	590	16
Doncaster	22	7	0	15	403	579	14
London C	22	5	2	15	384	606	12
Carlisle	22	3	2	17	351	723	8

13

*

1993-94

WE got our wish and the game reverted to a two-division structure. We didn't want the cull of teams that occurred but it happened anyway and Blackpool, Chorley and Nottingham were cast adrift into the amateur National Conference. The loss of Nottingham may have come as a blessed relief to Paul and Joan Thomlinson who ran the club. Certainly, I don't recall too many cries of anguish. The loss of Chorley, with its chairman a local MP, was seen as a much bigger blow to the game.

The passing of Blackpool Gladiators, a club with a string of antecedents as long as your arm was a puzzle to many. There had been a club in Blackpool since the Fifties. I think the reality was that the bloodline of the original Blackpool Borough resided in the other cast-adrift club, Chorley, and the Gladiators were perceived at that time as pretenders or non-family. I seem to remember their chairman creating embarrassment for the RFL too. Certainly few, if any, of the old sages on the RFL Council shed tears over their relegation.

In Carlisle, the amateur game continued to crumble, with the latest casualty being the biggest in the city, Dalston ARLFC. Superficially, Dalston had a lot going for them. They had their own ground and clubhouse a few miles to the west on land owned by the Nestlé corporation which still has a factory there. Carlisle Border Raiders played occasional pre-season friendlies at the venue and the bar was always lively.

A big step forward that summer had been the formation of a management support group who took it upon themselves to lend practical help to the board as we attempted to recover from the previous season's financial deficit. The group included my work colleague Jim Varah, former director Elsie Martlew, local farmer Eddie Wharton, our PA man Cyril Webber, local councillor Raymond Edgar, milkman Ian Reay and publican Peter Blake of Silloth. Their support lifted the spirits of the entire club and gave us the financial confidence to go out and sign players.

Our pre-season signings included three Aussies in Danny Russell, Adam Bertoli and Tony Coffey. Cameron Bell still recalls Danny Russell and Tony Coffey being picked up at Manchester Airport after a twenty-hour journey from Sydney. They were taken straight to Gillford Park, threw some kit on and played over half the game in a Cumbrian Cup pre-season fixture. 'Bloody marvellous,' said Cameron at the time.

Closer to home, we had recruited Paul Blake (brother of management support group member Peter Blake) from Wigton RU, Mark Chorley and Carl Henderson from Egremont ARLFC and about half of the Dalston ARLFC players including Chris and Geoff McManus who later, when their playing days were over, were to form an under-16s side in the city that played in 2007-08 under the name of Rickerby Saints. Geoff played his one and only first team game in a Raiders shirt at Bramley in the season's opening fixture. He claims to have had a hand in one of the tries when he came on, off the bench.

A few months after the start of the season, the former Great Britain international forward Hugh Waddell joined us from Sheffield. Hugh's professional career had actually started with Blackpool Borough in 1984 and had embraced spells that included Oldham and Leeds prior to joining the South Yorkshire outfit.

Willie Richardson's loan-spell from Whitehaven was made into a permanent transfer. It was as part of the deal that took Clayton Friend the other way. We gained at a stroke the safest full-back we'd ever had, a goal-kicker, a superb team motivator and a top guy all round.

The season opener was against Dewsbury at Batley's Mount Pleasant, their temporary home while a new stadium was being built following the devastating fire at Crown Flatt a couple of seasons before. We were dreadful and were hammered 48-6. We followed that with a couple of scratchy wins against Hunslet and Bramley and then, after a year's absence, we were back to derby games with the visit of Workington. We lost 28-12 but it was sheer relief to get a decent 2,000 gate after the previous season's offerings.

The Regal Trophy provided the first cup game of the season at Halloween, when Carcassonne were the visitors. Despite the poor gate of less than 600, this was a great occasion. Doc Haworth, our resident Francophile, wrote his usual programme piece, 'Doc's Deliberations', in French. Other programme contributors attempted to do likewise but fell short with their 'zut alors'-type contributions.

Our more waggish supporters wore Basque berets for the occasion. Mercifully there were no 'Onion Johnnie' types with pedal-cycles festooned with strings of onions.

We did manage to get an audio tape of *La Marseillaise* to

play prior to our own anthem before the match. Our lady mayor was present in her chain of office and was presented to the teams prior to kick-off. It was a ceremony that rivalled the scene in Gabriel Chevallier's satirical novel *Clochemerle* - scripted by Galton and Simpson into a hilarious 1970s TV series - where they opened the public *pissotiere*, or urinal.

The rugby was simply magnificent with an eighty-strong party of French supporters cheering to the echo every time the lead changed hands in their favour. Barry Williams, with two great tries, was the Carlisle star in our eventual 36-24 victory. Simon Knox also scored a brace with other tries coming from Paul Blake, Adam Bertoli and George Graham. Willie Richardson chipped in with four goals. This game was recalled by George as one of the highlights of his career at Carlisle.

The main beneficiary must have been the Railway Club, which was packed until late after the speechmaking had finished. We exchanged presents with the French officials. Their chairman, I remember, was a stereotypical Frenchman with a magnificent luxurious jet-black moustache. We gave them the usual pennants and club ties while they, in turn, presented us with some of their own wine and, for some mystifying reason, a tourist video of Carcassonne - in German! We all wished there could have been a return fixture. We'd have had a great time on the vin rouge.

The numbered balls in the cup draws were being really kind to us that season as we drew first division Wakefield Trinity at home next. Regrettably the Carlisle sporting public were as unimpressed with the prospect of watching higher division rugby as were the Wakefield faithful in making a trip to Carlisle. Just 750 supporters saw us pull off the shock of the season by beating the Regal Trophy winners of just two seasons earlier 28-12, courtesy of tries from Charlton, Coffey, Knox and Pape and six Willie Richardson goals.

Rodney Walker, later to become Sir Rodney and chairman of the RFL, was the chairman of Wakefield that year. He looked as sick as a parrot beneath his flamboyant fedora hat.

When we drew Bramley at home in the third round and slaughtered them 34-4 - tries by George Graham (3), Pape (2), Coffey and Russell, with Willie Richardson kicking three goals, our luck with the numbered balls began to embarrass us. It didn't last as we drew Castleford at Wheldon Road in the quarter-final and were duly hammered 44-4. Still, our share of the 4,500 gate plus the £3,000 prize money took away a bit of the disappointment. Then-chairman Eddie Ashton and his colleagues' courtesy and professionalism stay with me today. So much so that Castleford set a personal benchmark as to how visiting sides should be treated.

The Challenge Cup, later in the season, was somewhat less kind. After an easy home tie against the amateurs of Askam, which we won 42-8, we drew high-flying Workington at Gillford Park. Any further interest was extinguished as we lost an absolute cracker of a game 13-12, the difference being a Wayne Kitchin long-range drop-goal. We weren't complaining about a bumper 2,000-plus gate though. It set a new Gillford Park record, although Town's subsequent fifth-round tie at home to Bradford Northern with a 5,500 gate would have been even nicer.

Our performance in the league in that 1993-94 season was decidedly mixed as the coach familiarisation factor started to take effect. I've long since realised that as far as the British game is concerned, the optimum time of stay for coaching staff is two years, three at the most. Certainly after three, the motivational effect of a coach seems to wear off and some players start to lose that responsive hunger which gives them an all-important edge. Cameron Bell was still the same excellent coach that transformed Carlisle in 1990, but some of the players were looking for new leadership

Left: Carlisle's coaching
merry-go-round -
Cameron Bell, pictured
with Tammy the dog

instead of looking at their own performances and self-motivation.

It became common knowledge that season that Cameron wouldn't be returning in 1994-95 and it started to show on the pitch. Sad to say but amongst some of the players, it became an early case of 'The King is dead, long live the King'. The second half of our season was particularly bleak as we won just four out of seventeen league games and gates fell away alarmingly with a new low point of just 275 turning up to watch our fairly routine hammering of Highfield, 36-8, in late February.

Towards the end of that season, some of our better players were starting to get restless, none more so than Simon Knox, who we'd released on loan to first division Widnes. While there, Simon would start an apprenticeship at a higher level in their 'A' team; one that was ultimately to lead to him playing at the highest level with Brian Smith's Bradford Bulls in the Super League era. But not before another season at Gillford Park, once his spell at Widnes expired.

As the curtain finally came down, Carlisle languished in thirteenth position in a sixteen-team league. We were below

Border City Blues

Workington, who'd won it, Whitehaven and even Barrow. We'd recorded just nine wins from thirty league outings and shipped an average of nearly thirty points a game.

The only way was up, we felt, and appointed Hugh Waddell as player-coach, with Paul Charlton as his assistant, as we began to plan for the following term.

1993-94 CUMBERLAND AMATEUR RUGBY LEAGUE

Division Two

	P	W	D	L	F	A	Pts
Glasson Rangers	14	13	0	1	375	135	26
Westfield Hotel	14	10	1	3	449	208	21
Cockermouth	14	9	1	4	426	263	19
Flimby	14	8	0	6	280	279	16
Corkickle	14	7	0	7	316	237	14
Egremont	14	3	0	11	148	406	6
Linton Holme	14	3	0	11	165	530	6
Broughton Moor	14	2	0	12	148	249	4

Division Three

	P	W	D	L	F	A	Pts
Dearham	16	15	1	0	460	117	31
Distington	16	11	2	3	315	206	24
Wigton	16	10	0	6	413	204	20
Horse and Farrier	16	10	0	6	439	358	20
Westfield Welfare	16	8	2	6	410	337	18
St. Bees	16	7	1	8	364	288	15
Penrith	16	3	0	13	161	485	6
Aspatria	16	2	1	13	247	497	5
St. Nicholas Arms	16	2	1	13	207	524	5

1993-94 CUMBERLAND AMATEUR RUGBY LEAGUE ALLIANCE

Division Two

	P	W	D	L	F	A	Pts
Hensingham 'B'	14	14	0	0	626	105	28
Cockermouth 'A'	14	9	1	4	401	264	19
Westfield Hotel 'A'	14	9	0	5	300	338	18
Maryport 'A'	14	7	1	6	404	256	15
Flimby 'A'	14	5	1	8	170	251	11
St. Nicholas Arms 'A'	14	3	3	8	212	479	9
Linton Holme 'A'	14	3	0	11	119	289	6
Wigton 'A'	14	3	0	11	233	483	6

CARLISLE – 1993-94 – SEASON SUMMARY

Chairman:	Alan Tucker
Secretary:	Doug Fisher
Coach:	Cameron Bell (Feb 1990-Aug 1994), Hugh Waddell (Apr 1994-)
Records:	
Match	Goals: 10 by Barry Vickers at Nottingham C., 11 Mar 1990
	Tries: 4 by G. Peacham v. Workington T., 25 Jan, 1987
	and K. Pape v. Rochdale H., 11 Feb, 1987
	Points: 24 by B. Vickers v. Nottingham C., 11 Mar 1990
Season	Goals: 113 by S. Ferres, 1981-82
	Tries: 25 by M. Morgan, 1981-82, G. Peacham, 1984-85
	Points: 242 by S. Ferres, 1981-82
Career	Goals: 352 by Barry Vickers, 1988-92
	Tries: 184 by Kevin Pape, 1984-
	Points: 736 by Kevin Pape, 1984-
	Appearances: 317 by Kevin Pape, 1984-
	Highest Score: 60-0 v. Nottingham C., 1989-90
	Highest against: 112-0 v. St. Helens, 1986-87
Attendance:	5,903 v. Workington T. (Div 2) 6 Sept. 1981 at Brunton Park
	2,042 v. Workington T. (RL Cup), 30 Jan 1994 at Gillford Parkc

	App.	Tries	Goals	D/Gls	Pts		App.	Tries	Goals	D/Gls	Pts
Armstrong, Derek	13+1	1	-	-	4	McMullen, Alan	25	2	-	-	8
Armstrong, Ian	5+1	-	-	-	-	Manning, Phil	0+1	-	-	-	-
Bertoli, Adam	25	8	-	-	32	Murdock, Gary	11	2	-	-	8
Bethwaite, Kevin	7+3	6	-	-	24	Pape, Kevin	36	24	-	-	96
Blake, Paul	31+4	7	-	-	28	Paxton, Colin	7	4	-	-	16
Boucher, Philip	1	-	-	-	-	Richardson, Willie	36	3	99	-	210
Brierley, Steve	24+2	-	-	-	-	Russell, Danny	36	10	-	-	40
Charlton, Gary	19+2	5	-	-	20	Ryan, Mark	3	-	-	2	2
Chorley, Mark	2+7	-	-	-	-	Scott, Tony	16+6	-	-	-	-
Coffey, Anthony	19	9	-	-	36	Thomason, Malcolm	18	1	-	-	4
Crarey, Paul	15	5	-	-	20	Waddell, Hugh	17	5	-	-	20
Fox, Kevin	9+1	4	-	-	16	Westwood, Gary	8	-	-	-	-
Graham, George	24+1	9	-	-	36	White, Nigel	3	-	-	-	-
Harris, Grant	0+3	-	-	-	-	Wilkinson, Les	0+1	-	-	-	-
Henderson, Carl	7+2	-	-	-	-	Williams, Barry	5+17	7	-	4	32
Knox, Simon	27+3	9	-	-	36						
McCartney, Duncan	4	-	-	-	-	**TOTALS**					
McManus, Geoff	0+1	-	-	-	-	33 Players		123	99	6	696

1993-94 MATCH ANALYSIS

Date	Competition	Opponent	Result	Score	Tries	Goals	Attendance
329.8.93	SD	Dewsbury	L	6-48	Graham	Richardson	-
5.9.93	SD	Hunslet	W	24-20	Bethwaite (2), Blake, Knox	Richardson (4)	448
12.9.93	SD	Bramley	W	16-2	Bethwaite, Blake, Russell	Richardson (2)	-
19.9.93	SD	Workington T.	L	12-28	Bertoli, Bethwaite	Richardson (2)	1923
26.9.93	SD	Swinton	W	29-20	Coffey, Knox, Murdock, Pape, Richardson	Richardson (4), Williams (dg)	466
3.10.93	SD	Highfield	W	27-19	Coffey (2), Pape (2), Bertoli	Richardson (3), Ryan (dg)	-
10.10.93	SD	Doncaster	L	22-27	Bertoli, Pape, Williams	Richardson (4), Ryan (dg), Williams (dg)	-
24.10.93	SD	Batley	L	10-20	Coffey, Pape	Richardson	488

1993-94 MATCH ANALYSIS CONTINUED

Date	Competition	Opponent	Result	Score	Tries	Goals	Attendance
31.10.93	RT(1)	Carcassonne	W	36-24	Knox (2), Williams (2), Bertoli, Blake, Graham	Richardson (4)	593
7.11.93	SD	Keighley C.	W	26-24	Williams (2), Bertoli, Charlton, Knox	Richardson (3)	1092
14.11.93	RT(2)	Wakefield T.	W	28-12	Charlton, Coffey, Knox, Pape	Richardson (6)	746
21.11.93	SD	Huddersfield	L	16-42	Knox, Williams	Richardson (4)	-
28.11.93	SD	London C.	L	24-38	Graham (2), Coffey, Thomason	Richardson (4)	-
5.12.93	SD	Ryedale-York	L	26-32	Pape (2), Charlton (2), Graham	Richardson (3)	461
12.12.93	RT(3)	Bramley	W	34-4	Graham (3), Pape (2), Coffey, Russell	Richardson (3)	516
19.12.93	RT(4)	Castleford	L	4-44	McMullen	-	-
28.12.93	SD	Barrow	L	14-26	Coffey, Pape	Richardson (3)	-
2.1.94	SD	Whitehaven	L	12-34	Blake, Pape	Richardson (2)	937
5.1.94	SD	Rochdale H.	L	18-34	Pape (2), Blake, Crarey	Richardson	-
9.1.94	SD	Hunslet	W	18-16	D. Armstrong, Knox, Richardson, Russell	Richardson	-
16.1.94	CC(3)	Askam	W	42-8	Russell (2), Coffey, Crarey, Murdock, Pape, Richardson, Williams	Richardson (5)	521
23.1.94	SD	Bramley	W	20-16	Blake, Crarey, Pape	Richardson (4)	329
30.1.94	CC(4)	Workington T.	L	12-13	Crarey, Russell	Richardson (2)	2042
6.2.94	SD	Workington T.	L	16-23	Bertoli (2)	Richardson (4)	-
13.2.94	SD	Dewsbury	L	18-40	Knox, Pape, Waddell	Richardson (3)	480
20.2.94	SD	Swinton	L	6-38	Waddell	Richardson	-
27.2.94	SD	Highfield	W	36-8	Pape (2), Russell (2), Bertoli, McMullen, Waddell	Richardson (4)	275
6.3.94	SD	Doncaster	L	20-34	Fox, Pape, Paxton, Waddell	Richardson (2)	443
13.3.94	SD	Batley	L	6-56	Crarey	Richardson	-
20.3.94	SD	Keighley C.	L	12-50	Pape (2)	Richardson (2)	-
27.3.94	SD	Huddersfield	L	14-21	Charlton, Fox, Waddell	Richardson	600
1.4.94	SD	Barrow	W	29-24	Paxton (3), Blake, Russell	Richardson (4), Williams (dg)	398
4.4.94	SD	Whitehaven	L	4-46	-	Richardson (2)	-
10.4.94	SD	Rochdale H.	L	25-32	Pape (2), Russell, Trialist	Richardson (4), Williams (dg)	393
17.4.94	SD	Ryedale-York	L	22-34	Bethwaite (4), Fox, Trialist	Richardson (3)	-
24.4.94	SD	London C.	L	12-26	Fox, Graham	Richardson (2)	411

1993-94 SECOND DIVISION TABLE

	P	W	D	L	For Dg	Goals	Tries	Total	Agst Dg	Goals	Tries	Total	PTS
Workington T	30	22	2	6	4	114	132	760	7	54	54	331	46
Doncaster	30	22	1	7	11	99	130	729	8	67	86	486	45
London C	30	21	2	7	4	119	150	842	4	81	89	511	44
Batley	30	21	1	8	3	96	128	707	4	63	74	426	43
Huddersfield	30	20	0	10	3	107	111	661	10	76	89	518	40
Keithley C	30	19	1	10	4	104	161	856	8	66	83	472	39
Dewsbury	30	18	1	11	2	120	131	766	4	68	77	448	37
Rochdale H	30	18	0	12	10	101	123	704	4	72	96	532	36
Ryedale-York	30	17	1	12	12	89	118	662	6	73	91	516	35
Whitehaven	30	14	4	12	5	75	104	571	3	69	74	437	32
Barrow	30	13	1	16	13	82	101	581	7	104	132	743	27
Swinton	30	11	0	19	6	77	92	528	7	91	123	681	22
Carlisle	30	9	0	21	6	79	94	540	6	132	152	878	18
Hunslet	30	3	1	26	1	62	80	445	12	109	146	814	7
Bramley	30	3	0	27	4	40	73	376	1	132	173	957	6
Highfield	30	1	1	28	5	47	42	267	2	154	231	1234	3

1993-94 YOUNGER'S ALLIANCE - SECOND DIVISION

	P	W	D	L	For Pts	Agst Pts	Total
Oldham	22	21	1	0	844	287	43
Dewsbury	22	18	1	3	653	300	37
Doncaster	22	16	0	6	654	334	32
Hull KR	22	16	0	6	612	322	32
Rochdale H	22	14	0	8	599	441	28
Keighley C	22	13	1	8	561	372	27
Workington T	22	12	1	9	642	403	25
Leigh	22	11	0	11	536	440	22
Swinton	22	11	0	11	472	637	22
Huddersfield	22	9	1	12	427	460	19
Bramley	22	9	0	13	447	643	18
Sheffield E	22	8	0	14	424	392	16
Hunslet	22	7	0	15	490	643	14
Carlisle	22	4	1	17	393	780	9
London C	22	3	0	19	321	883	6
Barrow	22	1	0	21	299	1037	2

14

*

1994-95

DURING the previous season, we had done a lot of soul-searching to figure out a way forward. We were desperate to avoid the conclusion that a professional rugby league club could never work in the city. On the asset side, we knew how to run one on a shoestring. We had a good pool of players, were far more solvent than many, had a good lottery and a strong dedicated management team. On the negative side, the public of Carlisle was fickle, there was no heritage to draw on in terms of latent support, our ground was very basic and we were continually at war with our landlords in the Railway Club.

We concluded the obvious; that there were two ways to go. Either we gave up or found a way of negating the effects of our problems.

The die was partially cast anyway, as we had decided to accept the £150,000 sports and arts foundation grant originally intended to help us develop the Sheepmount Athletics Ground, but which was wholly insufficient for that purpose and renegotiated for use, along with our own funds, at Gillford Park instead. This proposal had eventually been accepted by all concerned and we therefore set about a major upgrade. At the same time we redoubled our efforts to peacefully co-exist with ground's owners and tried to get them to see the mutual benefits of a thriving rugby league club on their premises.

The first thing to go was the rickety corrugated steel-sheet fence that surrounded the ground. This had been standing for six years, originally as a 'temporary solution', and been badly damaged both as a result of strong winds and the actions of vandals. It was replaced by an eight-foot concrete block wall and topped with barbed wire.

The original wooden benches in the stand on the southern side of the ground were replaced by modern tipping bucket seats, and work began on a new building behind the goalposts at the western end. This new building, when finished, provided modern changing accommodation plus toilets, including full facilities for the disabled and a kitchen on the ground floor. The upper floor, an area of 2,000 square feet, was to be a gym or additional entertainment area and office. The sloping front of the structure provided covered seating for 150 spectators. It would enable us to dispose of those industrial cabins.

We thus had, within a few months, a completely secure ground with seated accommodation for 650 (although the new building's interior was still to be finished); total capacity somewhere between 2,500 and 3,600 (depending on which survey you accepted) and potentially excellent changing and entertainment facilities.

We didn't have the funds to both upgrade the ground and push the boat out on new players, so our pre-season signings were relatively low key and mainly amateurs from the local and West Cumbrian amateur game. Probably the most long-lived of these were Barry Quayle from Frizington, Gary Haile from Frizington, Matthew Lynch from Wigton RU and Jason Thurlow from The Horse and Farrier. Jason, who actually approached us on Christmas Eve at a party in the Crown Hotel in Botchergate, had previously had a spell at Barrow RLFC but hadn't made their first team. He'd also had an occasional game as a freelance in our Alliance side.

We'd lost our main derby, the lucrative home game with Workington, as they had achieved promotion to the first division with Leigh coming the other way, so we had a foreboding about finances before a ball was kicked.

The season started disastrously with just four wins from fifteen league games up to Christmas, and gates at an all-time low. We reluctantly concluded that having a player-coach wasn't working for us, relieved Hugh Waddell of the coaching duties and appointed his assistant, the vastly experienced Paul Charlton, to take his place.

It would be nice to record that Charlo immediately turned the situation around. Things were at too low an ebb for such a fairytale transformation however.

We adequately demonstrated that when your luck is out there's really not a great deal you can do to change it. As an example, we'd drawn and beaten the amateurs from Dudley Hill in both the Regal Trophy and the Challenge Cup. The sporting public of Carlisle responded to these draws with new record low attendances of 206 and 204 respectively to see us through to the next rounds with dismally supported home games against Dewsbury and Widnes. The gate against Widnes for example, the 1989 World Club champions and still a first division club at the time, was 614 as Carlisle bowed out of the Challenge Cup with a 40-2 defeat.

When the season ended to put us out of our misery, we'd recorded just eight wins from thirty games and finished in fourteenth position in the sixteen-club league with just perennial strugglers Barrow and Highfield below us. Of course, we'd always realised that we were treading a fine line by spending our resources on ground improvements rather than players but, maybe naively, we thought that by putting our supporters well in the picture, they would have stuck by us.

It wasn't just our supporters who had lost patience with our emphasis on ground improvements at the expense of new signings. Kevin Pape who had been with us since the 1983-84 season announced his disgruntlement with affairs and resigned, later to join first division Workington where he enjoyed a season or two at the top level before hanging up his boots.

Looking back on that wretched season, there were very few highs and an awful lot of lows. However, the positive things included Danny Russell maturing into a fine player and captain who would much later go on to play at the highest level for Huddersfield Giants. Another encouraging thing was the gracious and mature way in which Hugh Waddell took being relieved of the player-coach position and the cheerfully optimistic way in which Paul Charlton accepted the challenge.[1]

Paul Charlton was a fitness fanatic and a real workaholic who expected similar standards from his players. In fact his recommended cure for a dose of flu was to wrap up warm, mount a bike and spend a couple of hours riding furiously up in the West Cumbrian fells. His career had spanned twenty years and embraced nineteen full GB caps. He'd

---

[1]When his playing career in rugby league was over, Hugh Waddell settled in Carlisle, played rugby union for a while and actually turned back the clock to play half a game for Carlisle Centurions RLFC in 2005, alongside that other Raiders favourite George Graham. Hugh was 45 and George was 39. However it was Hugh who scored a trademark try from close in!

started his pro career in 1961 with Workington where he spent nearly nine seasons, played six seasons with Salford and then finally hung up his boots back at Blackpool after a further six seasons with Workington. He holds the record for appearances in a Workington shirt with 419.

Paul was and still is a most unassuming and impeccably polite man. Breathing fire in the dressing rooms and touchlines and wearing his heart on his sleeve at all times maybe, but a total gentleman for all that. His time as Carlisle coach is remembered with awe and respect by all who knew him.

Away from the dynamics of coaching, this was when the RFL published its proposals for the future of the professional game in a hard-hitting document called *Framing the Future*. It revealed some disturbing statistics including an analysis of member clubs' financial affairs that showed that thirty out of the thirty-two professional clubs in membership were technically insolvent. At a stroke, we started to understand how other clubs just seemed to defy economic logic and were willing to sign players willy-nilly and where we were 'going wrong'. Insolvency held no fears; many of them had been in that state for years! It seemed that the London Crusaders situation was endemic.

Other aspects of that highly critical report observed that the game barely existed in either professional or amateur conditions outside of the 'M62 corridor' and that the total combined attendance at all member clubs fell well short of being able to fill Old Trafford (in those days just 45,000). We all suspected that this report was just a forerunner of something bigger, but we never realised just how big until we were, along with other member clubs, summoned to two top-level meetings at Wigan's Central Park and then at a hotel just off the M62 near Huddersfield.

We had all heard a little about the struggles in Australia

between the media groups owned by Kerry Packer and Rupert Murdoch and how the Australian game featured in these politics. We'd also heard that Murdoch had British rugby league in his sights but few of us had any indication as to the financial implications of this.

In the first meeting at Central Park we were asked to agree to a series of mergers, including one between the four Cumbrian sides. The original intention was to create around fourteen Super League clubs, after the addition of Toulouse and Paris. There was also talk of new clubs in Leicester and Newcastle, the latter allegedly supported by Sir John Hall of Newcastle United. It was tentatively agreed that the 'Star League', as it was initially referred to, would be made up of: Wigan, St Helens, Leeds, Humber, Calder, London, Cumbria, Warrington and/or Widnes, Toulouse, Paris, Manchester, Halifax, Bradford and South Yorkshire. A new side was to be created in Cardiff and placed in Division One.

The new top-flight enterprises would share in about £75 million over five years. Any club that declined to join the new set-up would be given a parachute payment of £100,000 and ply its trade outside this new elite. The proposal seemed like a good idea to the cash-strapped clubs present, especially those not being asked to merge such as Leeds, St Helens, London and Wigan. Once the others took the merger proposals back to their boards and committees, however, they were rapidly rejected, in some cases almost violently, as angry supporters organised protest marches with numbers totally disproportionate to the usual match attendances.

The next meeting, three weeks later on the Sunday after the Challenge Cup final, was much more progressive. The meeting was held in the Hilton Hotel just off the M62 near Huddersfield and was clearly organised in a panic as we were only advised about it on the Friday. The ante had now increased to £87 million over five years.

Buried in the extensive minutes from that day is the following:

'Mr Tucker of Carlisle put forward three main proposals:
  1) That the lump sums to be distributed annually over 5
  years to the 3 Divisions be as follows:
      i)   £10.8 million to the Super League
      ii)   £5 million to the First Division
      iii)   £1.5 million to the Second Division
  2) That the nominated clubs in each of the 3 divisions be
  initially as listed in the minutes (of the RFL Board
  Meeting that preceeded the Clubs' Meeting)
  3) That there would be promotion and relegation from
  the end of season one, the numbers and basis of which
  would be subject to further debate.'

I barely remember making that proposal, which came about after a lot of side meetings with other members present and was purposely tailored to gain agreement from top to bottom. Eventually, clubs such as Carlisle in the second division would get a minimum of £100,000 per season with supplements for running alliance and academy teams. Nearly all clubs were anxious to get this deal signed and to start receiving the money to save them from insolvency's Grim Reaper.

On the face of it, this should have been manna from heaven for clubs who, in many cases, would see financial turnover increased by sixty per cent or more. What in practice happened was that most of the Sky money went out in transfer fees, wages and contract payments. Rightly or wrongly, after the most pressing debts were paid, the main beneficiaries of this windfall were players and their agents. The Cumbrian clubs were not immune to this factor and they found that to retain their players winning pay needed to increase dramatically. Player agencies developed into a growth industry until the RFL stepped in with rules including the need for substantial bonds as a prerequisite.

Thus the RFL's hope of massive infrastructure investment was largely sacrificed in favour of better playing terms for players and agents. This isn't the place to moralise about this; certainly players were underpaid compared to 'easier' and gentler sports like football, but the way the RFL just handed out the money with little in the way of controls as to how it should be spent was a scandal; a lost opportunity to develop the game's structure for the future. This was clearly realised because the next round of negotiations with member clubs a few years later saw very much smaller sums given to the lower echelons, and then only against certain criteria such as reserve and academy teams being in existence.

From that day onwards, professional rugby league began to change from being a mutually supportive organisation, wherein the minnows were equally respected, into a more hierarchical structure where wealth, volume of supporters and results were everything. In short, what was once an antidote to business became a cut-throat small-to-medium enterprise itself. Despite this coming of age, as we now realise from the depressingly recurrent instances of insolvency at all levels, lessons in financial prudence went unheeded.

1994-95 THE ALLIANCE - SECOND DIVISION

	P	W	D	L	For Pts	Agst Pts	Total
Sheffield E	22	19	0	3	720	406	38
Hull KR	22	17	0	5	601	335	34
Keighley C	22	16	1	5	769	303	33
Widnes	22	16	0	6	772	293	32
Workington T	22	14	2	6	511	424	30
Leigh	22	13	1	8	588	427	27
Batley	22	13	0	9	478	393	26
Doncaster	22	12	0	10	618	548	24
Rochdale H	22	12	0	10	526	485	24
Huddersfield	22	11	1	10	510	506	23
London B	22	10	0	12	499	530	20
Swinton	22	8	0	14	436	696	16
Whitehaven	22	6	0	16	410	636	12
Hunslet	22	2	1	19	387	633	5
Carlisle	22	2	0	20	262	811	4
Barrow	22	2	0	20	262	923	4

Border City Blues

CARLISLE – 1994-95 – SEASON SUMMARY

Chairman:	Alan Tucker
Secretary:	Doug Fisher
Coach:	Hugh Waddell (Apr 1994-Dec 1994), Paul Charlton (Dec 1994-)
Records:	
Match	Goals: 10 by Barry Vickers at Nottingham C., 11 Mar 1990
	Tries: 4 by G. Peacham v. Workington T., 25 Jan, 1987
	and K. Pape v. Rochdale H., 11 Feb, 1987
	Points: 24 by B. Vickers v. Nottingham C., 11 Mar 1990
Season	Goals: 113 by S. Ferres, 1981-82
	Tries: 25 by M. Morgan, 1981-82, G. Peacham, 1984-85
	Points: 242 by S. Ferres, 1981-82
Career	Goals: 352 by Barry Vickers, 1988-92
	Tries: 192 by Kevin Pape, 1984-94
	Points: 768 by Kevin Pape, 1984-94
	Appearances: 324 by Kevin Pape, 1984-94
	Highest Score: 60-0 v. Nottingham C., 1989-90
	Highest against: 112-0 v. St. Helens, 1986-87
Attendance:	5,903 v. Workington T. (Div 2) 6 Sept. 1981 at Brunton Park
	2,042 v. Workington T. (RL Cup), 30 Jan 1994 at Gillford Park

	App.	Tries	Goals	D/Gls	Pts		App.	Tries	Goals	D/Gls	Pts
Armstrong, Derek	10+8	3	-	-	12	Manning, Phil	14+2	4	-	-	16
Blake, Paul	3	-	-	-	-	Meteer, Paul	6+3	-	-	-	-
Brierley, Steve	32	1	-	-	4	Newell, John	6+4	2	-	-	8
Brookes, Mark	0+1	-	-	-	-	Pape, Kevin	7	8	-	-	32
Charlton, Gary	32	6	-	1	25	Paxton, Colin	22	3	-	-	12
Charlton, Jason	17+11	-	-	-	-	Quayle, Barry	20+3	6	-	-	24
Chorley, Mark	6+3	-	-	-	-	Richardson, Willie	34	4	96	-	208
Day, Glen	13+2	2	-	-	8	Robinson, Jeff	10+1	-	-	1	1
Dinsdale, Edwin	11+1	1	-	-	4	Ruddy, Gary	3	-	-	-	12
Gardner, Marc	6+1	3	-	-	12	Russell, Danny	34	14	-	-	56
Graham, George	29	7	-	-	28	Scott, Tony	7+6	-	-	-	-
Haile, Gary	4+2	3	-	-	12	Tait, Alan	0+2	-	-	-	-
Holt, Darren	2+2	-	-	-	-	Thurlow, Jason	11	7	-	-	28
Johnson, Willie	10	1	-	-	4	Underwood, Brian	0+1	-	-	-	-
Kavanagh, Mike	13	2	2	-	12	Waddell, Hugh	24	8	-	-	32
Knox, Simon	32	12	-	-	48	Wilkinson, Les	0+2	-	-	-	-
Knubley, Stuart	15+4	6	-	-	24	Williams, Barry	0+3	-	-	1	1
Lynch, Matthew	9	-	-	-	-	**TOTALS**					
McMullen, Alan	1	-	-	-	-	36 Players		106	98	3	623

1994-95 MATCH ANALYSIS

Date	Competition	Opponent	Result	Score	Tries	Goals	Attendance
21.8.94	SD	London B.	L	16-38	Pape, Graham, Knox	Richardson (2)	408
28.8.94	SD	Batley	L	16-44	G. Charlton, Knox, Russell	Richardson (2)	-
4.9.94	SD	Bramley	W	15-12	Pape, Waddell	Richardson (3), Williams (dg)	328
11.9.94	SD	Rochdale H.	L	32-42	Pape (3), Brierley, Russell	Richardson (6)	-
18.9.94	SD	Hunslet	W	26-22	Russell (2), G. Charlton, Pape	Richardson (5)	-
25.9.94	SD	Swinton	L	16-36	G. Charlton, Johnson, Pape	Richardson (2)	410
5.10.94	SD	Dewsbury	L	20-38	Graham (2), Richardson (2)	Richardson (2)	-
9.10.94	SD	Hull K.R.	L	0-52			-
16.10.94	SD	Highfield	W	28-8	Waddell (2), D. Armstrong, Pape	Richardson (6)	324
30.10.94	SD	Keighley C.	L	14-46	Knox, Waddell	Richardson (3)	-

1994-95 MATCH ANALYSIS CONTINUED

Date	Competition	Opponent	Result	Score	Tries	Goals	Attendance
6.11.94	SD	London B.	L	16-23	Quayle, Russell	Richardson (4)	-
13.11.94	SD	Batley	L	12-26	Knox, Russell	Richardson (2)	370
27.11.94	RT(1)	Dudley Hill	W	25-12	Newall (2), D. Armstrong, Knox	Richardson (4), Robinson (dg)	206
3.12.94	RT(2)	Dewsbury	L	16-30	D. Armstrong, Knox, Quayle	Richardson (2)	287
11.12.94	SD	Bramley	L	0-34	-	-	-
18.12.94	SD	Rochdale H.	L	16-18	Kavanagh, Knox	Richardson (4)	205
26.12.94	SD	Barrow	W	22-20	Graham, Knox, Knubley, Waddell	Richardson (3)	294
31.12.94	SD	Whitehaven	L	4-36	Waddell	-	-
8.1.95	SD	Huddersfield	L	20-26	Russell, Thurlow, Waddell	Richardson (4)	416
15.1.95	SD	Leigh	L	20-32	Graham, Knox, Russell, Waddell	Richardson (2)	-
22.1.95	CC(3)	Dudley Hill	W	34-4	Knubley (2), G. Charlton, Kavanagh, Quayle, Richardson	Richardson (5)	204
29.1.95	SD	Hunslet	L	12-32	Ruddy (3)	-	260
5.2.95	SD	Swinton	L	18-40	Dinsdale, Knox, Quayle	Richardson (3)	-
12.2.95	CC(4)	Widnes	L	2-40		Richardson	615
19.2.95	SD	Dewsbury	L	10-36	Russell, Thurlow	Richardson	287
6.3.95	SD	Hull K.R.	L	32-40	Quayle (2), G. Charlton, Graham, Thurlow	Richardson (6)	255
12.3.95	SD	Ryedale-York	L	22-49	Gardner (2), Knubley, Thurlow	Richardson (3)	-
19.3.95	SD	Highfield	W	56-14	Knubley (2), Thurlow (2), Day, Haile, Knox, Paxton, Russell	Richardson (6), Kavanagh (2)	Graham,
26.3.95	SD	Keighley C.	W	12-2	Manning, Russell	Richardson (2)	989
2.4.95	SD	Huddersfield	L	24-36	Manning (2), Paxton, Russell	Richardson (4)	-
9.4.95	SD	Leigh	W	22-20	G. Charlton, Haile, Paxton, Thurlow	Richardson (3)	219
14.4.95	SD	Barrow	L	6-14	Russell	Richardson	-
17.4.95	SD	Whitehaven	W	16-13	Gardner, Haile, Knox	Richardson (2)	624
23.4.95	SD	Ryledale-York (at Gateshead)	L	23-28	Day, Manning, Richardson, Russell	Richardson (3), Charlton (dg)	246

1994-95 SECOND DIVISION TABLE

	P	W	D	L	For Dg	Goals	Tries	Total	Agst Dg	Goals	Tries	Total	PTS
Keighley C	30	23	2	5	2	144	171	974	5	52	57	337	48
Batley	30	23	0	7	4	111	132	754	3	70	70	423	46
Huddersfield	30	19	3	8	4	121	156	870	5	87	90	539	41
London B	30	20	1	9	2	89	138	732	8	70	83	480	41
Whitehaven	30	19	0	11	4	113	134	766	3	76	88	507	38
Rochdale H	30	18	0	12	5	134	133	805	4	88	91	544	36
Dewsbury	30	17	1	12	4	114	128	744	6	82	92	538	35
Hull KR	30	16	1	13	2	125	143	824	6	79	88	516	33
Ryedale-York	30	15	2	13	14	99	127	720	6	84	107	602	32
Hunslet	30	16	0	14	7	88	107	611	5	109	140	783	32
Leigh	30	12	0	18	2	94	108	622	3	124	134	787	24
Swinton	30	12	0	18	2	85	101	576	2	121	131	768	24
Bramley	30	10	0	20	4	67	104	554	1	97	115	655	20
Carlisle	30	8	0	22	2	86	93	546	5	116	160	877	16
Barrow	30	6	0	24	7	79	71	449	3	122	141	811	12
Highfield	30	1	0	29	0	34	39	224	0	206	298	1604	2

Border City Blues

1994-95 CUMBERLAND AMATEUR RUGBY LEAGUE

Division Two

	P	W	D	L	F	A	Pts
Flimby	18	17	0	1	632	192	34
Cockermouth	18	15	0	3	501	239	30
Distington	18	13	0	5	400	257	26
Wigton	18	12	0	6	512	285	24
Great Clifton	18	11	0	7	404	393	22
Egremont	18	6	1	11	293	430	13
Maryport	18	6	0	12	236	440	12
Horse and Farrier	18	4	0	14	309	407	8
Dearham	18	3	1	14	221	506	7
Linton Holme	18	2	0	16	289	648	4

Division Three

	P	W	D	L	F	A	Pts
Ellenborough 'A'	18	16	0	2	736	242	32
Kells 'A'	18	16	0	2	461	295	32
Hensingham 'A'	18	14	0	4	549	296	28
Westfield Welfare	18	11	0	7	426	402	22
Wath Brown Hornets 'A'	18	8	2	8	386	402	18
Aspatria	18	7	0	11	393	490	14
St. Nicholas Arms	18	4	1	13	319	546	9
Frizington 'A'	18	4	1	13	232	638	9
Glasson Rangers 'A'	18	4	0	14	372	444	8
St. Bees	18	4	0	14	354	473	8

Division Four

	P	W	D	L	F	A	Pts
Seaton Rangers 'A'	16	15	0	1	402	168	30
Hensingham 'B'	16	13	0	3	493	308	26
Great Clifton 'A'	16	11	0	5	481	294	22
Flimby 'A'	16	10	0	6	349	285	20
Maryport 'A'	16	5	1	10	350	370	11
Penrith	16	5	1	10	288	319	11
Westfield Hotel 'A'	16	5	0	11	318	472	10
Wigton 'A'	16	3	2	11	257	499	8
Linton Holme 'A'	16	3	0	13	287	510	6

15

*

1995-96

THIS was the campaign in which 'truncated' entered the official RFL lexicon, the so-called truncated season in question bridging the gap between the end of the 1994-95 winter season in April 1995 and the start of the summer season in March 1996. As such, it was just twenty fixtures in length and ran from August 1995 until the end of January 1996. It contained one cup competition, the Regal Trophy. Bizarrely, the opening rounds of the following season's Challenge Cup were to be held in the latter stages of the current season's league competition.

As a result of the forthcoming Super League revolution, three divisions were back on the agenda but with eleven clubs in each of the lower divisions. The shorter term meant that there was no need for the double home and away formula that killed off the three division concept in 1992-93.

The 1995-96 campaign was also referred to as the game's centenary season, since rugby league had been born in The George Hotel, Huddersfield, one hundred years previously.

Sadly, the centenary element was never fully exploited, probably because the RFL was preoccupied with Super League and the resulting politics and distractions.

At Carlisle, it was Paul Charlton's first full season in command and we were able to supplement his squad with off-season signings such as Warren Rudd and Paul Meteer from West Cumbria, Stuart Rhodes and Mike Kavanagh from Barrow (both having played for us in earlier seasons) and local Limehouse schoolboy Darren Holt. The Junior Kiwi international half-back Tane Manihera was also to join us from Wellington a month in. Much later, another of Cameron Bell's recommendations, winger Richard Henare, arrived from Hawkes Bay RUFC.

With Workington enjoying their brief stay in the sunny uplands of Division One, Whitehaven in the table above us and no Challenge Cup, it was going to be, almost by definition, a badly-attended few months. The average for our league games turned out to be just 441.

Yet from a results point of view it was probably our best season since 1981-82, especially in September, October and November, when we won twelve games on the trot. Much of that success was owed to the on-field motivation of club captain Danny Russell, who became a model clubman as well as an inspirational leader. He formed a potent partnership with coach Paul Charlton.

Paul, who later had a spell coaching Barrow, now lives on Australia's Gold Coast with his wife Lillian. While he takes a keen interest in rugby both in Australia and in Workington, where his son Gary is now the joint coach, his main non-family preoccupation is his work as a carpenter engaged in the maintenance of retail outlets. Paul tells me he still remembers that winning sequence and, in particular, how it ended when we played Bramley with an injury-ravaged side at a rugby union ground in Leeds.

From a financial point of view the 1995-96 campaign was an unmitigated disaster - we paid out much higher winning bonuses from pathetically low gate receipts. We were forced into many economies even to stay afloat. One of the economies unfortunately saw long-serving assistant physio and sponge man Vic Semple leave us.

There are several key events and comings and goings which encapsulate that shortened season.

Tane Manihera, the 20-year-old Junior Kiwi international, arrived in late summer and after making his debut in the alliance side against Huddersfield, went on to be an ever-present, scoring nine tries in his debut year. One little known fact is that Tane was actually sent by Cameron Bell in place of the eventual New Zealand international skipper Stacey Jones, who had just upset our plans and signed for the newly-formed Auckland Warriors. Fourteen years on and Tane is still living in Cumbria with his wife, Gillian, and two young sons. His rugby career took in spells after Carlisle at Barrow, Widnes, Workington and Whitehaven, along with Wigton RUFC. Nowadays he works as a sales representative with a local manufacturer of sheet-steel roof-cladding products.

Tane remembers his time at Carlisle with deep affection: 'It was Cameron Bell who introduced me to Carlisle,' he says. 'I was living in Christchurch at the time and had been on a couple of tours with the Junior Kiwis, including coming to England in 1993 and also playing in Fiji. I arrived at Carlisle on 13th September 1995. I'd never heard of the place but quickly settled in. Carlisle is such a friendly place and I was sharing a house in Oswald Street with Danny Russell and Darren Holt, so that was a great help. The fans and my team-mates were great, so that also assisted. I can remember bits and pieces of my first game for Carlisle. It was an 'A' team match against Huddersfield. Mark Brookes, from Penrith, scored a couple of tries.

'I well remember my first team debut at home against Hunslet. I scored two tries, one off a George Graham pass. Carlisle had a great forward pack with Barry Williams, George and Steve Brierley outstanding. Danny Russell at hooker was a class act, as was Simon Knox in the second row.'

Later that season, another New Zealander arrived courtesy again of Cameron. Richard Henare was both an instant hit and a man of mystery. To say he kept his own counsel is an understatement. Richard was an enigma. He was probably the fastest wingman ever to play for Carlisle and scored ten tries in just seven appearances before he caught the eye of Alex Murphy, who was part of Warrington's management team at the time. To cut a long story short, Henare was transferred to Warrington very early the following season with a substantial cheque in compensation to Carlisle. In his new life at Wilderspool he scored seventeen tries at the rate of a try per game in 1996, until he left under a shadow due to off-field issues after the 1997 campaign. Another player to leave us in this season was Whitehaven lad Simon Knox, transferred to Bradford.

Off the field, we strengthened our management team by inviting local businessman and chartered accountant Dougal Kyle to join us. Dougal's financial aptitude and professionalism were to prove invaluable in assisting us to make sense of the somewhat chaotic financial records that had fallen well behind following director Frank Lowe's distraction by his new business interests and the resignation of the person we appointed to manage our finances in Frank's place. Thanks to Dougal, we soon had full sets of up to date accounts to frighten ourselves with.

Several games from Carlisle's history stick in the mind, but none as dramatic or in such sharp focus as our second-round tie against first division Castleford at Gillford Park that season. We'd despatched Doncaster in the first round quite comfortably 38-10 (Tane Manihera had a blinder) and expected little other than a gallant loss with a decent crowd after the magic balls drew us at home to first division Cas.

How wrong we were! The Carlisle lads played the game of their lives and were only trailing 18-10 at half-time, and this against the likes of Dean Sampson, Graham Steadman, Brendan Tuuta, Tawere Nikau and company. When we pulled level, 18-18, with twenty minutes to go, the tension was as unbearable as Carlisle's defence was impregnable. And when Bluey Kavanagh put over a drop-goal with ten minutes left on the clock, we all felt that history might be made, but we didn't want to endure the tension of the final countdown.

When the final hooter finally sounded, it felt as if we'd won the World Cup. The atmosphere in the Railway Club and the St Nicholas Arms later seemed to make up for the previous fourteen years of pain and disappointment. The beams of pride and joy on the faces of Paul Charlton and the players as they left the muddy field after that 19-18 victory were unforgettable to all.

The next morning, to a man, we all skived off work to go and relive it with Raymond Edgar our commercial manager-cum-groundsman at the ground. We were all disappointed with the measly attendance for such a prestigious fixture of 800 but Carlisle, a third division club now, had just defeated one of the best and biggest teams in the country. We even featured that Monday on BBC TV. We all agreed that the sporting public of Carlisle would have little choice other than to support us now. That sporting public repaid us with a gate of just 550 for the next home game.

Our efforts that Sunday earned us a plum draw against mighty Leeds at Headingley in the quarter-final a month later. Despite scoring the first try, we were well-beaten 44-22 by a team bristling with international superstars including Kevin Iro, Craig Innes, Francis Cummins, Graham Holroyd, James Lowes, Barrie McDermott and George Mann. Our scorers were George Graham and Phil Manning who grabbed a brace each and man of the match Willie Richardson slotted over our three goals. The defeat was sweetened by our share of the gate receipts from the 5,000-plus gate.

One other memory of that day that will forever stay with me was the Leeds RLFC hospitality. I'd taken my wife and daughter to the match with the intent of stopping off for a bar meal en route. Nowhere we passed looked decent so we resigned ourselves to a burger upon arrival. I asked the guy in the Headingley car park where we could get a bite to eat and he directed us to the reception office.

We duly went there to be met by Alf Davies, the Leeds chief executive, who I'd previously met at the RFL's HQ in Chapeltown Road. Alf airily dismissed our thoughts of a burger and rather grandly showed us to a sponsor suite where we were treated not to a burger or even a bar meal but to a slap-up three-course lunch. I was driving, so we declined the offer of wine. I remember thinking how good it would be if we could entertain visiting officials so well at Carlisle. The best we were able to offer them was a couple of biscuits and a cuppa.

Anyway, feeling well fed and grateful, I caught the waiter's eye to give him a generous tip and make a donation to Leeds costs. He beat me to it with a bill for £62.50. You never get owt for nowt in Yorkshire.

Tane Manihera still remembers that cup sequence well. 'Those cup games against Castleford and Leeds were the highlights of my Carlisle career,' he says. 'The Castleford team contained New Zealand legends such as Brendon Tuuta and Tawera Nikau, along with English stars like Colin

Maskill and Graham Steadman. To beat them was beyond my wildest dreams. When we went to Headingley to play Leeds in the next round and ran them close before going down 44-22, it really was something special. There was a stage where I thought we could have won against that team of world class players.'

Another former Carlisle player who remembers that cup run with absolute clarity is George Graham. 'The run where we beat Castleford and then I scored two tries at Headingley against a Leeds side full of international stars is a cherished memory of those Carlisle days,' he recalls. 'I also remember an illegal spear tackle on Derek Armstrong [currently coaching Hawick RUFC] that popped his shoulder out.'

One more landmark of Carlisle's 1995-96 season was when we were obliged, due to the tight scheduling of the shorter campaign, to play a couple of midweek evening matches. Gillford Park had no floodlights in those days so we accepted an invitation to play at the Carlisle RU club where there was adequate illumination.

The games were just ordinary league fixtures against York and Doncaster. But because the union club was situated in the city centre and next door to Brunton Park, where it all started in 1981, we were curious to see the extent to which the central venue might affect our gates. The RU club were all for the opportunity to accrue some good bar income.

The logistics of staging an all-paying game at that venue were quite difficult as the car park, which was used by members of both the RU club and an associated squash club, was within the precincts of the ground, so we relied heavily on supporters' honesty to offer payment as they entered.

We won both games and the organisation seemed to go well. The union people were gracious hosts, both teams and sets of supporters were well entertained and the bar did good trade. The few RU regulars who watched the alien sport professed to have enjoyed the experience. But the attendances at the two games - around 500 - were exactly what we would have expected that season had we played at Gillford Park.

It seemed, whatever the venue, after that initial euphoric first two seasons and without the lure of a first division club or a Cumbrian derby game, that there was some sort of natural law at play that limited attendances in Carlisle to just a few hundred. Certainly those sages who variously advocated returning to central Carlisle or playing at Penrith as the solution to our chronically low gates were exposed as clutching at straws.

What did emerge from this trial was that there was sufficient interest from both the RU club and ourselves to examine in detail the likely practicalities and advantages of a much longer term arrangement there. The venue might not have held the key to better attendances but it certainly had the advantage of being truly sports oriented. We had a number of frank meetings with various members of the committee there throughout 1995-96 but it became obvious that, for reasons with which we could sympathise, they wished to remain a rugby union only venue.

1995-96 SCOTTISH & NEWCASTLE CUMBERLAND AMATEUR RUGBY LEAGUE

Division Two

	P	W	D	L	F	A	Pts
Seaton Rangers	18	17	0	1	710	193	34
Distington	18	13	1	4	394	275	27
Maryport	18	12	0	6	502	343	24
Ellenborough 'A'	18	11	1	6	417	322	23
Wigton	18	5	2	11	372	374	12
Glasson Rangers	18	6	0	12	330	391	12
Great Clifton	18	6	0	12	332	442	12
Hensingham 'A'	18	6	2	10	277	397+50	11
Kells 'A'	18	5	1	12	228	627	11
Egremont	18	5	1	12	242	440+150	2

1995-96 SCOTTISH & NEWCASTLE CUMBERLAND AMATEUR RUGBY LEAGUE CONTINUED

Division Three

	P	W	D	L	F	A	Pts
Wath Brown Hornets 'A'	14	12	0	2	332	197	24
+	14	11	1	2	364	217	23
St. Nicholas Arms	14	10	1	3	216	140	21
Westfield Welfare	14	7	0	7	361	236	14
Flimby 'A'	14	6	0	8	230	341+100	6
Linton Holme	14	5	0	9	301	263+100	4
Seaton Rangers 'A'	14	4	0	10	184	310+150	-1
Frizington 'A'	14	0	0	14	101	385+200	-12

Division Four

	P	W	D	L	F	A	Pts
Maryport 'A'	16	16	0	0	545	180	32
Broughton Red Rose 'A'	16	11	1	4	608	238	23
St. Nicholas Arms 'A'	16	11	0	5	513	277	22
Lowca 'A'	16	10	0	6	352	319	20
Westfield Hotel 'A'	16	7	1	8	305	303	15
Distington 'A'	16	7	0	9	271	615	14
Penrith	16	3	0	13	158	365+50	3
Glasson Rangers 'A'	16	3	0	13	257	408+200	-6
Wigton 'A'	16	3	0	13	168	472+200	-6

1995-96 THE ALLIANCE - SECOND DIVISION

					For	Agst	
	P	W	D	L	Pts	Pts	Total
London B	18	12	2	4	597	273	26
Batley	18	13	0	5	458	305	26
Swinton	18	12	1	5	527	297	25
Huddersfield	18	12	0	6	421	380	24
Whitehaven	18	11	0	7	420	428	22
Rochdale H	18	9	0	9	440	413	18
Hunslet H	18	6	0	12	376	448	12
Blackpool G	18	6	0	12	352	525	12
Barrow B	18	5	0	13	300	539	10
Carlisle	18	2	1	15	281	564	5

Border City Blues

CARLISLE – 1995-96 – SEASON SUMMARY

Chairman: Alan Tucker
Secretary: Paul Scanlon-Wells
Coach: Paul Charlton (Dec 1994-)
Records:
Match   Goals: 10 by Barry Vickers at Nottingham C., 11 Mar 1990
                   Tries: 4 by G. Peacham v. Workington T., 25 Jan, 1987
                   and K. Pape v. Rochdale H., 11 Feb, 1987
                   Points: 24 by B. Vickers v. Nottingham C., 11 Mar 1990
Season   Goals: 113 by S. Ferres, 1981-82
                   Tries: 25 by M. Morgan, 1981-82, G. Peacham, 1984-85
                   Points: 242 by S. Ferres, 1981-82
Career   Goals: 352 by Barry Vickers, 1988-92
                   Tries: 192 by Kevin Pape, 1984-94
                   Points: 768 by Kevin Pape, 1984-94
                   Appearances: 324 by Kevin Pape, 1984-94
Highest Score: 70-0 v Highfield, 23rd Aug 1995
Highest against: 112-0 v. St. Helens, 1986-87
Attendance: 5,903 v. Workington T. (Div 2) 6 Sept. 1981 at Brunton Park
                   2,042 v. Workington T. (RL Cup), 30 Jan 1994 at Gillford Park

	App.	Tries	Goals	D/Gls	Pts		App.	Tries	Goals	D/Gls	Pts
Armstrong, Derek	10+5	5	0	0	20	Meteer, Paul	6+1	0	0	0	0
Blake, Paul	1	0	0	0	0	Quayle, Barry	2+1	1	0	0	4
Brierley, Steve	21+1	0	0	0	0	Rhodes, Stuart	24	13	0	0	52
Charlton, Gary	20	4	0	0	16	Richardson, Willie	24	6	96	0	216
Day, Glen	13+9	1	0	0	4	Rudd, Warren	10+5	0	0	0	0
Graham, George	20+1	4	0	0	16	Ruddy, Gary	17	13	0	0	52
Haile, Gary	3	3	0	0	12	Russell, Danny	20+1	12	0	0	48
Henare, Richard	6+1	10	0	0	40	Scott, Tony	0+1	0	0	0	0
Holt, Darren	0+1	0	0	0	0	Shackley, Mark	0+1	0	0	0	0
Kavanagh, Mike	24	3	2	1	17	Thurlow, Jason	21	9	0	0	36
Knox, Simon	9	8	0	0	32	Williams, Barry	1+15	6	0	0	24
Lynch, Matthew	24	9	0	0	36						
Manihera, Tane	15+1	9	0	0	36	**TOTALS**		126	98	1	701
Manning, Phil	21	10	0	0	40	25 Players					

1995-96 MATCH ANALYSIS

Date	Competition	Opponent	Result	Score	Tries	Goals	Attendance
20.8.95	SD	York	L	18-23	Richardson, Rhodes, Ruddy	Richardson (3)	-
23.8.95	SD	Highfield	W	70-0	D. Armstrong (3), Haile (3), Knox (3), Lynch (2), Ruddy, Kavanagh	Richardson (7)	340
27.8.95	SD	Barrow B.	L	20-21	Knox, Charlton, Graham	Richardson (4)	-
3.9.95	SD	Leigh C.	L	18-20	Knox, Ruddy, Rhodes	Richardson (3)	545
10.9.95	SD	Chorley	W	28-17	Thurlow (2), Graham, Manning, Russell	Richardson (4)	-
13.9.95	SD	Bramley	W	22-12	Kavanagh, Ruddy, Williams	Richardson (5)	400
17.9.95	SD	Doncaster D.	W	30-12	Rhodes (2), Knox, Manning, Richardson	Richardson (5)	-
24.9.95	SD	Hunslet H.	W	26-14	Richardson, Knox, Manning, Russell	Richardson (5)	550
1.10.95	RT(1)	Doncaster D.	W	38-10	Manihera (2), Williams, Charlton, Knox, Richardson	Richardson (7)	435

1995-96 MATCH ANALYSIS CONTINUED

Date	Competition	Opponent	Result	Score	Tries	Goals	Attendance
1.11.95	SD	Hull K.R.	W	14-12	Manihera, Lynch	Richardson (3)	-
5.11.95	SD	Swinton	W	34-16	Thurlow (2), Manning, Russell, Lynch, Ruddy, Rhodes	Richardson (3)	550
12.11.95	RT(2)	Castleford	W	19-18	Williams, Ruddy, Rhodes	Richardson (3), Kavanagh (dg)	850
15.11.95	SD	Highfield	W	48-22	Ruddy (2), Williams, Russell, Manning, Kavanagh, Lynch, Rhodes	Richardson (8)	-
19.11.95	SD	Chorley	W	62-10	Manihera (2), Rhodes (2), Ruddy (2), D. Armstrong (2), Charlton, Thurlow, Russell	Richardson (9)	550
26.11.95	RT(3)	Hunslet H.	W	22-17	Manihera, Thurlow, Russell, Williams	Richardson (3)	-
29.11.95	SD	York at Carlisle RU	W	40-8	Ruddy (2), Rhodes, Manning, Williams, Manihera, Day, Richardson	Richardson (4)	571
3.12.95	SD	Bramley	L	8-14	Lynch, Ruddy	-	-
10.12.95	RT(QF)	Leeds	L	22-44	Graham (2), Manning (2)	Richardson (3)	-
17.12.95	SD	Hunslet H.	L	14-21	Manning, Russell, Rhodes	Richardson	-
3.1.96	SD	Doncaster D. at Carlisle RU	W	42-4	Henare (4), Charlton, Manning, Rhodes, Thurlow	Richardson (3), Kavanagh (2)	450
7.1.96	SD	Hull K.R.	L	14-20	Lynch, Rhodes, Thurlow	Richardson	650
10.1.96	SD	Barrow B. at Carlisle RU	W	48-6	Henare (3), Russell (3), Manihera, Thurlow	Richardson (8)	350
17.1.96	SD	Leigh C.	L	22-33	Henare (2), Lynch, Manihera, Quayle	Richardson	-
21.1.96	SD	Swinton	L	22-24	Russell (2), Henare, Lynch	Richardson (3)	-

1995-96 STONES BITTER CENTENARY SECOND DIVISION

	P	W	D	L	For				Agst				PTS
					Dg	Goals	Tries	Total	Dg	Goals	Tries	Total	
Hull KR	20	18	0	2	4	114	128	744	5	31	41	231	36
Leigh C	20	16	0	4	8	82	105	592	7	52	56	335	32
Hunslet H	20	14	0	6	8	73	90	514	7	46	54	315	28
Swinton	20	13	0	7	3	67	96	521	3	44	60	331	26
Carlisle	20	12	0	8	0	82	109	600	5	56	48	309	24
York	20	10	1	9	8	69	74	442	5	65	70	415	21
Bramley	20	9	1	10	2	55	72	400	6	72	71	434	19
Barrow B	20	6	0	14	8	55	56	342	6	77	82	488	12
Chorley C	20	5	1	14	8	54	52	324	4	96	103	608	11
Doncaster D	20	5	0	15	4	52	60	348	6	86	117	646	10
Highfield	20	0	1	19	5	44	39	249	4	122	179	964	1

16

*

The 1996 Season

THIS was it, the real McCoy summer season that we had argued in favour of for so long. We were still in the third tier but, as the top level had been rechristened Super League, we were rebranded Division Two. A division of twelve clubs providing for just twenty-two league games per season plus the Challenge Cup, and the Regal Trophy kicked into touch.

This was also the year when professionalism in rugby union came out of the closet and boot money and spurious 'travelling expenses' became taxable income; much to the clubs' chagrin they had to introduce PAYE and NI systems for the players. It was the year, too, when the walls between the rugby codes were once and for all exposed as a creation of the RFU and the more pro-establishment media rather than the players or supporters.

Early that summer, this was truly emphasised when Bath and Wigan undertook a cross-code challenge involving eighty minutes of rugby league at Manchester City's Maine Road followed, two-and-a-half weeks later, by eighty minutes under rugby union rules at Twickenham. Of course, Wigan won the RL side of the leg quite easily, 82-6, while Bath were somewhat less convincing with their own 44-19 victory. The general view of the RU-oriented papers was that the whole episode was an irrelevant sideshow.

What was most certainly not an irrelevant sideshow was the 1996 Middlesex Sevens, when Wigan absolutely creamed Wasps 38-15 in the final. Given the teams that Saturday, it's small wonder that union clubs wasted little time in recruiting their tormentors. In future years, the likes of Jason Robinson, Gary Connolly, Va'aiga Tuigamala, Shaun Edwards, Andy Farrell and Henry Paul would all switch codes to their financial benefit once they'd lost either the fitness, sharpness or hunger - or all three - necessary for the thirteen-a-side code.

It seemed amazing and almost surreal that until that season, the heinous crime of even trialling with a rugby league club could - and frequently did - attract a lifetime ban from the fifteen-a-side game.

In Super League, 1996 saw the introduction of squad numbers, rather than the old-style one-to-thirteen positional numbering. In theory, this would boost sales of replica shirts. Whether or not it ever did achieve this aim has never been proved. It certainly made comprehension of the game's positional tactics difficult for the uninitiated.

More unpalatable for the lower division clubs was the introduction of a weighted voting structure on the Rugby League Council. Until 1996, one club one vote was a well-established principle. Following the introduction of Super League, that was changed. Super League clubs had four votes, first division clubs two votes and clubs like Carlisle in the Division Two just the one. Thus the twelve top-flight clubs, provided they acted in unison, effectively controlled the entire professional game.

Daft appendages to club names also became the norm. Thus Wigan Warriors, Barrow Braves, Wakefield Trinity Wildcats, Hull Sharks and, daftest of all, Halifax Blue Sox temporarily entered the arena before public outrage and ridicule forced a rethink in some quarters anyway.

Back at Carlisle, behind the scenes we had a new man looking after our administrative affairs in Jim Thoburn, formerly of Carlisle United. Our new clubhouse, complete with changing rooms, was up and running. Danny Russell was again team captain and he formed a great motivational team with coach Paul Charlton. In fact Danny and Paul, both time-served carpenters, had worked wonders in finishing off and equipping the changing rooms. Danny had also taken it upon himself to sort out a chronic Gillford Park bugbear by recruiting, training and organising our small band of matchday ball boys. Paul Charlton still eulogises about Danny, both as a player and as a colleague.

Raymond Edgar, as always, was looking after the ground, ensuring that the kit was laundered, collecting the lottery money, organising the draw and ensuring winners were notified. In between times he was acting as mentor to those players who needed it, travelling with the 'A' team on Saturdays and the first team on Sundays and generally holding the whole thing together. Pat Conway, owner of Conway Vauxhall, the local Vauxhall car dealership, and our sponsor, was co-opted into running the PR and promotional side of our affairs.

The rules about overseas signings had been considerably tightened since the latitude of Cameron Bell's days and we were only allowed one such additional player. After an earlier high-profile target - Poasa Vasakicakau, a Fijian international - had fallen through due to work permit issues, we eventually signed a wingman for whom Paul Charlton seemed to have a high regard, Matt Nable from South

Sydney. Matt was certainly an unlucky traveller. Firstly his plane from Sydney was diverted and delayed by ten hours due to an engine failure. Then his train from the airport to Carlisle broke down. Finally, the coach bringing him back from his debut game at Doncaster did likewise.

Other signings for the new season included Alasdair Bell from Fylde RU, Sean Cusack from Broughton ARL and David Warwick, Tane Manihera's future brother-in-law, from Wigton RU.

Looking back, the division we were in was the division from hell. There were no derby games to whet the public's appetite and the nearest club to us was Barrow, a two-hour coach trip away. The only club with any appreciable support was Hull KR and it was an optimistic daydream to expect many of their fans to make the seven-hour round haul to the far North West. The furthest club, South Wales, might as well have been in France as Cardiff, such was the journey time and cost of the trip.

Talk of a Cumbrian merger, too, came back to the table after its brief and abortive appearance during the original Super League discussions in early 1995.[1] This time the talk was a bit more structured, initiated by the Government-sponsored West Cumbria Development Fund and co-ordinated by a firm known as Drivers Jonas, a multi-million pound commercial property consultancy with several offices

---

[1] A little know fact is that a merger between Workington and Carlisle had been actively considered by the late Tom Mitchell, former GB manager and ex-chairman of Workington RLFC, several years earlier in the late 1980s. Tom invited us through a trusted intermediary to meet with him at his house, in a cloak and dagger arrangement. The plan was that Frank Lowe, Don McDowall and I were to follow this intermediary's car to Tom's house, a picturesque little cottage that had the grand name of Salmon Hall just outside Workington, as he wished to engage in merger talks. However, I can't remember any meaningful discussion and we left bewildered and bemused after an hour of fairly meaningless chit-chat. I now believe that this meeting was over-sold to both Tom and us by his intermediary.

in the UK. Dougal Kyle and I, with our opposite numbers from the two West Cumbrian clubs, had a very enjoyable working dinner in West Cumbria hosted by Drivers Jonas to discuss the subject. However, while we were open-minded about it, we felt that the prospect of the Workington and Whitehaven clubs' supporters, or even their boards, giving up autonomy to a yet-to-be-formed Super League entity playing out of a yet-to-be-built stadium in no-man's land between Workington and Whitehaven, or in Penrith or Kendal, was pie in the sky. Events proved us correct. The project was put quietly to sleep in 1997.

The 1996 season actually began with the Challenge Cup in the middle of a wintry January, when Bradford amateurs West Bowling were summarily dismissed 36-6 at Gillford Park in the third round. First division Wakefield were the visitors for the next round and they dumped us out 36-6 in front of a pathetic 550 gate.

The league season kicked off at the end of March (two months after the Wakefield cup game, such was the quality of the RFL's fixture planning) with three straight wins over Chorley (H), Barrow (A) and Leigh (H). The win against Chorley saw Willie Richardson set a new Carlisle points in a game record with 26. 'Fossil', as he was affectionately known, actually went on to set three more club records that year for goals in a career (405), points in a season (254) and points in a career (902). And he added to all the above tallies in 1997. Not bad for a lad born in October 1960!

After a narrow 16-14 loss at York, we were straight back into winning ways with comfortable victories against Bramley (H), Doncaster (A) and Prescott (H).

The wheels fell off a little with five straight losses including an 37-18 reverse to South Wales in Cardiff. We broke new ground for this Saturday game by travelling the round-trip by train. It was reckoned much more comfortable for the players as they could wander up and down the train and eat from the buffet car as they wished. It was also considerably cheaper than overnight accommodation.

Unfortunately, the fixture in the shadow of the soon to be completed Millennium Stadium played second fiddle to a Super League 'On the Road' clash between St Helens and Sheffield. We were the curtain-raisers and relegated to some inferior changing rooms. The refreshment arrangements post-match were also a disgrace and the whole organisation treated us as a distraction from the Super League fare on offer later that afternoon. 'What goes around comes around,' was how we consoled ourselves. We were determined to reverse the result at home and show an otherwise excellent Welsh side decent hospitality for the rematch at Gillford Park.

More happily, we then hit a six-match winning streak against Barrow (H), Leigh (A), York (H), Bramley (A), Doncaster (H) and Prescot (A), the latter being a personal triumph for captain Danny Russell, who bagged three tries on the Prescot Cables FC ground.[2] But as seemed to be customary with Carlisle, that winning streak came to an abrupt end with three losses on the trot against Swinton, Hull KR and Hunslet. The Hunslet game was particularly hard to stomach as we were run ragged at the South Leeds Stadium by ex-Hull player Paul Sterling, who crossed four times in a 52-6 hammering.

The final game of that season, was the eagerly anticipated visit of South Wales, our opportunity both to set the playing record to rights and to show the officials of the Welsh club some decent organisation and hospitality. We needn't have bothered.

---

[2]Prescot was essentially the same club with the same management as that which had operated at various venues in Merseyside under the names of Huyton, Runcorn Highfield and Highfield for the previous fifteen years. They had very few stars in their latter stages and seemed to rely solely on fringe or out-of-favour players from other South Lancashire clubs.

Border City Blues

Even though the formal notification of their resignation from the game was several weeks away, the officials of South Wales at least had already given up the ghost, probably because their hopes of a fast-track into Super League were now bound to be vetoed due to low attendances. As a result, we got no pleasure whatsoever from our 58-6 victory. That game, incidentally, was a Danny Russell masterclass in acting-half-back play. It closed our first season of summer rugby league and left Carlisle in a creditable fourth position.

1996-97 YOUNGER'S SCOTCH BITTER CUMBERLAND AMATEUR RUGBY LEAGUE

Division Two

	P	W	D	L	F	A	Pts
Glasson Rangers	18	14	0	4	494	286	28
Frizington	18	14	0	4	404	253	28
Wigton	18	11	1	6	414	314	23
Ellenborough 'A'	18	11	0	7	437	327	22
Great Clifton	18	10	1	7	449	355	21
Maryport	18	10	0	8	493	368	20
Wath Brown Hornets 'A'	18	8	0	10	376	542	16
Hensingham 'A'	18	4	0	14	334	524	5
Cockermouth	18	5	0	13	349	591	4
Aspatria	18	2	0	16	316	656	4

Division Three

	P	W	D	L	F	A	Pts
Smiths R.U.	16	12	1	3	560	236	25
Westfield Hotel 'A'	16	12	0	4	391	210	24
Egremont	16	11	0	5	436	279	22
St. Nicholas Arms	16	11	0	5	326	322	22
Kells 'A'	16	10	1	5	536	231	21
Linton Holme	16	9	0	7	252	380	15
Seaton 'A'	16	3	0	13	233	587	3
Maryport 'A'	16	3	0	13	181	540	-3
Flimby 'A'	16	0	0	16	126	806	-18

Division Four

	P	W	D	L	F	A	Pts
St. Nicholas Arms 'A'	18	14	0	4	611	253	28
Lowca 'A'	18	13	1	4	563	249	27
Glasson Rangers 'A'	18	10	0	8	417	397	20
Great Clifton 'A'	18	10	0	8	424	416	17
Penrith	18	8	1	9	450	418	14
Distington 'A'	18	7	0	11	359	586	14
Wigton 'A'	18	0	0	18	212	867	-3

CARLISLE – 1996 – SEASON SUMMARY

Chairman:	Alan Tucker
Coach:	Paul Charlton (Dec 1994-)
Records:	
Match	Goals: 10 by Barry Vickers at Nottingham C., 11 Mar 1990
	Tries: 4 by G. Peacham v. Workington T., 25 Jan, 1987
	and K. Pape v. Rochdale H., 11 Feb, 1987, Richard Henare v. Doncaster, 3 Jan 1996
	Points: 26 by Willie Richardson v. Chorley, 31 Mar 1996
Season	Goals: 113 by S. Ferres, 1981-82
	Tries: 25 by M. Morgan, 1981-82, G. Peacham, 1984-85
	Points: 254 by Willie Richardson, 1996
Career	Goals: 403 by Willie Richardson, 1992-
	Tries: 192 by Kevin Pape, 1984-94
	Points: 902 by Willie Richardson, 1992-
	Appearances: 324 by Kevin Pape, 1984-94
	Highest Score: 70-0 v Highfield, 23rd Aug 1995
	Highest against: 112-0 v. St. Helens, 1986-87
Attendance:	5,903 v. Workington T. (Div 2) 6 Sept. 1981 at Brunton Park
	2,042 v. Workington T. (RL Cup), 30 Jan 1994 at Gillford Park

	App.	Tries	Goals	D/Gls	Pts		App.	Tries	Goals	D/Gls	Pts
Armstrong, Derek	1+8	0	0	0	0	Manning, Phil	2+3	1	0	0	4
Armstrong, Mike	0+3	0	0	0	0	Meteer, Paul	8+8	2	0	0	8
Bell, Alasdair	4+2	5	0	0	20	Nable, Matt	16	4	0	0	16
Brierley, Steve	17+5	0	0	0	0	Quayle, Barry	5+2	1	0	0	4
Charlton, Gary	16+1	1	0	0	4	Rhodes, Stuart	20+1	9	0	0	36
Charlton, Jason	9+7	1	0	0	4	Richardson, Willie	24	10	107	0	254
Chorley, Mark	0+1	0	0	0	0	Rudd, Warren	8+9	0	0	0	0
Cusack, Sean	15+1	6	0	0	24	Ruddy, Gary	16+1	10	0	0	40
Day, Glen	2+2	1	0	0	4	Ruddy, Wayne	5	0	0	0	0
Farrimond, Jonathan	0+1	0	0	0	0	Russell, Danny	24	17	0	0	68
Graham, George	11+2	3	0	0	12	Scott, Tony	0+5	2	0	0	8
Henare, Richard	2	2	0	0	8	Stoddart, Stephen	0+1	0	0	0	0
Hetherington, Gary	3+1	0	0	0	0	Tait, Alan	0+1	0	0	0	0
Holt, Darren	4+3	0	0	0	0	Thurlow, Jason	18+1	6	0	0	24
Kavanagh, Mike	16+2	7	0	0	28	Warwick, Dave	3	1	0	0	4
Lynch, Matthew	22	8	0	0	32	Williams, Barry	19+1	11	0	1	45
Manihera, Tane	22	15	0	1	61	**TOTALS**					
						33 Players					

1996 MATCH ANALYSIS

Date	Competition	Opponent	Result	Score	Tries	Goals	Attendance
14.1.96	CC(3)	West Bowling	W	36-3	Kavanagh, Henare, Quayle, Rhodes, Richardson, Thurlow, Williams	Richardson (4)	350
4.2.96	CC(4)	Wakefield T.	L	18-34	Day, Henare, Thurlow	Richardson (3)	550
31.3.96	SD	Chorley C.	W	66-16	Cusack (3), G. Ruddy (2), Richardson (2), Kavanagh, Lynch, Manihera, Rhodes, Russell	Richardson (9)	500
5.4.96	SD	Barrow B.	W	30-10	Russell (2), Lynch, Manihera, G. Ruddy	Richardson (5)	-
8.4.96	SD	Leigh C.	W	42-34	Manihera (2), Russell (2), Kavanagh, Lynch, Meteer	Richardson (7)	650
14.4.96	SD	York	L	14-16	Manihera, Richardson	Richardson (3)	-

Border City Blues

1996 MATCH ANALYSIS CONTINUED

Date	Competition	Opponent	Result	Score	Tries	Goals	Attendance
21.4.96	SD	Bramley	W	26-6	Lynch (2), Graham, Kavanagh, Williams	Richardson (3)	500
5.5.96	SD	Doncaster D.	W	35-10	Manihera (2), Russell (2), Williams, Lynch	Richardson (5), Williams (dg)	-
12.5.96	SD	Prescot P.	W	38-6	Richardson (2), Cusack, Kavanagh, Manihera, Manning	Richardson (7)	517
19.5.96	SD	Swinton L.	L	22-30	Williams (2), Manihera	Richardson (5)	-
26.5.96	SD	Hull K.R.	L	22-28	Graham, Richardson, Thurlow, G. Ruddy	Richardson (3)	917
2.6.96	SD	Hunslet H.	L	16-23	Russell (2)	Richardson (4)	720
8.6.96	SD	South Wales	L	18-37	Richardson, Russell, G. Ruddy, Williams	Richardson	-
16.6.96	SD	Chorley	L	14-28	Williams, Graham	Richardson (3)	-
23.6.96	SD	Barrow B.	W	50-18	Thurlow (2), Nable, Manihera, Rhodes, Russell, Scott, Warwick, Williams	Richardson (7)	517
30.6.96	SD	Leigh C.	W	27-20	Rhodes, Lynch, (2) J. Charlton, Williams	Richardson (3), Manihera (dg)	-
7.7.96	SD	York	W	20-19	Bell (2), G. Ruddy, Nable	Richardson (2)	589
14.7.96	SD	Bramley	W	48-12	Rhodes (3), Manihera (2), Bell, Richardson, Russell	Richardson (8)	-
21.7.96	SD	Doncaster D.	W	22-16	Bell, Manihera, Richardson, G. Ruddy	Richardson (3)	615
28.7.96	SD	Prescot P.	W	56-24	Russell (3), G. Ruddy (2), Bell, G. Charlton, Kavanagh, Manihera, Nable	Richardson (8)	-
4.8.96	SD	Swinton L.	L	12-32	Nable, G. Ruddy	Richardson (2)	743
11.8.96	SD	Hull K.R.	L	12-43	Meteer, Scott	Richardson (2)	-
18.8.96	SD	Hunslet H.	L	6-52	Thurlow	Richardson	-
25.8.96	SD	South Wales	W	58-6	Russell (2), Cusack (2), Rhodes (2), Lynch, Manihera, Williams, Kavanagh	Richardson (9)	457

1996 DIVISION TWO CHAMPIONSHIP

	P	W	D	L	For Dg	Goals	Tries	Total	Agst Dg	Goals	Tries	Total	PTS
Hull KR	22	21	0	1	1	152	176	1009	2	46	50	294	42
Swinton L	22	18	0	4	3	119	136	785	3	44	51	295	36
Hunslet H	22	18	0	4	8	95	133	730	10	58	50	326	36
Carlisle	22	13	0	9	2	100	113	654	8	79	80	486	26
Doncaster D	22	13	0	9	6	69	89	500	4	84	92	540	26
South Wales	22	12	0	10	10	69	95	528	2	73	100	548	24
Leigh C	22	10	0	12	12	98	98	594	6	76	88	510	20
York	22	9	0	13	13	70	75	449	5	85	107	603	18
Chorley	22	6	0	16	16	51	62	354	5	101	129	723	12
Barrow B	22	5	0	17	17	61	57	354	3	96	114	651	10
Bramley	22	5	0	17	17	55	62	360	7	120	128	759	10
Prescot P	22	2	0	20	20	51	49	301	3	128	156	883	4

Above: The 1996 Carlisle ladies rugby league team

1996 THE ALLIANCE - SECOND DIVISION

	P	W	D	L	For Pts	Agst Pts	Total
Hunslet H	18	16	0	2	644	274	32
Keighley C	18	13	0	5	623	310	26
Huddersfield G	18	13	0	5	596	364	26
Whitehaven	18	12	1	5	521	400	25
Rochdale H	18	11	0	7	469	338	22
Blackpool	18	7	1	10	441	441	15
Carlisle	18	6	0	12	340	534	12
Doncaster D	18	5	0	13	321	516	10
Barrow B	18	3	0	15	213	588	6
Chorley	18	3	0	15	280	683	6

17

*

The 1997 Season

THERE were ongoing tensions with our landlords at the Railway Club even before the season started. Looked at with mature hindsight, the situation was never likely to improve. There were deep personality conflicts that transcended mere logic.

The issue in question on that occasion was rental arrears built up over the close-season. We brought the arrears up to date but, with extraordinary prescience, left the notice to quit (in those days a first response to any dispute by their treasurer), unchallenged. There was even at that early stage a conviction that a further season at Gillford Park was unlikely and that it would be far easier to leave without the burden of having to give the otherwise required six-months' notice with full rental payments.[1]

---

[1] Since the formation in 2003 of Carlisle Centurions and return to Gillford Park, it has to be said that we have enjoyed a very good and constructive relationship with the Railway Club based on mutual respect and trust. The people who now run the Railway Club were not part of the situation in those days.

We had formed an executive club, the main perk of which being use of the newly-fitted-out upstairs lounge in the stand, erected the previous season. This in itself was to create further upset with the landlords, who originally agreed to obtain a licence to enable us to sell alcoholic beverages provided they were bought from them. This promised licence never materialised, leaving the rugby club in the position of having fully paid-up executive club members without licensed premises for them to frequent on matchdays. Every attempt at resolving the situation ended in friction and eventually turned out to be the final straw as far as we were concerned.

Our board of directors was also wearing thin following the resignations, for business reasons, of Brian Whittaker, Frank Lowe and John Pattinson. Maybe there was a little prescience at play there too.

There was plenty of player movement behind the scenes before the season began. Danny Russell was head-hunted by Super League aspirants Huddersfield, who enjoyed the backing of multi-millionaire Ken Davy. Danny had been a great ambassador and captain for Carlisle, so we were reluctant to release him. However, as his previous contract had expired and we were unable to match the Huddersfield offer, we shook his hand and wished him all the best. He went on to have a long and distinguished career.

Also making his exit that winter was Barry Williams, whose subsequent season with Workington Town was the polar opposite of Danny Russell's. Workington, having been relegated from Super League in 1996, continued their downward slide and were relegated to Division Two at the end of 1997.

George Graham, our Scottish prop, took advantage of rugby union's switch to open professionalism and joined the former England international fly-half Rob Andrew at

Newcastle Falcons. In so doing, he launched an international career of his own, with twenty-five full Scottish caps to his credit. These days, after a diverse career - including spells on the Scotland coaching staff and a period as a head coach in Italy with Petrarca RU in Padua in 2008-09 - he is back on home soil and enjoying a second go as coach at Galashiels in the Scottish Borders.

Of the rest, winger Matty Nable, who had been on just a season's contract, returned to Australia, and Tane Manihera, despite numerous articles linking him variously with Salford and Castleford, stayed put. Afterwards, it appeared that Tane's agent had been, naively maybe, trying to play Castleford off against Salford in the hope of raising his contract fee. Unfortunately, for both he and Tane, the ploy didn't work and both Castleford and Salford declined. We were happy to retain Tane for another season, but there is no doubt Tane was disappointed.

On the acquisition side of the balance sheet, we recruited well that winter. Chris Whitely, a prison officer at Wymot Prison, near Preston, had been recommended to us by Gary Charlton. Chris, a superbly fit PT trainer at the prison, had enjoyed a mixed career that included spells with London Broncos when he was working in the South East and Doncaster. He was a well experienced prop-second row forward. Just what we needed to replace George.

Another incomer was Jamie Stevens, a talented young Kiwi recommended to us by Cameron Bell, who'd spent the Christmas holiday period with his daughter and family in Carlisle and given our livers a work-out in the process!

Before the season began, we signed two more Kiwis, centre Jonathan Hughes and winger Darryl Menzies. Darryl, who'd never before played league, was actually playing union with Ayr RU. The highly experienced Whitehaven prop Willie Burns joined us about the same time.

The 1997 season structure was a contrived one. With the RFL's commitment to a three-division professional game, there were insufficient fixtures within the two lower leagues of eleven clubs each to produce a meaningful campaign. The RFL's solution was to create an end-of-season competition entitled the Divisional Premiership whereby, in the early stages, clubs played other Division One and Two clubs from their own locality before progressing through to the latter stages, culminating in a Divisional Premiership Final to be played at Old Trafford as a curtain-raiser to the main Super League event. In Carlisle's case, this was to be a home and away competition against Workington, Whitehaven, Barrow, and Lancashire Lynx. It started in late July with the winners playing their equivalents from other areas. It was to be a hopelessly unpopular, dog's breakfast of a competition that for most clubs just served as an unnecessary end-of-season expense.

Carlisle's season opened with the early rounds of the Challenge Cup. First up was an amateur Yorkshire Premier League club, BRK, from Leeds. They were delightful company after the game and surprisingly difficult to beat during it. We duly progressed to the next round, though, following a fairly tough 34-8 victory at Gillford Park.

Playing us in the next round at Gillford Park were the Bradford-based amateurs Dudley Hill, who had just disposed of York at the Ryedale Stadium and who, after the usual fisticuffs, we beat 62-2. The gates for both these games were pathetically low and left the participating clubs with financial losses. Not so for the fifth round, when first division Featherstone Rovers were our opponents and we shared a decent 1,100 gate but went down 32-20.

The Division Two league competition got underway the following weekend when Batley came to town. Carlisle, whose debutant wingman Daryl Menzies scored a brace of tries, won 22-14 in front of just 450 supporters. The following weekend it got better when we beat Doncaster at the Meadow Court Greyhound Stadium 32-12 with Menzies trumping his previous performance and picking up three tries. When we beat York 23-0 at Gillford Park the following week and Menzies added another couple of tries to his tally, we were really flying; that is until we checked the gate receipts to find that just 437 souls could be bothered to support us.

Another player going well that season was Millom-based wingman Gary Ruddy. Without a doubt Gary was blessed with pace to burn and could certainly score tries but his main problem was putting in regular training sessions. This was probably a lot to do with the relatively inaccessible location of Millom, midway on the coast between Whitehaven and Barrow. But in those two wingers, Carlisle had the best in the division; they each scored twenty-two tries that season.

A 26-6 defeat to Lancashire Lynx at their new Deepdale home broke the sequence. Deepdale is the impressive home of Preston North End FC and Lynx's gate of 295 inside a 22,000-seater stadium looked quite ludicrous and totally out of place with a stark appearance of impermanence about it. Still, we'd have swapped places with them and left our own home at the drop of a hat.

After that disappointment we put together wins against Barrow at home (44-8), Leigh away (34-4) and, best of all, at home by 34-4 to league-leaders Hunslet in front of an encouraging 600 gate. It indicates how low our expectations were by then that we considered 600 to be encouraging.

The following week, as if to punish us for having high hopes, we were rewarded with our lowest league gate ever - just 240 to watch us go down 20-10 to Rochdale. We knew then that nothing short of a miracle would persuade us to see out another season at Gillford Park. We'd spent our own as well as public money upgrading the place; we'd put a competitive side on the pitch and good professional management off it. The conclusion was that we'd see out the season giving it the best shot we could and then take a rational decision as to the club's future in the close-season. With no fairy godmothers or sugar daddies waiting to take our place and at best fickle spectator support in the city, we knew the decision was ours and ours alone to make.

We went on to have a decent season, finishing fifth in the eleven-team league. We had the division's top try-scorers in Menzies and Ruddy and were just two wins off a promotion spot. The sporting public had rewarded us with an average attendance of just 420. Only Prescot Panthers and Lancashire Lynx got less.

The first decision - whether or not to leave Gillford Park - was made easy. It was the last game of the season and Workington were the visitors in that unwelcome cup competition that had been tagged on at the season-end. We'd planned a thank-you party for the players of both sides and laid on a barbecue for them. Despite earlier assurances to the contrary, however, we discovered from talking to the club steward on the day before the game that the Railway Club had that week surrendered the appropriate licence to prevent us from reselling their drink in the stand-lounge. They had obtained it only a few weeks previously. We therefore bought a keg of beer with which to treat the players and members of the executive club by giving them a drink with our compliments.

During the game we were astounded when the police turned up following a complaint that we were selling drink without a licence. They informed us the name of the Railway Club official who had made the complaint. The name held few surprises! After satisfying themselves that no money

Above: The new stand at Gillford Park that was the source of so much trouble

other than my 50p for a glass of lemonade had changed hands, the police apologised and left somewhat bemused. It appeared that our landlords, or at least one of their committee, despite our assurance before the game started that the only drink dispensed by us would be as a gift to the executive committee and players of both teams, couldn't understand such generosity.

Events that afternoon left us with no agonising decision to make. By common accord before we even left for home, we all agreed that was our last ever game at Gillford Park.

When we later met with the Railway Club committee to formally wind up our affairs there, we had to smile as their apoplectic treasurer sought to remind us that we were due to pay six months rent in lieu of notice, completely forgetting that it had been *he* who had served notice on *us* earlier in the year.

1997-98 YOUNGER'S SCOTCH BITTER CUMBERLAND AMATEUR RUGBY LEAGUE

Division Two

	P	W	D	L	F	A	Pts
Flimby	17	15	0	2	595	191	30
Wigton	18	14	0	4	580	309	28
Great Clifton	18	11	0	7	362	362	22
Wath Brown Hornets 'A'	18	11	1	6	459	374	20
Smiths RU	18	10	1	7	436	429	18
Seaton	18	8	0	10	352	340	16
Hensingham 'A'	17	5	0	12	173	520	10
Maryport	18	3	0	15	276	534	6
Ellenborough 'A'	18	7	0	11	313	508	5
Westfield 'A'	18	4	0	14	267	596	2

Division Three

	P	W	D	L	F	A	Pts
Seaton Pack Horse	14	13	0	1	479	115	26
St. Nicholas Arms	14	11	0	3	352	218	22
Egremont	14	9	0	5	334	257	18
Kells 'A'	14	8	0	6	263	313	10
St. Nicholas Arms 'A'	14	5	0	9	320	404	10
Lowca 'A'	14	5	0	9	209	348	10
Aspatria	14	3	0	11	207	548	-3
Seaton 'A'	14	2	0	12	113	674	-17

Division Four

	P	W	D	L	F	A	Pts
Penrith	16	15	0	1	494	152	30
Great Clifton 'A'	16	12	0	4	400	179	24
Flimby 'A'	16	10	0	5	275	267	19
Seaton Pack Horse 'A'	16	8	0	8	349	312	13
Wigton 'A'	16	6	0	10	235	482	12
Maryport 'A'	16	8	1	7	224	403	5
Distington 'A'	16	2	1	13	148	632	5
Glasson 'A'	16	6	0	10	272	462	3
Broughton Red Rose 'A'	16	3	0	13	159	617	-24

1997 THE ALLIANCE - SECOND DIVISION

	P	W	D	L	For Pts	Agst Pts	Total
Huddersfield G	20	18	0	2	849	229	36
Keighley C	20	15	1	4	666	275	31
Rochdale H	20	15	1	4	710	347	31
Hemel Hempstead	20	14	2	4	800	352	30
Whitehaven W	20	9	1	10	508	471	19
Doncaster D	20	9	1	10	465	565	19
Carlisle BR	20	7	2	11	527	570	16
Lancashire L	20	7	0	13	408	516	14
Barrow B	20	7	0	13	342	645	14
Blackpool G	20	3	0	17	247	842	6
Prescot P	20	2	0	18	231	941	4

CARLISLE – 1997 – SEASON SUMMARY

Chairman:	Alan Tucker
Coach:	Paul Charlton (Dec 1994-)
Records:	
Match	Goals: 10 by Barry Vickers at Nottingham C., 11 Mar 1990
	5 by Darryl Menzies v. Prescot P., 20 July 1997, Gary Ruddy v. Prescot P., 20 July '97
	Points: 26 by Willie Richardson v. Chorley, 31 Mar 1996
Season	Goals: 113 by S. Ferres, 1981-82
	Tries: 30 by Gary Ruddy, 1997
	Points: 254 by Willie Richardson, 1996
Career	Goals: 509 by Willie Richardson, 1992-97
	Tries: 192 by Kevin Pape, 1984-94
	Points: 1149 by Willie Richardson, 1992-97
	Appearances: 324 by Kevin Pape, 1984-94
	Highest Score: 70-0 v Highfield, 23rd Aug 1995
	Highest against: 112-0 v. St. Helens, 1986-87
Attendance:	5,903 v. Workington T. (Div 2) 6 Sept. 1981 at Brunton Park
	2,042 v. Workington T. (RL Cup), 30 Jan 1994 at Gillford Park

	App.	Tries	Goals	D/Gls	Pts		App.	Tries	Goals	D/Gls	Pts
Anderson, Phil	0+3	0	0	0	0	Massey, Richard	0+1	0	0	0	0
Armstrong, Derek	11+12	6	0	0	24	McCall, Simon	1	0	0	0	0
Brierley, Steve	21+4	0	0	0	0	Menzies, Darryl	22	22	0	0	88
Burns, William	5+7	1	0	0	4	Meteer, Paul	12+6	1	0	0	4
Charlton, Gary	27	8	0	0	32	Quayle, Barry	2	0	0	0	0
Clark, Neil	4	0	0	0	0	Rhodes, Stuart	16+2	7	0	0	28
Cusack, Sean	2	0	0	0	0	Richardson, Willie	31	9	105	1	247
Day, Glen	8+11	1	0	0	4	Rudd, Warren	3+11	1	0	0	4
Farrimond, Jonathan	4+5	0	0	0	0	Ruddy, Gary	28	30	0	0	120
Frazer, Neil	1	0	0	0	0	Scott, Tony	8+14	1	0	0	4
Haile, Gary	0+1	0	0	0	0	Stevens, Jamie	21	6	0	0	24
Holt, Darren	30	4	5	1	27	Stoddart, Stephen	7+6	6	0	0	24
Hughes, Jonathan	25	7	0	0	28	Tait, Alan	0+2	1	0	0	4
Jackson, Steve	1+3	0	0	0	0	Thurlow, Jason	26+3	9	0	0	36
Johnstone, Jake	2+8	2	0	0	8	Underwood, Brian	0+1	0	0	0	0
Lynch, Matthew	20+1	8	0	0	32	Warwick, Dave	4+1	2	0	0	8
Magorian, Stewart	8+3	4	0	0	16	Whiteley, Chris	23	0	0	1	1
Manihera, Tane	29	19	0	0	76	**TOTALS**		156	110	3	847
Manning, Phil	1	1	0	0	4	36 Players					

1997 MATCH ANALYSIS

Date	Competition	Opponent	Result	Score	Tries	Goals	Attendance
26.1.97	CC(3)	BRK	W	34-8	Ruddy (3), Manihera, Rhodes, Stoddart, Thurlow	Richardson (3)	452
9.2.97	CC(4)	Dudley Hill	W	62-2	Manihera (3), Ruddy (2), Stoddaty (2), Charlton, Lynch, Richardson, Thurlow	Richardson (9)	523
23.2.97	CC(5)	Featherstone R.	L	20-32	Charlton, Lynch, Manihera, Richardson	Richardson (2)	1062
2.3.97	SD	Batley B.	W	22-14	Menzies (2), Lynch, Ruddy, Richardson	Richardson	449
9.3.97	SD	Doncaster D.	W	32-12	Menzies (3), Ruddy (2), Thurlow	Richardson (4)	-

1997 MATCH ANALYSIS CONTINUED

Date	Competition	Opponent	Result	Score	Tries	Goals	Attendance
16.3.97	SD	York	W	22-0	Menzies (2), Rhodes, Thurlow	Richardson (3)	437
21.3.97	SD	Lancashire L.	L	6-26	Hughes	Richardson	-
28.3.97	SD	Barrow B.	W	44-8	Menzies (2), Armstrong, Hughes, Manihera, Meteer, Rhodes, Thurlow	Richardson (6)	485
31.3.97	SD	Leigh C.	W	34-4	Rhodes (2), Thurlow (2), Manihera, Menzies	Richardson (5)	-
6.4.97	SD	Hunslet H.	W	30-14	Charlton, Lynch, Manihera, Ruddy	Richardson (6, dg), Holt (dg)	600
20.4.97	SD	Rochdale H.	L	10-20	Ruddy, Thurlow	Richardson	240
27.4.97	SD	Bramley	W	22-16	Lynch (2), Menzies, Richardson	Richardson (3)	-
11.5.97	SD	Prescot P.	W	34-6	Holt, Manihera, Menzies, Rhodes, Richardson, Ruddy	Richardson (5)	-
18.5.97	SD	Batley B.	L	20-21	Armstong, Manihera, Menzies, Stevens	Richardson (2)	-
23.5.97	SD	Doncaster D.	W	26-21	Hughes, Lynch, Manihera, Menzies, Ruddy	Richardson (3)	400
26.5.97	SD	York	L	16-37	Armstrong, Johnson, Stevens	Richardson (2)	-
1.6.97	SD	Lancashire L.	W	46-33	Charlton (2), Manihera (2), Magorian (2), Menzies, Stevens	Richardson (7)	406
8.6.97	SD	Barrow B.	W	32-6	Richardson (2), Ruddy (2), Burns, Charlton	Richardson (4)	-
15.6.97	SD	Leigh C.	L	12-24	Hughes, Menzies, Ruddy	-	611
22.6.97	SD	Hunslet H.	L	12-26	Johnstone, Ruddy	Richardson (2)	-
29.6.97	SD	Bramley	W	44-20	Ruddy (3), Holt, Magorian, Manihera, Menzies, Stoddart	Richardson (6)	320
6.7.97	SD	Rochdale H.	L	28-66	Ruddy (3), Hughes, Manihera	Richardson (4)	-
20.7.97	SD	Prescot P.	W	72-10	Menzies (5), Ruddy (5), Armstong (2), Lynch, Manihera, Rudd	Holt (4), Richardson (2)	297
27.7.97	DP	Barrow B.	W	38-20	Stevens (3), Rhodes, Tait, Richardson	Richardson (7)	311
30.7.97	DP	Lancashire L.	W	26-22	Charlton (2), Ruddy (2)	Richardson (5)	-
3.8.97	DP	Whitehaven W.	L	19-34	Hughes, Manihera, Richardson	Richardson (3), Whiteley (dg)	621
13.8.97	DP	Workington T.	L	12-28	Ruddy, Manihera	Richardson (2)	-
17.8.97	DP	Barrow B.	L	16-64	Manning, Stoddart, Warwick	Richardson (2)	-
22.8.97	DP	Lancashire L at Hawick RU	W	32-6	Holt (2), Armstrong, Warwick, Manihera, Thurlow, Stoddart	Richardson, Holt	424
3.9.97	DP	Whitehaven W.	L	0-40	-	-	-
7.9.97	DP	Workington T.	L	24-34	Day, Hughes, Magorian, Scott	Richardson (4)	453

1997 DIVISION TWO CHAMPIONSHIP

	P	W	D	L	For				Agst				PTS
					Dg	Goals	Tries	Total	Dg	Goals	Tries	Total	
Hunslet H	20	15	0	5	4	85	127	682	6	41	42	256	30
Rochdale H	20	15	0	5	6	91	123	680	3	52	60	347	30
Leigh C	20	15	0	5	8	83	93	546	2	56	58	346	30
Batley B	20	14	0	6	2	89	105	600	5	69	73	435	28
Carlisle BR	20	13	0	7	2	71	105	564	4	54	68	384	26
Lancashire L	20	12	0	8	6	73	100	552	2	60	68	394	24
York	20	8	0	12	3	80	85	503	7	71	92	517	16
Barrow B	20	7	0	13	3	52	57	335	4	90	112	632	14
Bramley	20	5	1	14	1	50	63	353	5	64	95	513	11
Doncaster D	20	3	1	16	5	29	46	247	0	90	122	668	7
Prescot P	20	2	0	18	1	43	40	247	3	99	154	817	4

18

✳

Post-1997

ALTHOUGH we had burned our boats at Gillford Park, we still wished to keep the professional game alive in the city if possible. We met again with the RU club but they remained uninterested. We even met Michael Knighton at Carlisle United, but as the conversation evolved around the soccer club acquiring the RL club, all its gate receipts and other income streams, plus the author of this book joining the Carlisle United board and the purchase of £40,000 worth of football shares for the privilege, it came to nought.

The obvious business solution then was to follow either the lead of Workington Town and Keighley Cougars, who had just gone into an insolvency arrangement, or Prescot, Oldham Bears and Paris St Germain, who had simply wound up. Had our only creditors been institutional bodies such as the Inland Revenue and the bank, we may well have chosen one of these routes. As matters stood however, many creditors were local traders and businesses who had extended credit based on our own assurances and personal reputations for probity. Strangely, the answer came from the south of the county.

During one of our many several conversations, Alan Stoker, a director of Barrow and its CEO, expressed the idle thought that if only Barrow had a team of Carlisle's quality, they could drag themselves out of the deep mire they had been in for the previous seven or eight years. Barrow, a club with a massive history, had huge latent support; rugby league was the town's major sport. In any event, despite their dire performances, their gates were three times as high as ours. Added to that, they were totally self-sufficient. They owned their Craven Park ground.

We then had several discussions with Maurice Lindsay, head honcho at the RFL, to check if such a venture would be supported by the game's board of directors. The answer came back positive, provided that Carlisle's creditors would agree to be partially repaid by an independent trust set up to receive and distribute the money that an independent Carlisle would have received as its share of the Sky sponsorship deal. It was also a voluntary pre-condition suggested by Carlisle that Carlisle directors write off their own shares in Carlisle RLFC and any loans made to it. This was a not insignificant sum and well into six figures.

Another precondition included the proviso that sufficient players from the Carlisle club would agree to move their allegiance to Barrow. Barrow, in turn, insisted that they would not be held responsible for any claim arising from the arrangement, however spurious. This demand was as outrageous as it was impractical and led to some acrimonious moments in the Craven Park boardroom before resolution.

Former Carlisle players Darren Holt, Mike Kavanagh, Stewart Magorian, Tane Manihera (via a brief spell at Widnes), Stuart Rhodes, Gary Ruddy, Jamie Stevens, Jason

Thurlow and Hugh Waddell thus joined the Furness Club for the 1998 season. Of these, a couple left soon after but Darren Holt, for example, at the time of the merger a newcomer into first-team rugby at Carlisle, went on to become Barrow's all-time points and goal scorer. Directors Mally Cooper and I also served on the Barrow board for several years. I was elected chief executive in 1999 through to 2001, and chairman in 2002.

Were Carlisle Border Raiders RLFC missed in the city? Well, although the visible sum total of opposition to the merger amounted to a couple of very moderate letters in the *Evening News and Star*, we have been made aware that the club found a place in the hearts of its sporting population. We still meet people who claim to have seen every home game. Whilst there were indeed such committed supporters, I believe that most of our spectators saw actively supporting the Border Raiders as a secondary passion to be shelved when times were rough.

It is maybe revealing that the most vocal opposition to the merger was in Barrow itself, where disgruntled local supporters wondered why their club needed players and directors from the north. Given the success of Barrow in the years 2007 to date, it's a very pertinent question!

To bring the Carlisle rugby league story right up to date, Carlisle Saints ARLFC, originally St Nicholas Arms ARLFC in the days of the Carlisle and District ARL competition, continued successfully in the Cumberland ARL and after a season playing at Carlisle's Sheepmount moved into Gillford Park.

Theirs and the other original Carlisle and District League club records are summarised in the following end-of-season league tables:

1998-99 CUMBERLAND AMATEUR RUGBY LEAGUE

Division Two

	P	W	D	L	F	A	Pts
Ellenborough	18	17	0	1	882	184	34
Wath Brow Hornets	18	15	0	3	418	286	30
Kells	18	14	0	4	749	270	28
Hensingham	18	12	0	6	574	270	24
Westfield	18	10	0	8	376	404	20
Broughton Red Rose	18	8	0	10	335	437	13
Distington	18	6	0	12	322	652	9
Wigton	18	4	0	14	324	534	8
Lowca	18	2	0	16	224	822	-2
Flimby	18	2	0	16	210	955	-8

Division Two

	P	W	D	L	F	A	Pts
Seaton	17	15	0	2	475	186	30
Smiths R.U.	18	13	0	5	434	292	23
Glasson Rangers	18	11	0	7	475	302	22
Ellenborough 'A'	18	12	0	6	444	327	21
St. Nicholas Arms	18	9	1	8	364	297	19
Wath Brow Hornets 'A'	18	9	1	8	382	307	16
Seaton Pack Horse	18	7	0	11	318	352	14
Great Clifton	18	5	0	13	142	522	10
Maryport	18	3	0	15	174	505	6
Hensingham	17	3	0	14	128	696	-12

Division Three

	P	W	D	L	F	A	Pts
Kells 'A'	20	18	0	2	650	142	36
Penrith	19	15	0	4	508	274	30
Egremont	20	14	1	5	546	306	29
Seaton 'A'	20	13	0	7	475	364	26
Westfield 'A'	20	9	0	11	475	468	15
St. Nicholas Arms 'A'	20	6	0	14	328	570	12
Distington	20	6	0	14	314	814	12
Wigton 'A'	20	7	1	12	393	539	6
Seaton Pack Horse 'A'	20	9	0	11	336	513	6
Glasson Rangers 'A'	20	7	0	13	304	615	-1
Lowca 'A'	19	4	0	15	231	855	-7

1999-2000 CUMBERLAND AMATEUR RUGBY LEAGUE

Division One

	P	W	D	L	F	A	Pts
Wath Brow Hornets	16	15	0	1	595	192	30
Hensingham	16	13	0	3	516	191	26
Egremont	16	11	0	5	384	222	22
Ellenborough	16	9	0	7	414	363	15
Kells	16	7	0	9	394	324	14
Westfield	16	7	0	9	231	374	14
Broughton Red Rose	16	5	1	10	274	334	11
Seaton	16	3	0	13	180	452	6
Wigton	16	1	1	14	137	723	3

Border City Blues

1999-2000 CUMBERLAND AMATEUR RUGBY LEAGUE CONTINUED

Division Two

	P	W	D	L	F	A	Pts
Maryport	18	15	1	2	693	208	31
Pack Horse	18	12	2	4	315	254	26
Lowca	18	11	0	7	504	368	22
St. Nicholas Arms	18	11	0	7	514	396	22
Glasson Rangers	18	11	0	7	365	308	22
Great Clifton	18	9	0	9	336	364	18
Penrith	18	7	2	9	331	427	16
Distington	18	8	0	10	279	466	16
Cockermouth	18	1	1	16	200	721	-12
Flimby	18	2	0	16	190	815	-17

Alliance League

	P	W	D	L	F	A	Pts
Wath Brow Hornets 'A'	20	19	0	1	766	112	38
Kells 'A'	20	17	1	2	461	154	35
Hensingham 'A'	19	14	0	5	378	254	28
St. Nicholas Arms 'A'	19	8	0	11	205	669	13
Egremont 'A'	20	11	0	9	484	485	10
Westfield 'A'	20	11	0	9	297	488	10
Maryport 'A'	20	10	1	9	383	594	6
Broughton Red Rose 'A'	20	7	0	13	180	697	5
Wigton 'A'	20	5	0	15	192	640	1
Pack Horse 'A'	20	5	0	15	140	668	-20
Glasson 'A'	20	1	0	19	115	790	-25

2000-2001 CUMBERLAND AMATEUR RUGBY LEAGUE

Group A

	P	W	D	L	F	A	Pts
Wath Brow Hornets	7	7	0	0	362	50	14
St. Nicholas Arms	8	5	0	3	240	180	10
Kells	8	5	0	3	178	202	10
Wigton	7	1	0	6	94	266	2
Distington	8	1	0	7	82	358	-4

Division Two

	P	W	D	L	F	A	Pts
Seaton	8	7	0	1	189	81	14
St. Nicholas Arms	8	5	1	2	139	128	11
Kells	8	4	1	3	137	138	9
Maryport	8	3	0	5	252	242	3
Flimby	8	0	0	8	34	462	-15

Division Three

	P	W	D	L	F	A	Pts
Glasson	6	5	1	0	153	53	11
Wigton	6	4	1	1	59	34	9
Salterbeck	6	2	0	4	88	207	1
Broughton Red Rose	6	0	0	6	36	242	-9

2000-2001 CUMBERLAND AMATEUR RUGBY LEAGUE CONTINUED

Alliance League

	P	W	D	L	F	A	Pts	
Wath Brow Hornets 'A'	14	14	0	0	360	75	28	
Kells 'A'	14	10	0	4	221	235	17	
Hensingham 'A'	14	9	1	4	225	262	16	
Egremont 'A'	14	7	1	6	295	393	9	St.
Nicholas Arms 'A'	14	3	0	11	113	486	6	
Wigton 'A'	14	3	0	11	98	601	-12	
Westfield 'A'	14	4	0	10	190	481	-13	
Ellenborough 'A'	14	5	0	9	197	466	-14	

2001-2002 CUMBERLAND AMATEUR RUGBY LEAGUE

Division One

	P	W	D	L	F	A	Pts
Wath Brow Hornets	18	17	0	1	889	147	34
Hensingham	18	12	1	5	389	250	25
Ellenborough	18	12	0	6	387	273	24
Kells	18	10	0	8	430	347	20
Seaton	18	10	0	8	384	311	20
Westfield	18	10	0	8	376	465	20
Egremont	18	6	0	12	279	387	12
St. Nicholas	18	5	0	13	275	491	10
Glasson Rangers	18	5	0	13	246	633	7
Wigton	18	2	1	15	230	631	5

Alliance League

	P	W	D	L	F	A	Pts
Hensingham 'A'	12	12	0	0	363	66	24
Kells 'A'	12	9	0	3	232	122	18
Seaton 'A'	12	7	0	5	252	220	14
Egremont 'A'	12	6	1	5	205	272	10
Glasson Rangers 'A'	12	5	0	7	130	338	1
St. Nicholas 'A'	12	1	0	11	130	518	-4
Wigton 'A'	12	1	1	10	76	502	-18

AT the end of the 2001-02 season, St Nicholas Arms ARLFC's former player and secretary, Andrew Hodgkinson (42 years old at the time), won the amateur game's top award, the Tom Keaveny Memorial Award, for his commitment to the game since the club's formation in 1982. The citation recorded that during this time the club had risen to the Cumberland ARL Division One and developed a thriving youth set-up with teams from under-8s up. In addition to his role in running St Nicholas Arms, Andrew played a major role in setting up the Carlisle and District ARL, where he served as chairman and secretary. He was also a member of the management committee of the Cumberland ARL for five years.

His enthusiasm for rugby league in the city continues unabated and he continues to play a full and practical role in the running of Carlisle Centurions RLFC, often taking time out from his busy management job to mark the pitch etc.

2002-03 CUMBERLAND AMATEUR RUGBY LEAGUE

Division One

	P	W	D	L	F	A	Pts
Hensingham	18	18	0	0	552	134	36
Kells	18	14	0	4	519	292	28
Seaton	18	14	0	4	412	269	28
Ellenborough	18	9	0	9	337	329	15
Carlisle Saints	18	7	1	10	279	469	15
Wath Brow Hornets	18	8	0	10	301	381	13
Egremont	18	7	1	10	374	394	12
Westfield	18	7	0	11	285	423	8
Broughton Red Rose	18	3	0	15	241	477	6
Glasson Rangers	18	2	0	16	246	628	4

Division Two

	P	W	D	L	F	A	Pts
Lowca	22	19	0	3	837	313	38
Maryport	22	18	0	4	845	297	36
Wigton	22	16	0	6	547	378	32
Hensingham 'A'	22	15	0	7	600	404	30
Kells 'A'	22	15	0	7	640	431	27
Salterbeck	22	10	0	12	499	517	20
Great Clifton	22	8	0	14	372	616	16
Penrith	22	8	0	14	390	657	16
Flimby	22	7	1	14	383	539	15
Egremont 'A'	22	7	1	14	532	566	9
Glasson Rangers 'A'	22	4	0	18	290	901	8
Lowca 'A'	22	2	2	18	226	1042	-15

2003-04 CUMBERLAND AMATEUR RUGBY LEAGUE

Division One

	P	W	D	L	F	A	Pts
Hensingham	18	15	0	3	651	265	30
Seaton	18	14	0	4	594	208	28
Kells	18	13	0	5	632	368	26
Egremont	18	13	0	5	531	364	26
Wath Brow Hornets	18	9	0	9	463	459	18
Ellenborough	17	9	0	8	438	355	15
Lowca	17	7	0	10	344	639	14
Westfield	18	4	0	14	284	527	8
Broughton Red Rose	18	2	0	16	236	635	4
Carlisle Saints	18	3	0	16	225	678	3

2003-04 CUMBERLAND AMATEUR RUGBY LEAGUE CONTINUED

Division Two

	P	W	D	L	F	A	Pts
Maryport	19	17	0	2	732	301	34
Glasson Rangers	20	14	1	5	602	285	29
Wigton	20	13	1	6	581	246	27
Great Clifton	20	12	1	7	474	396	25
Seaton 'A'	20	8	0	12	322	'507	16
Egremont 'A'	20	7	0	13	468	723	14
Flimby	20	7	1	12	304	492	12
Salterbeck	20	8	1	11	304	492	11
Ellenborough 'A'	19	7	0	12	284	519	11
Kells 'A'	20	9	0	11	440	639	3
Penrith	20	3	1	16	298	750	1

2004-05 CUMBERLAND AMATEUR RUGBY LEAGUE

Division Two

	P	W	D	L	F	A	Pts
Carlisle Saints	18	16	0	2	564	186	32
Glasson Rangers	18	14	1	3	436	179	29
Kells 'A'	18	12	0	6	439	257	24
Salterbeck	18	11	0	7	387	353	22
Wigton	18	11	1	6	526	323	20
Great Clifton	18	9	2	7	444	359	20
Egremont 'A'	18	6	0	12	441	595	9
Flimby	18	2	1	15	264	784	2
Westfield 'A'	18	3	1	14	274	720	-2
Salterbeck 'A'	18	3	0	15	199	668	-3

SEASON 2004-05 turned out to be the last ever season of Carlisle Saints or St Nicholas Arms as they were originally known. When Carlisle Centurions reformed for the 2006 season, the clubs effectively merged and to this day the backbone of the Centurions owe their pedigree to the St Nicholas Arms-Carlisle Saints clubs.

In 2002, Andrew Hodgkinson was asked by former dual code international player Bev Risman whether there was any interest in Carlisle putting a club in the up and coming summer conference. I was Barrow RLFC chairman at that time but wearying of the twice-weekly return journey. When approached by Andrew on behalf of Bev regarding my joining this new venture, I jumped at the chance.

At a very early stage, Dougal Kyle and I attended a summer conference annual meeting at the Willows home of

Salford City Reds. This coincided with the 2002 Super League Grand Final, so we went straight from there to Old Trafford.

I hadn't expected too much from that meeting as I was well aware of the political bureaucracy that existed within the British Amateur Rugby League Association. However, this was the RFL - totally unlike BARLA in its approach to bureaucratic matters. The meeting was well chaired by Niel Wood of the RFL who ensured us that there would be no politics and very little bureaucracy. The whole event seemed to be a celebration of rugby league in non-traditional areas. There were so many clubs, old and new, looking to participate that the main challenge for the RFL people present seemed to be how to create fixtures for all of them. This was the very antithesis of the shrinking number of participants presided over by BARLA.

As soon as possible we convened a getting together of like-minded rugby league folk in the city and started to meet under Bev's leadership. Our initial team included former Border Raiders people such as Doc Haworth, leaders of the amateur code like Andrew Hodgkinson and Craig McCullough, people from the original youth organisation like Ann Underwood, Doc Mackay and Trevor Easton, the former referee Mike Rayson and many more.

There were several main issues to be addressed such as where we would play, what we would call ourselves, who would coach us, from where would we recruit players and so on. Bev made it clear that he would only be involved as long as it took to get the club running and reasonably stable, so it rapidly became clear that we were building something with which we all had to be comfortable for the long term.

The decision as to what we'd be called was a true test of democratic reasoning. We'd toyed with names that evoked Carlisle's railway heritage such as Carlisle Lokomotif but we homed in on the Roman connection and all felt comfortable with Carlisle Centurions RLFC.

Gradually the other issues were put to bed including the slightly contentious one as to our venue. I'll admit to serious misgivings when the committee homed in on Gillford Park, the spiritual home of Carlisle rugby league until we vacated it six years earlier, leaving it to be used in the winter by Carlisle Saints ARLFC, the one remaining club from that once thriving Carlisle amateur scene. I needn't have worried. We were welcomed with open arms by the new Railway Club committee, who were anxious to distance themselves from the old adversarial politics of the Eighties and Nineties. And they have been as good as their word.

On the subject of a coach, we were fortunate in Bev's recommendation and recruitment of former Carlisle Border Raiders and Workington Town player Gary Murdock, who'd gained an immense amount of coaching experience in the West Cumbrian amateur game. Gary was able to recruit some of the best West Cumbrian amateurs around who, combined with the North Cumbrian talent, in particular from Carlisle Saints, looked a potentially formidable team.

The new club was launched in style at the old Officers Mess bar in Carlisle Castle. Guests of honour included the BBC's Ray French (who was also the keynote speaker and had us all in hysterics with his stories and anecdotes); Bev Risman; Dean Bell, complete with the Challenge Cup that Wigan had won in the previous spring; his father Cameron - Carlisle coach of 1990-94, who was also visiting in Carlisle at that time; John Courtney, chairman of Carlisle United; directors from Whitehaven RLFC; officials from the Cumberland Amateur Rugby League; and several members of Carlisle City Council.

Since then, Carlisle Centurions have had modest success. In 2003, having emphatically disposed of Leeds Akademiks

68-2 in the quarter-final and then Birmingham Bulldogs 44-2 in the semi-final played at Sheffield, we were narrowly defeated finalists in the Harry Jepson Trophy at Wilderspool, Warrington. Bridgend Blue Bulls, the team who beat us 33-26, boasted several former professional RL internationals including Kevin Ellis, Allan Bateman and John Devereux, plus future Celtic Crusaders Super League players Karl Hocking and Lenny Woodard.

The Carlisle team that day was: Craig Stalker (T); Andy Sawyers, Jamie Watson, Martin Stalker (c), Dean Haney (2G); Dale Semple, Mike Marsden; Richard Nicholson, Steve Brough, Paul McGee (2T), Richard Campbell (T), Richard Massey, Eddie Robinson. Subs: Ross Stewart, James Mackay, Chris Sawyers (T), Gary Murdock.

I am indebted to Phil Caplan who was reporting the match on behalf of both the RFL and *Rugby League World* magazine. 'In a magnificent game, the power and dexterity of Bev Risman Medal winner Karl Hocking, the midfield solidity of Allan Bateman, industry of Marcus Sainsbury and superb kicking of John Williams allied to Kevin Ellis's guile and passion was just enough to beat the Centurions for whom two-try Paul McGee was outstanding,' wrote Phil.

'The Warrington crowd who came early in numbers for their Super League encounter with Halifax witnessed a classic and their passionate enthusiasm, principally for their former favourites, produced the perfect backdrop. A fantastic tackle by Dean Haney forced Geraint Lewis to knock on and from the resultant scrum Dale Semple ghosted through the Welsh defence to lay on a perfect pass for Mc Gee to score. On the 35th minute with the scores 10-10 it looked as if the Bulls were wobbling but they hit back immediately after Haney was deemed to have caught the restart with a foot in touch, Ellis's cut-out ball allowing Bateman's long pass to put Mike Davies in at the corner,

Williams again converting. A minute after the break and the lead was extended, Carlisle surrendering position on their own "40" and Hocking producing another magical pass to send Dan Shore powering over in the corner.'

Murdock's reassuring arrival off the bench signalled three tries in ten minutes to put Centurions into the lead for the first time. Phil Caplan's report went on: 'McGee's break and chip which forced a drop-out set the position and Murdock, Robinson and Semple freed Campbell whose nimble foot-work on the inside took him across. Before Bridgend could regroup, Murdock's great pass on the inside sent McGee stepping effortlessly to the line to make it 22-20 and on a Murdock inspired power play Semple chipped over, hacked on and Chris Sawyers won the race to the ball to put the Centurions in front at 26-22.'

Sadly, a tiring Carlisle made a couple of forced errors in the closing stages and with Ellis in superb form for the Welshmen, a couple of Bridgend tries combined with a drop-goal saw them home. It had been a memorable final. On returning to Carlisle, we were pleasantly surprised when the Mayor, Judith Patterson, and Council Leader Mike Mitchelson invited us all to a buffet and drinks reception at the civic centre to celebrate the event.

Despite a consistently high level of results and spectacle, the club has never quite recaptured the public's interest of that 2003 season in general and that final in particular. Most notable has been the drop in matchday income to a half of the level achieved in those early days. A case of Carlisle RLFC post-1981-82 *déjà vu* perhaps? Or, maybe, we were just repeating the early experiences of all the other new clubs such as Cardiff, Fulham and Scarborough etc in non-traditional areas, where the gates rapidly declined after the initial interest.

The league table for that initial season was:

2003 TOTALRL.COM CONFERENCE - NORTH WEST

	P	W	D	L	F	A	Diff	Pts
Carlisle Centurions	10	10	0	0	554	105	450	20
Chester Wolves	10	8	0	2	398	258	140	16
Bolton le Moors	10	6	0	4	335	267	68	12
Liverpool Buccaneers	10	3	0	7	210	371	-161	6
Blackpool S Eagles	10	2	0	8	200	476	-276	4
Lancaster	10	1	0	9	162	383	-221	2

FOLLOWING the retirement of the 2003 coach Gary Murdock, long-serving former Carlisle Saints player Mike Marsden stepped up to take the reins and Centurions were promoted to National League 3 (NL3) for 2004 and 2005. They finished the 2004 season twelfth in a fourteen-team league. Disappointingly they, along with Birmingham, failed to finish the 2005 season. The excessively long-distance journeys to Essex, St Albans, Hemel Hempstead and Coventry took an inevitable toll on players. The two clubs withdrew from the competition and their results were expunged from the records. In subsequent seasons many other clubs, including Coventry, Bradford, Sheffield, St Albans, South London, Manchester and Essex, dropped down into the regional competitions due to travel and other difficulties.

2004 NATIONAL LEAGUE THREE

	P	W	D	L	F	A	Diff	Pts
Coventry Bears	20	17	0	3	831	385	446	34
Bradford-Dudley H	20	16	0	4	942	317	625	32
Warrington-Woolston	20	15	1	4	764	232	532	31
Sheff-Hillsborough	20	13	1	6	631	334	297	27
Bramley Buffaloes	20	13	1	6	592	368	224	27
Hemel Stags	20	13	0	7	721	424	297	26
St Albans C	20	12	0	8	724	406	318	24
Birmingham B	20	10	0	10	620	624	-4	20
Huddersfield-U'bank	20	9	1	10	671	519	152	19
South London S	20	8	2	10	496	510	-14	18
Manchester Knights	20	5	0	15	467	625	-158	10
Carlisle Centurions	20	3	0	17	290	948	-658	6
Gateshead Storm	20	2	0	18	290	1041	-751	4
Essex Eels	20	1	0	19	186	1492	-1306	2

THE year 2006 saw Centurions with another new coach in former Carlisle Saint Geoff Greaves. They were also back in the NE regional summer conference, where they became northern regional champions, beating Copeland for the dubiously nick-named 'Cock of the North' title before falling 38-12 to Liverpool Buccaneers in the regional semi-finals at Ince Rosebridge, near Wigan. The Carlisle line-up was: Stephen Moss; Matt Rodgers, Tony Palmer, Andy Holcroft, Gavin Davis; Phil Hewitt, Joe Crowther; Richard Nicholson, Steve Brough, James Mackay, James Stainton, Craig Richardson, Mike Dodd. Subs: Craig Rumney, Mike Scott, Gavin Mooney, Steve Mattinson.

2006 TOTALRL.COM CONFERENCE REGIONAL LEAGUES

NORTH

	P	W	D	L	F	A	Diff	PTS
Copeland Athletic	12	10	0	2	608	232	376	20
Carlisle Centurions	12	10	0	2	515	196	319	20
Peterlee Pumas	12	8	0	4	370	290	80	16
Jarrow Vikings	12	6	0	6	332	321	11	12
Sunderland Nissan	12	2	0	10	164	548	-384	4

ALSO in 2006, a new under-16s venture made a brief appearance, organised by Chris McManus (former Dalston and Carlisle alliance team), his son Grant and a handful of friends. This kick-about escalated until twenty players were regularly turning up after school on Thursday afternoons.

Geoff Macmanus, another former Dalston and Carlisle alliance team player and the brother of Chris was co-opted into assisting with running the team. Home games were played at Creighton RUFC, on the southern edge of the city. Geoff recalls: 'Friendlies were arranged with North East junior teams and then, to give the lads regular rugby, they were entered into the West Cumbrian League in 2007-08. This was a hard introduction and several hammerings were suffered.

'However, credit to the lads and the coaches. The end of

the season brought a great improvement in form with much closer games and the season climaxed with a fantastic win over a strong Kells side followed by wins against the Scottish under-16s champions Easterhouse Panthers.

'Notable player successes that filled the coaching staff [Chris and Geoff McManus, John Parry and Barry Sharrock] with pride include Reece Bone, Ross Allen, Gavin Campbell and Nathan Morris, all of whom went on to represent Scotland at under-16 and under-18 level. Sadly, the venture died a death once the boys turned sixteen as there was no suitable league available to them.'

In 2007, Centurions again made the regional semi-final and took on Coventry Bears at Rochdale Mayfield in early September. The team was well beaten, 40-14, by a much bigger Midlands outfit. The Carlisle team was: Steve Moss; Chris Fairclough, Tony Palmer, John Haughey, Gavin Davis; Mike Dodd, Martin Stalker; James Mackay, George Graham, Richard Nicholson, James Stainton, Steve Jackson, Andy Holcroft. Subs: Craig Rumney, Andy Dalton, Stuart Bulman, Carl Bateson.

2007 NORTHERN PREMIER

	P	W	D	L	F	A	Pts
Carlisle Centurions	14	13	0	1	744	128	26
Billingham Lions	14	10	0	4	638	310	20
Peterlee Pumas	14	8	4	2	546	282	20
Copeland Athletic	14	8	1	5	452	429	17
Newcastle Knights	14	7	2	5	421	336	16
Sunderland Nissan	14	7	0	7	350	459	14
Jarrow Vikings	14	5	1	8	431	346	11
Durham Tigers	14	4	0	10	215	539	8
Gateshead Storm 'A'	14	2	0	12	200	426	4
Whitley Bay Barbarians	14	1	0	12	128	850	2

IN 2008, Carlisle made it three semi-finals in a row for coach Geoff Greaves when they once again made the regional semi-finals and earned the right to take on Nottingham Outlaws, at Rochdale Mayfield. Again we saw the shortcomings of competing and winning easily in a

Above: Rickerby Saints Under-16s in 2007-08. Back row: Chris McManus (coach), Kate Hudson (physio), Mark Sykes, Ben Reid, Leon Cowx, Grant Lyndsley, Adam Telford, Nathan Morris, Ross Allan, Dean Learmount, Tom Reay, Ian Martin. Front row: Preben Mykland, Alan Shaw, Michael Barber, Chris Humpleby, Danny Bell, Grant McManus, Steve Grieve, Steve Robinson

Northern competition when the Centurions met a well-drilled and battle-hardened team from a much stronger league. We were well beaten 47-22 by the East Midlanders. The Carlisle team was: James Sanderson; Tony Palmer, Martin Stalker, Steven Potter, Craig Atkinson; Craig Stalker, George Graham; Richard Nicholson, Mike Scott, Steve Jackson, Mike Stevens, Andy Holcroft, Mike Dodd. Subs: Dennis Bibby, Dan Holmes, Gavin Davis, Stuart Graham.

2008 NORTHERN PREMIER

	P	W	D	L	F	A	Diff	Pts
Carlisle Centurions	14	14	0	0	900	100	800	28
Leeds Akkies	14	10	0	4	672	198	474	20
Jarrow Vikings	14	10	0	4	565	363	202	20
Newcastle Knights	14	9	1	4	606	275	331	19
Peterlee Pumas	14	6	1	7	492	406	86	13
Sunderland Nissan	14	4	0	10	315	660	-345	8
Durham Tigers	14	1	0	13	162	642	-480	2
Whitley Bay Barbarians	14	1	0	13	64	1132	-1068	2

THE pattern of games from 2006 through to 2008, i.e. easy passages in the regional league competitions and then heavy defeats against teams from other regional leagues in the play-off rounds leading to the national grand final, was inhibiting development. The team needed greater intensity throughout the season to develop. Accordingly, Centurions management applied to rejoin the stronger national competition - the former NL3, now renamed Rugby League Conference National. In 2009 our application was accepted and Centurions won five out of their allotted twenty league games, having travelled to such non-traditional locations as Hemel Hempstead, Nottingham and Liverpool. It's fair to say that while the national competition had lost its developmental feel when teams like Essex Eels, South London Storm, St Albans and Coventry dropped out with only three expansion clubs still remaining at that level, its standards were greatly improved by the retrenchment to more traditional areas. Whether or not this is a good thing for the long-term future of the code is the subject of much debate, especially on the various rugby league website forums. Personally, I feel that the game took a backward, but maybe unavoidable, step with the loss of three of its southern-based clubs from the elite competition. Maybe there is future scope to regionalise this level into north and south and bring the southern clubs back into the elite fold.

2009 THE CO-OPERATIVE RUGBY LEAGUE CONFERENCE NATIONAL

	P	W	D	L	Bonus	F	A	Pts
Bramley Buffaloes	20	17	1	2	2	833	332	55
Huddersfield Underbank	20	15	1	4	3	722	330	50
Featherstone Lions	20	13	2	5	3	795	414	46
Nottingham Outlaws	20	15	0	5	0	746	474	45
Hemel Stags	20	13	0	7	5	776	415	44
Warrington Wizards	20	12	0	8	2	714	599	38
Liverpool Buccaneers	20	8	0	12	7	602	593	31
Dewsbury Celtic	20	5	0	15	3	417	774	18
Carlisle	20	5	0	15	1	411	983	16
East Lancashire Lions	20	3	0	17	2	356	895	11
Gateshead Storm	20	2	0	18	2	294	857	8

SO what of the future? One very positive development is the recent action taken by the RFL to re-establish the post of rugby league development officer in Carlisle schools. This is a major step for the code in North Cumbria and should once again establish a conveyor belt to feed the open-age game and such clubs that emerge in the future. I suppose the big

Above: 2008 Northern Premier League champions having just beaten Leeds Akkies 38-20 in the regional final at Gillford Park. Standing: Geoff Greaves (coach). Kathryn Osborne (physio), Adam Pate, Dennis Bibby, Tom Armstrong, Steve Moss, Tony Palmer, Mike Stevens , Steve Jackson, Martin Stalker, Trevor Easton (team manager), James Stainton, Craig Stalker. Kneeling: Andy Holcroft, Richard Nicholson, Mike Dodd (captain), George Graham, James Sanderson, Craig Atkinson, Dan Holmes

question is whether there will ever again be a top-flight professional rugby league club in Carlisle.

My honest opinion is that it would take a fairly significant event, such as the coming together of several very determined, energetic, comparatively youthful and driven rugby league zealots along with a capital investment of many hundreds of thousands of pounds. I don't think it's feasible any longer to form a semi-professional club, capitalised as the old Carlisle Border Raiders RLFC was, with around £200,000 of unsecured (and ultimately written-off) loans and share-capital, and to be both competitive and financially stable. Since rugby union has become openly professional, talented rugby players need no longer take the one-way ticket to rugby league in order to earn money. This alone has pushed up the entry cost of a new professional club.

Will such rugby league zealots come forward in Carlisle once more in the future? Well, they did at regular intervals in the 1980s and '90s. So why not again? And, if they do, they will find the start-up capital for sure.

Appendix

*

The Early Days

HARRABY PARK STADIUM
CARLISLE

Greyhound Racing every Monday, Thursday, and Saturday.

NORTHERN RUGBY LEAGUE.—CARLISLE CITY will play during the Season all the Lancashire League Clubs and some Yorkshire HARRABY PARK STADIUM can accommodate 70,000 spectators, and is the Largest and Most Beautiful Ground in the North-West

THE late Tom Clark, a very loyal and knowledgable Carlisle fan, prepared the following account of the Carlisle City pro club that briefly existed in 1928 and played at Harraby Greyhound Stadium, believed to be where Gillford Park now stands. Tom carried out his research from contemporary newpaper reports held at Carlisle Library and passed this to me in about 1988, at one of our earliest Carlisle Border Raiders games at Gillford Park. I wish he was still around to see it appreciated by a much wider readership

*

A Short History of Carlisle City
June - November 1928
by Tom Clark

ON Wednesday afternoon, 28th April, 1928, a conference was held in the County Hotel, Carlisle, between the directors of the Carlisle and Cumberland Greyhound Racing and Sports Ltd and representatives of the Rugby League to discuss the formation of a first class rugby league team for the city. It was attended by Mr John Wilson, secretary of the Rugby League and by three Cumberland Commissioners, Mr Brown (Silecroft), hon secretary, Mr G. Plummer and Mr T. Banks (Siddick). The chair was taken by Mr E. Summerside, a director of the company, in the absence of Major English through illness.

The feeling was expressed that there was room for the introduction for the first time in the city's history of a rugby league team. The financial side of the project was thoroughly examined and consideration given to the acquisition of a team sufficiently strong to play a worthy part in the league. It was thought that the nucleus would be obtained from the clubs in West Cumberland and Furness districts. These areas have always been productive of fine forwards.

There was no intention to compete with Carlisle United for spectators; fixtures would be arranged to avoid clashing. It was also thought that the introduction of rugby league into the city would strongly assist United to get into the Third Division of the Football League. An all-round improvement in the status of both codes was envisaged.

The League authorities undertook to give the new team every possible assistance, particularly in team building. It was also stated that arrangements could be made for the playing of international and county matches on Harraby Park, the company's ground, which, it was claimed, could accommodate 30,000 spectators, 6,000 of whom would have grandstand seats. As the ground was alongside the railway a special siding for use by spectators would be erected.

At an extraordinary meeting of the Northern Rugby League which followed the annual meeting in Leeds on Wednesday 16th June, Carlisle were admitted to the League for the 1928-09 season by twenty votes to two. Leeds and Featherstone Rovers voted against.

In July, thirty-six representatives of all the clubs attended a meeting of Cumberland Rugby League at Workington. After reviewing last season, Mr. Plummer, the secretary, said the formation of the new club would prove an asset to the game in Cumberland and if they met with a measure of success on the field he believed they would be financially viable. The fact that the club had been granted fixtures with Lancashire clubs was the finest start it could possibly have, and in his opinion the club could not have been formed at a better time.

Among the players signed were R. Scott (native of Aspatria, aged 26, 5 feet 6 inches, 10 st 7 lbs. Played for Warrington, Batley and Huddersfield); J. F. Peel (born at Flimby. Descendant of the famous John Peel. Aged 23, 5 feet 8 inches and 11 st 7 lbs. Played for Flimby and Fothergill and

Huddersfield); George Ellis (played for Millom and Wigan. Aged 24, 5 feet 7 inches and 11 stones); H. James (from Welsh RU. 1927-08 played for Leeds); W. Gunson (former Great Clifton. Aged 20, 5 feet 8 inches and 11 stone); Isaac Southward (from a rugby family, his brother played for Salford six seasons. Isaac played for Dearham Wanderers and in 1926-07 he played against Dewsbury in the Challenge Cup. Aged 21, 5 feet 9 and 10 st 7lbs)[1]; W. Irving (5 feet 6 and 10 st); O. W. Errington (played for Cumberland and Huddersfield. From Aspatria. Reputed to be the best hooker in rugby league at the time.); R. Lowery (former St Bees. Transferred from Bradford Northern. 5 feet 9 inches and 12 st 7 lbs.)[2]; F. S. Railton (from Dearharn Wanderers. 5 feet 10 inches and 12 stone 7 lbs. Much sought after by other clubs.); R. Sandham (5 feet 11 inches and 13 stone); E. Howe (Workington. Had a trial with Leeds. 5 feet 11 inches and 13 stone.); H. Buglass (aged 27, 5 feet 10 inches and 12 stone 7 lbs.)

A trial game was played at Harraby Park on 18th August, 1928 when the referee was J. Ackerly of Maryport and the touch judges were R. Fenwick and J. Nelson from the Cumberland Rugby League Commissioners. By this time 'Ted' Hodgson, the former Maryport, Brookland Rovers, Hull Kingston Rovers, Barrow, Bramley and Cumberland three-quarter, had been appointed trainer.

1928-29 SEASON

August 25 - City 3 Wigan Highfield 10, home lost, att: 2,000
R. Scott: James, Peel, Gunson, Key, Ellis, Fairfax; Green, Errington, Tweedie, Railton, Sandham, Lowery (try)

---

[1]This particular Isaac Southward is the uncle of the late Workington and Salford international Ike Southward.

[2] Thanks to Keith Nutter's excellent book *Keeping the Dream Alive*, we understand that Robert Lowery signed originally for Bradford Northern from St Bees ARLFC in 1926, returned there after Carlisle folded, and then played a season in 1930 back in the professional game for Barrow.

1928-29 SEASON CONTINUED

8 September City 5 St. Helens 8, home lost att: 1,000
R. Scott: James, Peel (goal and try), Key, Gunson; Ellis, Fairfax; Green, Errington, Tweedie, Railton: Sandham, Lowery

15 September Wigan Highfield 27 City 3, away lost
Peel: James (try), Fairfax, Key, Gunson; Ellis, Owen; Green, Errington, Tweedie, Railton, Sandham, Lowery

22 September St. Helens Recs 20 City 12, away lost
R. Scott: James (try), Fairfax, Key (try), Peel (2 goals); Ellis (goal), Irving; Green, Errington, Tweedie, Sandham, Railton, Lowery

29 September City 8 Keighley 2, home won att: 3,000
R, Scott: James, Fairfax, Key, Peel (try); Ellis, Irving (try); Green, Errington, Tweedie, Sandham, Railton (goal), Lowery

6 October Widnes 16 City 6, away lost
R. Scott (try): James, Peel (try), Fairfax, Southward; Ellis, Irving; G. Scott, Errington, Green, Sandham, Railton, Lowery

13 October City 3 Salford 12, home lost att: 650
Fearon; James, Peel, R. Scott, Gunson ; Ellis, Fairfax ; Denwood, Errington, Little, Raiiton (try), Green, Lowery

20 October - Leigh 23 City 3, away lost
Fearon; Peel, James, Fairfax, Gunson(try) ; Ellis, Irving; Green, Denwood, Little, Tweedie, Sandham, Lowery

27 October - City 13 Warrington 36, home lost att: 450
R. Scott (2 goals); Fearon, Peel, Key, James(try); Ellis (2 tries), Fairfax; Green, Errington, Denwood, Sandham, Little, Lowery

3 November, Rochdale H. 12 City 3, away lost
R. Scott ; James, Peel, Fairfax (try), Gunson; Ellis, Irving; Little, Denwood, Errington, Green, Tweedie, Lowery

ALTHOUGH Carlisle were defeated in their first match, City were considered a good average side, as Wigan Highfield were the only club to have a 100 per cent record after the first five matches. The game clearly indicated the need for a good goal kicker and far more weighty forwards.

One outstanding weakness was that of high-tackling, and the stand-off and centres came in for some criticism due to their kicking away possession. Most of the weakness, however, was put down to a lack of match practice and the game was said to have been an enjoyable one which gave general satisfaction to the spectators.

The critics were strangely at variance with regard to Carlisle's performance at St Helens Recs where they lost 20-12 in front of a crowd of 4,000. Some commended City on their display for which they received a standing ovation at the end of the game, but one inferred that the Recs took things easy, 'not desiring for a cricket score'.

Trailing 13-0 at half-time, City gained two tries through well executed moves. In the first, Fairfax was the mainspring, taking a pass from the scrum and faced with an apparently impenetrable defence he put the ball to his feet and dribbled through. Key followed up and touched down for a great try. It was generally agreed that with a bit more weight in the pack and more practice Carlisle would improve.

The following week at Harraby Park, City earned their one and only victory at the expense of a struggling Keighley. The Lawkholmers' following of 1,500 numbered half the attendance. With both sides tackling well, the greater part of the game was played with the ball on the ground, and in the loose rushes the light Carlisle forwards, led by Lowery, Railton and Errington were repeatedly dangerous. Carlisle scored their two tries through individual efforts rather than any combination of their three-quarters, however, with the wings, Poole and James, being starved of the ball.

Trailing by six points at Widnes, Carlisle drew level and put up fine resistance against the better side until the last five minutes when the Chemics added two late tries. County full-back Scott, who was in the Cumberland team chosen to meet Glamorgan and Monmouthshire at Whitehaven on 20th October, once broke through from his own 22 and was only stopped after a desperate tackle by Topping. The new three-quarter, Southward, made his debut on the wing but got few chances with City persisting in their tendency to kick when on attack.

After an attractive first half, when Salford's three-quarters had most of the play, the game deteriorated and rough play was all too common. Solitary points came when Railton got over from close range after a fine solo run by James.

Without Scott and Errington, who were both in the Cumberland side, Carlisle were overrun in the second half at Leigh. At half-time the scores were level with a try each, but City's lack of stamina again told and the scoreline flattered the hosts. Leigh's county scrum-half Houghton was in brilliant form and outplayed Irving. The Leigh correspondent considered that Carlisle were a much better team than the then-defunct Pontypridd, but they needed strengthening in certain positions. No accounts of the last two games are available except the scores and scorers.

The decision to disband was made at a meeting of the club officials on Thursday afternoon, 8th November, 1928, following what would be the last match away to Rochdale.

The main reason for this was clear. Support had dwindled to only 400 spectators by the final home game, when Warrington were the visitors. After debating the prospect of transferring the club to Workington, it was decided to apply to the Rugby League for permission to change the venue of upcoming home matches from Harraby Park to Bradbury Avenue, Maryport, home of Brookland Rovers. The ground was owned by the Rugby League, having been bought two years previously with the intention of it being developed as the county ground.

Support was thought to be more forthcoming in West Cumberland while the success of Carlisle United offered no prospects for professional rugby league in the city. This application was considered at a Rugby League Management Committee meeting in Leeds on Wednesday 14th November 1928, but it was refused after being strongly opposed by Mr Brown of the Cumberland Commission.

It was then decided, on Thursday morning, to play the next fixture at Harraby Park on Saturday against Leigh, and a team was selected. At a further meeting in the afternoon, however, this decision was reversed and steps taken to disband the club.

At a meeting of the Rugby League on 21st November 1928, the following Carlisle players were transfer-listed at a fee to be decided: Scott, James, Peel, Ellis, Errington and Lowery. On 1st December, the club records were expunged and the players not belonging to any club were declared free agents with no fee payable.

Player movement after disbandonment: R. Scott to Swinton; W. H. James to Oldham; G. Ellis to Rochdale Hornets; S. V. Fairfax to Bradford Northern; A. Green to Barrow; Denwood to Hunslet.

THE UNCOMPLETED FIXTURE LIST

1928

Aug	25	Wigan Highfield	home	3-10	Lowery try
Sep.	1	No Fixture			
	8	St Helens	home	5-8	Peel try & goal
	15	Wigan Highfield	away	3-27	James try
	22	St Helens Rec.	away	12-20	James, Key tries: Peel 2 gls, Ellis
	29	Keighley	home	8-2	Peel, Irving tries, Railton goal
Oct.	6	Widnes	away	6-16	Peel, Scott
	13	Salford	home	3-12	Railton, try
	20	Leigh	away	3-23	Gunson try
	27	Warrington	home	13-36	James, Ellis 2 tries, Scott 2 goals
Nov.	3	Rochdale	away	3-12	Fairfax try
	10	Leigh	home		
	17	Warrington	away		
	24	Barrow	home		
Dec.	1	Castleford	away		
	8	Rochdale	home		
	15	St Helens	away		
	22	Wigan	home		
	25	Barrow	away		
	26	Oldham	home		

Border City Blues

1929

Jan.	1	Widnes	home
	5	Salford	away
	19	Keighley	away
	26	Swinton	away
Feb.	2	Swinton	home
	16	Oldham	away
Mar.	2	Broughton	home
	9	Wigan	away
	16	Castleford	home
	23	Broughton	away
	30	St Helens Rec	home
Apr.	1	Bramley	home

4 Matches with Yorkshire clubs have yet to be arranged.
Played 10; Won 1; Drawn 0; Lost 9; For 59, Agst 166.

PLAYER STATISTICS

Player	Appearances	Goal	Tries	Points
Denwood	4			
G. Ellis	10	1	2	8
OW. Errington	9		1	3
SV. Fairfax	10		1	3
S. Fearon	3			
A. Green	10			
W. Gunson	6		1	3
W. Irving	5		1	3
WH. James	10		3	9
H. Key	6		1	3
Little	4			
R. Lowery	10		1	3
Owen	1			
JF. Peel	10	3	3	15
FS. Railton	7	1	1	5
R. Sandham	8			
G. Scott	1			
R. Scott	8	2	1	7
J. Southwaite	1			
Tweedie	7			

Author's Note: There is speculation as to the whereabouts of Harraby Greyhound Stadium. From studying the only photograph we could find, the proximity of the railway embankment and the railway footbridge suggests the Gillford Park area, home to Carlisle Border Raiders RLFC between 1988 and 1997 and present home to Carlisle Centurions. It took Alex MacKenzie, long-time committee member of the Carlisle Railway Club, to solve the mystery and confirm what his own dad had told him; Gillford Park and Harraby Stadium occupied the same piece of ground. This is given credence by the area of wide cinder-track that occasionally gets exposed in front of the goal posts at the eastern end of the ground. Alex further recounted that the huge wooden stand had been dismantled and sold to Gateshead Football Club in 1929 when Cowans acquired the land. Fittingly, it was transported by rail.

*

Amateur Carlisle City RLFC
1950-52
by Graeme Harker

I AM indebted to my colleague at Carlisle Centurions, Graeme Harker, for the following well-researched article on the 1950-52 amateur Carlisle City RLFC. The photograph of this team overleaf is courtesy of another colleague, former headmaster Malcolm Jackson, of Heads Nook.

I also thank the late Joe Creighton's daughter, Mrs Olwen Hill, who lives in the delightful hamlet of Parton, about seven miles to the west of Carlisle, for the info on the extended caption regarding her father and the team.

Graeme Harker writes: Rugby league as an organised sport in Carlisle died with the 1928 experiment at Harraby Greyhound Stadium, until the early 1950s when an amateur side, also called Carlisle City, played two seasons in the Cumberland League from 1950 to 1952.

Two of the men behind the new club, Jimmy Haslam and Joe Creighton, then living in the city, were veterans of the game in West Cumberland from before the First War. Haslam

Border City Blues

Back row: The gent at the extreme left of the photograph is Mr Fulton, who lived near the Pedestrian Arms in Newtown Road. Next along is Mr Lupton also from Newtown Road. The third suited gent is Mr J Scott, club chairman, who had some sort of engineering business at the Bridge Lane end of Caldewgate. Then the players; first and second unknown, third along 'Chicken' Armstrong, unknown ex-Carlisle RUFC, Duggie Creighton, Hodgson, 'Ikie', surname unknown but confirmed as not being the late Ike Southward, Joe 'Jobby' Creighton who'd played for Aspatria Hornets and who was a ganger with Laings, and the unknown referee.

Front row: Raymond or Dennis Creighton, 'Ginger' Ivison, Unknown, Pop Shearman, Georgie Grayson and Porthouse. Mrs Hill recalls that the team played just to the west of Morton Manor in a field that bordered the south side of Wigton Road. Their playing strip was light green and white stripes. Each month the team held a pie and pea supper in the Temperance Hall to raise money for playing strip and travel costs.

It seems probable that maybe three factors contributed to the club's early demise. Lack of interest due to the strength of the rugby union code in Carlisle; the code incidentally that Joe Creighton was wont to refer to as the 'boys' game' compared to rugby league the 'men's game'; and Joe's own work commitments, which took him all over the country. Another factor may very well have been the transient nature of the country's young men due to National Service commitments in those post-war years.

---

played for Workington in the very early 1900s and Creighton had been involved with the successful Aspatria Hornets club for many years. City's chairman was J. Scott, and J. Barwise filled the position of secretary. Undertaking the coaching duties was former Workington Town centre G. Armstrong, who apparently rejected an approach by Hunslet and instead threw in his lot with Carlisle.

The club's Headquarters were in the Temperance Hall in Wigton Road, opposite Carr's factory and the now demolished Holy Trinity church.

The club made an inauspicious start when they called off their very first game at Maryport because of lack of numbers - only telegraphing their hosts on the morning of the match! Fortunately, things improved the next week and they entertained Great Clifton at Gillford Park. The newcomers lost 13-2 but according to press reports the young team acquitted themselves well against their more experienced opponents. City played the first two matches at Gillford Park while waiting for the completion of their permanent home at Morton Bridge, which was sited on what is now the Richard Rose Academy. The team met and changed at the Temperance Hall before walking up Wigton Road to the pitch.[1]

After only three games, City entered the Challenge Cup and the rookies couldn't have received a tougher draw in the first qualifying round - the famous Brookland Rovers. The Maryport club were renowned cup fighters and had famously qualified for the competition proper on numerous occasions. Against all the odds City prevailed courtesy of a splendid goal-kicking performance by centre J. Hodgson. His five successful penalty conversions - including one mammoth effort from ten yards inside Carlisle's half - sealed a notable 10-2 win. In the next round, Seaton proved an impossible nut to crack and the city team's first Challenge Cup adventure ended in a heavy 33-2 defeat, though by all accounts the team was not disgraced.

---

[1] This information re Morton Bridge venue is disputed by Mrs Hill, see pic caption

In a bid to promote the game to a wider audience City organised a lecture and film show in the Co-operative Hall in Botchergate. The event was hosted by Trevor Foster, the Rugby League's chief coach and himself a Welsh international. Also in attendance were several Workington Town players, including Gus Risman, Tony Paskins and Billy Ivison, and Whitehaven's up-and-coming star Bill Garrett. Foster lectured the three-figure audience on the rules and tactics of the code and introduced the Rugby League's promotion film *Rugby in Focus*. The event was deemed a huge success.

There was also an attempt to organise an exhibition game at Brunton Park involving two of the country's leading professional clubs, but Carlisle United rejected City's overtures.

At least two Carlisle schools – Creighton and Robert Ferguson - appear to have taken up the game and at one school match the Rugby League's man at the top, Bill Fallowfield, was in attendance to present prizes to the boys. An under-18s team entered the Benevolent Cup and reached the second round.

City's side was a blend of locals, young West Cumbrians and forces personnel stationed in the district. While performances were encouraging, actual wins were harder to come by. The closest they came to it was a 3-3 tie against Workington United Steel in a game played in driving wind and a snowstorm. Tinnion levelled the scores late on for City but Thurlow was unable to convert the relatively simple kick in the severe conditions.

All in all, the first year was judged a success and the club set about preparing for the 1951-52 season. They made a number of impressive signings - a mix of young and seasoned players including 'Pop' Shearman, a well respected Maryport player; W. McKendry, ex Liverpool City;

the teenage Martlew brothers, originally from Wigan and then resident in Carlisle[2]; Porthouse - an England under-18 international from Flimby; and 18-year-old national serviceman George Grayson - formerly on York's books.

As expected, City were a more competitive team and registered, initially at least, some impressive performances against their more experienced Cumberland League opponents. One early success came at Kells, 9-7, with Grayson well to the fore. The *Carlisle Journal* reported: 'It was a victory snatched from the blue... by their eighteen-year-old centre, George Grayson, of the RAF, playing his first game for the city.' With City trailing and the game entering its final stages... 'Grayson collected the ball well in his own half and went away with 'Pop' Shearman and Barwise in support. Ducking and sidestepping, he left five players clutching the air and scored about ten yards out. Barwise converted.'

In mid-November, City defeated Distington at Morton Bridge and the full-back that day was a raw seventeen year-old from Maryport - one Ike Southward!

The *Cumberland News* lauded the debutant's

---

[2] As an interesting aside, it turns out that the two Martlews, Ron and Dennis, who played for Carlisle City RLFC, were the elder brothers of Carlisle MP Eric Martlew. Dennis was nineteen at the time and Ron, twenty-one, was just out of National Service with the RAF. It seems that their father, George Martlew, was a train driver in Wigan who was offered a position in Carlisle that came with a house in Petterill Terrace, just off London Road in Harraby.

Prior to moving north, Ron and Dennis had played rugby league in Wigan and Ron had actually trialled as a professional for Leigh RLFC, so playing their chosen sport in their new hometown of Carlisle was a natural progression.

Following the demise in 1952 of the fledgling amateur Carlisle City, the brothers briefly played rugby union for Carlisle before word of their heinous transgression of playing the thirteen-a-side code reached the club committee and they were promptly banned *sine die*. A not uncommon fate that was still invoked until the mid-1990s for those who chose to play the forbidden game, whether as an amateur or professional.

performance, writing: 'Southward, handling the greasy ball well, initiated several attacks on the Distington line, and on this form he is definitely going to be an acquisition to the City team.' Southward was outstanding for Carlisle until the end of the season but he was destined for higher things. The following summer he signed for Workington Town, the Challenge Cup holders, and he later won eleven caps for Great Britain, including all three Tests in the famous 1958 series.

Results fell away towards the end of the season although the club enjoyed a couple of wins in the Cumberland Cup after losing their first-round match! United Steel fielded a suspended player and a replay was ordered at Morton Bridge, which City won. The club ended the season with pride intact, a support that impressed many visiting clubs, and a reasonably healthy financial balance. To the modern eye it is surprising that the club didn't survive the summer.

END